BRidGes to a holy time

NEW WORSHIP FOR THE SABBATH AND MINOR FESTIVALS

BRidGes to a holy time

NEW WORSHIP FOR THE SABBATH AND MINOR FESTIVALS

Edited by
Alfred Jospe and Richard N. Levy

KTAV PUBLISHING HOUSE, INC.
NEW YORK, N.Y.
1973

SBN 87068-226-1

LIBRARY OF CONGRESS CATALOG CARD NUMBER 73-6095
MANUFACTURED IN THE UNITED STATES OF AMERICA

CONTENTS

FIVE SETTINGS FOR CREATIVE WORSHIP

TRADITION AND INNOVATION IN WORSHIP

I. *Some Fundamental Questions*

by Alfred Jospe

Numerous observers and students of the religious scene in America feel that a new religious intensity has begun to make itself felt among young people. It rejects the standard forms of worship and religious expression but seems to reflect a genuine religious quest and, in some instances, actually possesses all the elements of a religion which accompany the counter-culture that has developed among a substantial segment of the nation's youth.

A

Several features characterize these new modes of worship and religious expression.

1) They differ radically from the traditional and conventional forms of worship. Some employ a multi-media approach; others experiment with jazz music and masses, calls to worship accompanied by a twelve-string guitar, dances on the pulpit, seating in concentric circles on the floor, long periods of silent meditation, prayers taken from newspaper headlines or reflections on them, changing light effects. Nevertheless, some observers and many participants feel that the rejection of the conventional forms and symbols of religion does not imply a rejection of religious faith itself; it simply constitutes a search for new ways of expressing it more meaningfully. As one rabbi put it, "We need the expression of religious ideas through media which are familiar to our young people." The *depositum fidei* remains valid and vital. The old wine is still potable and heady. Only new bottles are needed. For this reason, worship today must learn to use the language, symbols and images of contemporary culture in order to express and communicate religious ideas more effectively.

1

2) Others feel, however, that more than a rejection of the conventional forms and language of religion is called for. They insist that western religion is bankrupt—its intellectual affirmations have become untenable; its moral posture is hypocritical; its identification of social ideals with bourgeois aspirations is unsupportable; its emotional appeal is emasculated by its dessicated moralizing stance that ignores vital dimensions of human experience. Precisely for this reason young people seek new worship patterns in order to find more adequate ways for the expression of these dimensions—their sense of love, their emphasis on celebration, their quest for community, their groping for new certainties, their search for the experience of the mystical. Indeed, their new life style and worship patterns frequently embody a special emphasis on the mystical. The use of drugs is justified as an aid to the achievement of the mystical experience, characterized by a new self-knowledge, an unsuspected sense of the presence of the divine, an overwhelming feeling of unity with God and the cosmos, an ability to perceive and evaluate things more clearly than ever before. There is also a growing tendency on the part of young people to turn to Eastern religions and models of expression. Enrollment in college courses of religion has increased substantially in the past few years. But it is significant that the increase has been primarily in courses devoted to the study of the Eastern religions.

3) There is a heightened emphasis on the role of symbolism and liturgical elements in unconventional forms. The Woodstock Festival has been described as an example of a "new religious culture" precisely because of the numerous cultic elements that were evident at the Festival—the use of incense, candles, bright costumes, hymn singing, loud music, convulsive dances, and similar elements which must be classified as liturgical.

4) Behind these trends one can frequently sense or discern a rejection of the "myth of rationalism" which, many young people maintain, has long characterized much of higher education—the claim (I am not judging its validity) that the only reliable road to truth is the morally neutral and emotionally detached analysis of

reality. They feel that reality is too alive and multi-layered to be captured by this one-dimensional approach. Drugs and other stimulants can open up dimensions of experience, vision and mysteries previously unknown.

5) Services of this kind are generally conducted outside the synagogue and church structure. The advocates and practitioners of the new approach feel that the existing institutions of the various faith communities are incapable of instituting the kind of radical change that would be required to accommodate their emphasis on love, their new modes of celebration, their unconventional liturgies and use of symbolism, their heightened concern with the mystical.

6) While some individuals and groups feel that religious quest and activity are most meaningful when pursued privately, others place a strong emphasis on a new sense of community—generated by "sharing experiences," by public discussion of one's private thoughts, emotions, and concerns, and by "closeness" not only in spiritual but also in physical terms including hand-holding, touching, hugging, and other forms of physical relationship.

B.

Numerous young Jews share these views. For reasons which have frequently been analyzed and need to be only briefly recapitulated here, they reject the synagogue and what it stands for in Jewish life. Some reject it because they have come to reject "religion" in any form—worship, belief, observance—as intellectually untenable and culturally unacceptable for modern man. They feel that a religious posture is incompatible with their intellectual integrity and that religion has nothing meaningful to contribute to their search for spiritual fulfillment and moral significance. Others reject the synagogue not as a matter of principle; they reject what is going on in the synagogue or, to be more precise, in the synagogues they know. They reject the synagogue as a social club; they criticize its frequent mediocrity and substitution of social and entertainment values for genuine spiritual quest. Still others no longer feel at

3

home in services that are conducted in accordance with the patterns of the community institutions in which they have grown up and which, they believe, do not offer them a setting for the expression of their own religious quest. And still others do not reject religion *per se;* they reject organized religion because, for them, religion is something highly private and intimately personal. Whatever the reasons—whether they reflect a total or merely a partial rejection of the religious enterprise of the community—they stay away.

Nevertheless, numerous young Jews continue to ask questions of ultimate concern and attempt to find or create a setting in which their quest might find meaningful expression in the language of contemporary thought and culture.

Jewish institutions—some congregations, youth organizations, Hillel Foundations, summer camps and similar groups—attempt to meet this need by introducing experimental or "innovative" worship patterns in order to attract young people who, in all likelihood, cannot be reached by any other approach and who may find an opportunity for religious self-expression in such services.

Creative or experimental worship can be found in three dominant formats. One, the least "experimental" format, long used by and for young people in youth conclaves, summer camps and junior congregations, generally follows one of the standard *minhagim* but supplements it, minimally, with readings from Jewish or general literature or, more elaborately, with specific liturgical insertions such as singing of *l'kha dodi* to the tune of "Scarborough Fair" or of *Adon Olam* to the tune of "Yellow Submarine." Still more elaborate efforts will utilize drama, poetry, dance, play-acting, or audio-visual media such as psychedelic films or taped sounds to illustrate the joy of common celebration or the agony of human suffering. I believe the use of these media raises basically not a religious question but primarily a question of taste and style.

A second kind of creative liturgical effort is the sort of "original" services which are based on scripts or readings written or selected for Shabbat or such special occasions as Shabbat Hanukkah, Yom Ha'Atzmaut, the commemoration of the anniversary of the Warsaw Ghetto Uprising, Jewish Music Month, and similar occasions. Several examples of this type of service are contained in Section II of this volume.

The most radical type of experimentation in the form and content of worship is represented in Section IV of this book which we have called "Five Settings for Creative Worship." The formats of such services vary greatly. The lighting of the Sabbath candles can be followed by readings from the Sidrah of the week or poetry from other religious (especially oriental) traditions, the presentation of folk or rock music, dramatizations of contemporary issues by the use of devices such as two sound tracks running simultaneously, one featuring a song of quiet and serenity, the other presenting the evening news with its reports of war and brutality. In other settings, the "congregation" sits on the floor; candles constitute the only source of light; and lengthy periods of meditation are interspersed with discussions of a variety of subjects. The participants are encouraged to bring their own "gifts" of readings or thoughts that press for expression at the moment, after which all drink from a common Kiddush cup, gaze at flowers, and perhaps sing a *nigun*.

All three of these liturgical developments are challenging in what they reveal about the problems of our religious institutions as well as about the concerns and needs of many of our young people today. They must be taken seriously because they frequently are the expression of a genuine and deeply felt religious quest. Yet they also raise several fundamental questions about the nature and meaning of Jewish worship as such:

1) There is the question of religious authenticity: To what extent can what happens in some of these "experimental" services be defined as "religion"? Granted that new experimental forms of worship can make religious ideas more meaningful, can what seeks expression here be defined *ipso facto* as "religious" ideas? Are an emphasis on love and celebration, a search for community, a quest

for meaning automatically "religious" by definition? They may and often do involve an act of faith. But are all types of acts of faith "religious" in the established sense of the word?

Young people frequently speak of God in such settings. But speaking *of* God may not, or at least not yet, be speaking *to* God or listening to Him. And listening to one's own voice is precisely that—and nothing more.

I know, of course, that God can be addressed and worshiped in many ways and not only in words or actions hallowed by the past. Every attempt to express in word or thought the nature of God is ultimately but a human attempt to state in rational terms or symbolic form what according to its very essense must remain hidden from us. Nevertheless, must we not guard against the danger of reducing ontology to psychology, worship to poetry, the prayerful affirmation of the divine to meditation about our humanity? It is precisely this danger against which Max Scheler cautioned us when he said that the common error of contemporary religious thought is its claim that you can grasp or determine an ontological reality by analyzing your emotions. And Franz Rosenzweig rejected the same reduction of ontology to psychology when he compared a certain psychologist of religion with an astronomer who, with the seriousness and ingenuity worthy of a Chelmite, takes the telescope apart in the hope of finding the stars in it.

2) A second question: What is authentic worship? Does speaking of God already constitute worship? Reading poetry to one another or singing folk songs on a Friday evening may be a beautifully satisfying aesthetic and emotional experience. But does it constitute authentic worship even when it takes place on *Erev Shabbat*? I submit that there is a need to be cautious about any forms of worship in which the participants seem to examine only the telescope and do not even look for the stars—in which they speak only of themselves and describe their private emotions, beautiful, touching, and moving as they may be, without relating them to a search for or awareness of an ultimate. To be sure, Hasidism, for instance, also

6

expresses a joyous affirmation of the glory of life; yet the Hasid always sees and experiences life as the creation of the Master of the universe. This is precisely the point of reference which seems to be missing in some of these experimental services—a quest for or sense of an ultimate reality beyond ourselves, no matter what name we give to it. In short, the question is whether the verbalization of private emotions can and should rightfully be defined as worship.

3) A third question: To what extent and in what ways can this kind of worship be defined as *Jewish?* Jewish experience is connected with a time dimension. Our symbols and observances, our rituals, celebrations and modes of self-expression embody and carry with them a sense of history and continuity that can protect the individual against utter subjectivity, privatism, and unhistorical individualism. Is there perhaps the danger that developments of this kind may lead to a new unhistorical sectarianism? What is distinctly and distinctively Jewish about private prayers of the kind frequently uttered in these services? Could they not conceivably also be said by a young Hindu, Christian or Buddhist? Until now, as Daniel Bell wrote recently, the characteristic of self-explorations has been that they have grown out of a sense of the past, out of the awareness that others had had similar experiences, and that there was not only a tradition of self-questioning and alienation but also a tradition of continuity. If everything emerges only out of myself and the situation in which I find myself, as if the past had never existed, what links me to the time dimensions of Jewish experiences?

4) Finally, there is the question of *community* or, more precisely, of Jewish *peoplehood.* What is taking place in these services can undoubtedly create a sense of community among those directly involved. But to what extent can these approaches be naturalized into the larger Jewish community? Vice versa, as long as the proponents of this type of experimental worship insist on remaining outside the institutions of the Jewish community, do they not pursue a course that sets them apart so utterly from the thought and life patterns of other Jews that they might simply become a privatistic

sect divorced from the rest of the Jewish people and its historic modes of self-expression? The historic forms and content of Jewish worship—Hebrew, the Shema, the Kiddush, the Torah reading—carry a sense of community not only in time but also in space. Does an approach to worship that is concerned primarily with the needs of a small group and the quest for its private satisfaction not involve the very real danger of separatism that may ultimately evolve into a complete sectarianism?

How valid, then, are these questions and considerations? Do such experiments and innovations as are included in this volume represent modes of authentic religious expression in a Jewish context? Are there any criteria by which such a judgment can be made? Do they constitute authentic worship? Can they succeed in bringing young people closer to Jewish thought, life, experience and self-expression? Vice versa, how real is the danger that they may lead to a radical discontinuity with Jewish life and the Jewish community both in time and space? If these risks exist, are they justified and should they be taken? If not, is it still possible to create an innovative approach to worship which will do justice to the needs and predicaments of our young people yet, at the same time, safeguard and maintain our continuity with the millenial patterns of Jewish life?

It is easier to ask these questions than to answer them. We should certainly not reject traditional patterns merely because they are old. At the same time, we must not blindly use tradition to justify a rejection of the symbols, images, or media in which our own time searches for truth and enduring values. We must not permit today's worship of "relevance" to erode or destroy the relevance of worship. The best answer may be a sensitive approach that orchestrates the language of tradition with the language of contemporary thought and culture.

We have compiled this volume because the services it contains represent a variety of attempts to achieve a successful orchestration of

8

tradition and innovation. We hope their publication will stimulate creative experimentation with similar or additional patterns and approaches that will satisfy the religious needs and aspirations of young Jews and, at the same time, safeguard the creative unity and continuity of the Jewish people.

II. *Creativity: Pathway to Tradition*
by Richard N. Levy

I shall reverse my colleague's procedure and attempt to deal with his questions before presenting some general observations on the goals of the kind of worship represented by this volume.

Alfred Jospe asks whether "an emphasis on love and celebration, a search for community, the quest for meaning (are) *ipso facto* 'religious' by definition." I believe they can be seen as *dimensions* of religiosity. The point is whether the manner in which they are articulated or evoked is a specifically religious mode. I have seen all those values emerge out of a discussion on Shabbat based on Abraham Heschel's *The Sabbath,* which preceded one of the services included in this anthology. I agree that we do our students a disservice when we emphasize only love, community, "meaning," etc.; however, when we employ techniques whereby aspects of Jewish tradition can lead to the creation of those values, we do them a great boon.

Clearly, to encourage the development of these values through the rubric and concepts of the Jewish prayer structure is also a way of avoiding the great danger of which my colleague rightly warns— a tendency toward separation from the wider Jewish community. Yet through what forms is that community expressed? Expression through its texts is the most valid, I think, because the texts are unspoiled by the diseases of institutionalization. The community is much less validly expressed through its institutions, and merely to continue conducting services out of the standard prayer books because otherwise students will not be able to be fed back into the organized community upon graduation, is an inappropriate response to the value of *klal Yisrael.* Rather, knowing how sterile most of the institutions in the Jewish community are, it is our duty to encourage students to develop alternative models while on campus, encouraging them to continue after graduation, or assisting students

11

to introduce them into existing synagogues and other structures. Knowing how desperately older Jews (including rabbis!) caught in the toils of these institutions want them to become more responsive, I am convinced that we shall be benefitting the wider Jewish community and not harming it by our encouragement of models for alternative structures of prayer, study, and action.

The question is, of course: Must these models conform to any criteria at all in order to be considered "Jewish"? The issue is not the use of specific techniques—free expression of feelings, introduction of flowers, touching, dance, candlelight, etc. Obviously there is nothing in these techniques that is intrinsically religious, worshipful, Judaic, or Jewish. If these techniques are used to increase the significance of the themes in a traditional prayer structure, the *matbea' ha-tefila*, the techniques do not detract from, and indeed may greatly enhance, the Jewishness of the service. The problem is whether the use of these techniques without any traditional undergirding provides for authentic celebrations of Jewish occasions.

There are those who argue that it is enough merely to bring alienated Jews together on Shabbat to read statements of sentiments and aspirations in keeping with their present lifestyles and convictions. The assumption is that they will know they have come together as Jews, in a Jewish place, for a celebration of a Jewish event. If it is a good experience, they will return; and as they feel more and more at home, their resistance to the introduction of specifically Jewish texts and rituals will disappear. But what is likely to be bothering most of these alienated worshippers, as we shall indicate more fully below, is not so much the Jewishness of a text as their early experiences with it. If they are permitted to express their feelings about some of these experiences and about the texts themselves, the group may then realistically help them move from negative to positive feelings. If we delay the process of confronting the texts whose associations are the main source of their alienation, we shall thereby delay the process whereby the alienated come to feel at home in a *Jewish* environment of their own creation. Too often a totally nonstructured service, lacking any Jewish elements, helps a worshiper relate only to those parts of himself with which he feels at ease. Unless we help him relate to the Jewish part of himself as well, we shall not help him work toward the fullest integration of his being.

What is the relation between personal integration and the worship of God? One of the most useful aspects of Alfred Jospe's questions is his insistence that we confront the problem of God-language in creative prayer: "Speaking *of* God may not, or at least not yet, be speaking *to* God or listening to Him." It is often very difficult to write prayers treating God in the second person, perhaps deriving from an awareness of other people's difficulty in speaking directly to God. My colleague takes note of this in his important Rosenzweigian words, "not yet." For people who have not experienced a responsive presence at the other end of their prayers, the third person is often a less obstructive means of creating a mood in which they might approach such a presence by talking about it. The use of the third person in Jewish prayer is hardly untraditional, and to leave a person free to feel himself into that presence, letting him walk slowly around and around and finally enter in, is preferable to throwing him in, gagging and struggling, by the obtrusive use of the second person.

It is, surely, a mistake to confuse communion with oneself and communion with the divine. Yet the first is often a prerequisite for the second, if one is ever to develop the trust to reach out beyond oneself, enter into relationship with divinity, and yet know that one will not lose one's own identity there, but may return to normal life because he is too strong and worthwhile and integrated a person ever to lose his identity. Moreover, while it is important to know that we shall not find the stars by taking apart the telescope, it may be important to take it apart first in order to learn enough about the instrument to trust the image of reality it will present to our eye. The danger is, of course, that we may become so entranced with the instrument that we lose sight of the reality beyond, which is the ultimate goal of prayer.

I have already alluded to some of the negative feelings about past experience which often obscure the reality which the worshiper is seeking. No creative service will begin to develop positive feelings for prayer unless it enables the worshiper to come to grips with at least three of these negative attitudes: 1) *doubt* regarding the value of prayer in his life; 2) *ignorance* about the meaning of the Jewish prayer service; 3) *anger* that too often public worship forces him into the role of a passive spectator, accentuating the impotence he feels in life rather than helping him to overcome it.

To deal with the first, a good service should include prayers which articulate some frequently encountered doubts (e.g., about God, the purpose of prayer, the role of suffering and compassion) and so encourage the worshiper, by joining other doubters in voicing his doubts aloud, to eliminate much of his guilt about his doubts. It should also include some new interpretations of the prayers which are the subject of his doubt so that he may find significant meanings there for himself and realize that he can participate wholeheartedly in a service which both recognizes doubt and encourages a struggle toward a modus vivendi with it.

One of the pitfalls of many creative liturgists is their assumption that a "creative" service in and of itself will dispel the doubts which arise through the use of printed prayerbooks. But clearly a liturgist may write a service which beautifully expresses his own theology, but which will cause as many problems to others who read his service, each of whom has his own theology, as the most theistic printed liturgy. To be truly "creative", a service must include opportunities for each individual to respond to the prayers and express his own feelings either aloud or to himself.

Aside from theological doubts, the service should take account of an ethical doubt as well: What right have we to sit here praying when the world around us is in flames? The service could convey that understanding of prayer which is an essential of non-Orthodox worship: the end of prayer is not only in itself (as it is for Jews who retain the binding character of the *mitzvot,* one of which is prayer), but can be seen as well to lie in the ethical actions to which the service should impel the worshiper after he has left the prayer room. At the service's end, therefore, the Reader might well desire to make that impulsion specific by scheduling a discussion or an action workshop after the Kiddush has been recited and refreshments have been served. The problem of *ignorance* should be confronted through the retention of the traditional prayer structure and the inclusion of contemporary interpretations of much traditional material. It is important that the worshiper feel that this is not a "substitute" service, but a way into understanding the regular Jewish prayer service. Each traditional section (e.g., *Kabbalat Shabbat, Shma u'Virkhoteha, Amida, Aleynu*) should include sufficient interpretive material so that a worshiper who has participated in this service for several months (though not, ideally, the same format every week) should be able to enter a regular service and read into its prayers the understandings internalized at the creative service.

Why should we adhere to these traditional forms? Is not the main purpose of "creative," experimental worship to break away from old forms, to enable people to pray free from restrictive words and theologies? It is my feeling that the Jewish service with the most profound meaning is the traditional service, davened in the traditional manner. But those profundities are denied worshipers who lack a knowledge of the Siddur sufficient to infuse the words they read in Hebrew or English with the meanings with which the traditional prayers overflow. Our purpose in "creative" worship should be to enable those not now accustomed to traditional prayer to participate in its profundity. Our aim, therefore, should not be to replace permanently any prayer book now extant, but to infuse the worshiper with both a knowledge of the possibilities of the prayers and a confidence that he can be at home in a service and has the right to participate in his own way. We should furnish him with sufficient contemporary treatments of traditional prayers that when he learns how to daven he can read in some of the interpretations contained in our service so that he can transcend the literal meaning of words and concepts that may repel him, to find his own meanings behind the common words he may wish to retain as a reminder of his bond with his people and their common past.

Thus another purpose of creative worship should be to teach a student how to daven; but for this we need not write a new service, but rather help a worshiper ease himself into the rhythmic mood of concentration that davening demands. Rabbi Zalman Schachter has helped many of us to do this not only in Hebrew but in English as well, and opportunities are presented in this volume for "Non-Unison Davening" of vernacular prayers rendered in the laconic, poetic, and repetitive style of the original Hebrew.

It is also important to develop the realization in young, socially concerned Jewish worshipers that through Jewish texts they can be helped to articulate some of their social concerns, that their *prayer* can articulate them, not merely expressing that which they have derived from other places, but offering new insights into social problems and their solutions. Many of the services included in this volume contain teaching material which can illuminate not only the nature of Jewish prayer, but the depth of Jewish social ethics as well. A Jewish service begins by reminding Israel that God is One and concludes with the hope that all the world will come to know His Oneness; such worship is a most fitting vehicle for an experience of the interrelatedness of all of life's concerns, and of the integrated facets of the Jewish human person. If those who pray the services in this book come no closer to an understanding of traditional prayer than a realization of that unity, we shall be more than content.

For this reason the third purpose of creative worship is also of great importance, namely the confrontation with the sense of *alienation* which so much mass worship produces. In addition to an integrated experience contained in the written text, a service should offer many opportunities for silent prayer, which encourage the worshiper to explore his own thoughts and yearnings; and there should be repeated opportunities for sharing those private thoughts with others, which can break down the sense of isolation from other worshipers which most large-group worship creates. People may be asked at the start of a service to introduce themselves to those sitting near them; alternate rows may be asked to turn around to face those behind them for discussions, or to share prayers with each other. This obvious sharing of thoughts and ideas can create a very important mood in the service, not merely of good feeling as is the case with some unstructured creative prayer, but of participation as well in the content of Jewish prayer. Even when the congregation is merely reading printed prayers in unison, they may be helped to experience each other's presence through what we have called "antiphonal readings," in which half the congregation (males or females, right side or left side) reads a paragraph and the other half responds.

One of the elements promoting the alienation of worshipers in the usual service is the sense of remoteness of the rabbi or reader. By participating in the introductions, discussions, and a concluding blessing in which each worshiper expresses a Sabbath blessing to his neighbor, the reader should create a model not for an isolated, rigid worshiper, but for a participant free to move about, to share his own feelings of the service (though not to let his feelings dominate—hence he should offer his interpretation of reading last, in emulation of Sanhedrin procedure), to come out from behind the pulpit and demonstrate that he is, after all, but another worshiper. A strolling cantor with his guitar can provide another model of a participating worshiper.

A word is in order about the texts of creative prayers. The Siddur is an anthology compiled over the centuries. Our services should attempt to reflect something of that, through a mixture of Biblical, rabbinic, traditional liturgical, and contemporary readings. But it should not stop there. Some prayers can be composed especially for the service, representing an anthology of feelings of the worshipers themselves, underscored by the opportunities to express those feelings in silence or within the congregation. Not only will there be a juxtaposition of traditional and contemporary, of others' prayers and private prayers, but also a juxtaposition of Hebrew and English, seldom in exact translation, usually in paraphrase, hopefully arousing in the Hebraically ignorant the realization that the purpose of Hebrew is not the mere incantation of pro forma syllables, but the opening of a door into some very old experiences through a language whose words convey some profound ideas. While we do not wish the new prayers we write to be too prolix, we must also be aware that too simplistic a style and vocabulary can cause a worshiper to tire after but a few readings of the service. On the other hand, long, rolling periods are less suitable for davening than are the short, often laconic prayers which more faithfully reflect the style of the Hebrew.

Behind all work in creative liturgy must lie the conviction that we are heirs to a brilliant and profound tradition. But we work with Jews who not only have learned precious little about that tradition, but who often have tried to cut their heritage out of themselves, because poor Jewish education and a seemingly more attractive non-Jewish, "universal," society turned the Jewish part of them to dross. Happily, the surgery has not been successful—or rather, as to poor young Isaac, the angel of insight has come just in time. Young Jews are coming increasingly to realize that they must contribute something special of their own to universal society, else they shall be parasites upon it; they are coming to realize that the solution to the poor education and uninspiring worship that so often marked their childhood now lies, as for Job, in the creativity of their own right hand. Concrete cities, choking air, frightened authorities, endless warfare without and within are not—cannot be—the only realities in our lives. Young Jews, and not-so-young, wish to relate to a higher reality whatever its nature, whatever its name. The services in this book are a sample of the responses to this desperate realization. The world around us is in flames; we offer here some words and gestures, music and silence as well as calls to action, through which each of us might gain the courage and the faith to help save it.

All the services included in this volume were originally written for use in Hillel Foundations around the country. They are the work of students and Hillel directors, separately or in partnership.

We have attempted to include a wide variety within each of the three basic categories of creative worship—insertions into a traditional service, completely new texts, and free-flowing unstructured formats in a variety of settings.

The central part of this volume presents new service texts, which we have arranged in three categories: Sabbath evening services, services on special themes, services for Purim and Hanukkah. Though virtually all of these services were written for use on Friday evenings, most are suitable for Shabbat morning as well with the addition of a Torah reading ("New Windows on an Ancient Day" already includes one). With the omission of some specific references to Shabbat the services for Purim and Hanukkah may be used independent of a Shabbat service.

A word about the individual service texts:

General Sabbath Evening Services

1) "New Windows on an Ancient Day." Commissioned and published by the Central Conference of American Rabbis, this service was written by Rabbi Richard N. Levy. It is made up of material originally used at the Hillel Council at UCLA. Some of its material will also be found in its original form in other services in this volume. It follows the basic outline of the *matbea' ha-tefila,* while at the same time interpreting traditional prayers both in the light of other traditional material and contemporary social concerns. It offers several opportunities for worshipers to express their own prayers and feelings.

2) "The Spark". A new service, this text was written by Rachel (Mrs. Moshe) Adler originally for use at Hillel at San Fernando Valley State College in Los Angeles. It consists of many poetic

translations and interpretations of the basic prayers of a traditional service, woven together around the kabbalistic theme of the liberation of the divine spark from the material shells in which it has become encased. Since all Hebrew prayers are transliterated, it is designed to be used by worshipers with no knowledge of Hebrew, as well as those interested in the mystic strain of Jewish tradition.

3) "The Sabbath Bridge." Written by Robert Ganz, a student at the University of Rochester, this service intends to meld worship with action—the building of a bridge out of wood beams and cinder blocks as a symbol of the bridge between the holy Sabbath and the ordinary weekdays. While traditional prayers are used, they are not found in their accustomed order. The worship, construction, and final walking across the bridge that all have built provides a unique experience of worship as the creation of a Shabbat community.

4) "Silence." An original script written and coordinated by Debra Sowald, a student at Case-Western Reserve University, and including material written by Susan Edison, a senior at Eastmoor Senior High School in Columbus, Ohio. "Silence" is not a service in itself but a dramatic reading to be inserted into one of the conventional structures of worship.

5) "Noah's Sabbath." Compiled by Rabbi Richard N. Levy and presented originally at UCLA, this service attempts to relate a Biblical tale with contemporary overtones through the course of a Friday evening service, arranged according to the traditional order of prayers. Communication between worshippers is provided, and the readings following Noah's sending out of raven and dove are intended to stimulate reflection on the position of blacks, Jews, and other whites in contemporary society. Folk and contemporary songs dealing with the Noah story, rain, and animals are included.

6) "A Visit to Sodom: A Torah Reading in Mixed Media." Arranged by Rabbi Richard N. Levy, this script is a utilization of the Sodom and Gomorra account in *Parasha Vayera* (Gen. 19) through a dramatic reading, recorded music, slides, and film. The

service requires a reader and a cantor who will chant selected sections of the Torah portion either in Hebrew or in English, as the text indicates. Though there are no specific provisions for it in the script, dance may also be introduced into the dramatization at several points. The intent of the text is to press middle-class Jews into confronting the eternal question of those contemplating a society in chaos, "What can I do?"

7) "Havdalah." The Havdalah service offers a unique setting for an extemporaneous response to symbols and to Shabbat. As a result the responses written in this service should be used primarily as suggestions. If the reader substitutes his own words for those of the printed text, he will allow a more natural mood to develop, creating an impressive experience of sharing. Much of the warmth of Havdalah comes from turning aside from printed materials and creating instead a more simple climate of relating to symbol, to Shabbat, to self and to others. Participants should not be required to hold a printed text.

Through the twisted candle, wine, and spices, the appeal of Havdalah is to all the senses, and these symbols can be shared so all present feel themselves to be true participants. The reader may begin by lighting the candle, talking about Havdalah and Shabbat, and then go to the wine and the spices. The blessings are sung together, and can be taught orally very quickly. Most already know the beginning of each blessing. After the spices are shared, a blessing is sung for the light of the candle, and then all share the wine. The candle is put out, and the service concluded. The reader may also incorporate comments about the kind of experience Shabbat has been for his group, and the expression of appropriate hopes for all in the week to come. The script was written by Rabbi Theodore G. Falcon, of the California State University at Northridge.

Sabbath Evening Services on Special Themes

1) "The American Jew." Presented by students at UCLA, this service involves the congregation in the confrontation between Jewish values and American culture. The lengthy Kabbalat Shab-

bat consists of a number of texts describing the early experiences of Jewish settlers in the United States, culminating with Charles Reznikoff's lament: "How difficult for me is Hebrew . . . how far have I been exiled, Zion", after which Kabbalat Shabbat concludes and the traditional service continues with untransliterated Hebrew and only slightly periphrastic translations of the Shema and its Blessings, reminding us of the unity of the Jewish people with itself and its tradition against the onslaught of all cultures. The Amidah is a compilation of prayers and aspirations for a different kind of American Jewish community, built by those who are now its children, concluding with the hope that is the Vay'chulu: as the Sabbath culminates the building of the world, so may that Sabbath come when the society we desire shall also have been completed. The service concludes with Aleynu and Kaddish, and includes two original songs on the theme in the contemporary mode. The service was compiled by Rabbi David M. Berner with the assistance of Karen Fox, Mitch Corber, Gerald Fisch, Evelyn Graziani, David Rosner and Suzanne Weiss.

2) "A Service for Israel." Written by Rabbi Stanley Ringler, Hillel Director at the University of Miami, this non-liturgical service evokes the historical experience of the Jew as he moves from his inception in his own land to landless exile, culminating in the Holocaust of European Jewry, to the rise of the Jewish state which emerges from the ashes of exile into "a complete unit of existence and experience," albeit to the accompaniment of continuing war yet also of unceasing hope for peace. The service conveys these themes through quotations from important documents and writers, solo readings and appropriate musical selections. Traditional prayer material is thus replaced by readings from different ages, reflecting the continuity of the hope for Zion throughout Jewish history. The service is suitable for Israel Independence Day observances regardless of whether they are conducted on Shabbat or on weekdays.

3) "A Day of Witness: A Service for Soviet Jews." Written by Rabbi Joel Poupko, Associate Hillel Director at the University of

Michigan, the script was prepared as a stage presentation of a trial of God for "crimes against the Jews of Russia." Although written in stage format, it is intended to be a form of prayer. The stage directions are intended only as suggestions and are not meant to limit future participants.

4) "A Service of Remembrance for the Six Million: On the Occasion of the Warsaw Ghetto Anniversary." Written by the late Rabbi Sheldon Gordon for the students at the University of Arizona and used in Hillel Foundations throughout the country, this is a moving compilation of readings on the theme of the Holocaust, confronting the problem of praying to God in its aftermath. The service follows the traditional order of prayers, interspersed with various readings from the Shoa literature.

5) "A Service of Jewish Giving." Written by Rabbi Richard Levy for a Pacific Regional Leadership Training Institute for Hillel participants in the United Jewish Appeal-United Jewish Welfare Fund campaign, the service attempts to provide opportunities not only for worship, but for the learning about traditional Jewish ideas of tzedakah, that kind of giving which is "justice". In addition, since the recipients of our gifts are Jews in all parts of the world, the service presents texts and music from the struggles of Soviet Jews, Israelis, and young American Jews trying to create a new kind of Jewish life on our own shores.

6) "A Service of Peace and Brotherhood." This text combines material from a service used at San Fernando Valley State College, originally written by Rabbi Aaron Opher for the Pacific Association of Reform Rabbis, with prayers written by students at the University of Arizona. The service contains several powerful litanies and poetic readings, offering opportunities for a number of readers to participate in the service.

7) "The Earth He Gave to Man." This service begins with an interpretation of Psalm 104 and continues with an expansion of a contemporary description of the Creation (or man's perversion of

it), written by Paul Flucke, into which are interwoven some contemporary songs and the basic elements of the traditional service. The Amidah is a series of readings on the interdependence of man, animals, and nature, followed by the traditional Vay'chulu which in context becomes not only a Biblical description of God's rest from the Creation, but a contemporary prayer that man might rest from his destruction of that Creation. This service was compiled by Rabbi David Berner of Hillel at UCLA, with the assistance of the following students: Gerald Fisch, Carrie Small, Suzanne Weiss, Bruce and Monica Devons, Evelyn Graziani, and Karen Fox.

Services for Hanukkah and Purim

1) "An Anticipation of Purim." Written by Rabbi Richard N. Levy at UCLA, this service with but a few excisions can become a service for the Eve of Purim itself. It attempts to interpret some of the themes and rituals of Purim in terms of contemporary problems, including a paraphrase of the Avot prayer in the Amidah which tries to relate that prayer to the changing needs and roles of women. In the middle of the service there is room for a Megillah reading or a creative retelling of the story by members of the congregation, each of whom might add a sentence to what has gone before, accompanied by greggers, if desired. Humorous folk songs of Purim are included to temper the serious themes of the service.

2) "A Hanukkah Service of Lights." Originally written for students at the University of Arizona to accompany the lighting of the Hanukkah candles, we have inserted appropriate portions of a regular service to enable it to be used as a complete Friday evening or Hanukkah service. If desired, the liturgical insertions can be omitted and only the responsive readings for each of the eight candles used.

3) "Service for Shabbat Hanukkah." This service emphasizes some of the antinomies present in the Hanukkah season: darkness and light, war and opposition to war (including the singing of the Vilna Partisans' Song and *lo yisa goy*), fidelity to Jewish culture and the seduction of other cultures, the unity of God and the multiplicity of approaches to Him, etc. The service concludes with the lighting of Hanukkah candles. It was compiled by Rabbi Richard N. Levy for students at UCLA.

Selections may be taken from any of these services and included in a traditional service, or completely new services may be compiled from readings selected herein. For example:

Kabbalat Shabbat	*from*	"The Spark" (which includes
	"	versions of the rest of the
		prayers as well)
Maariv Aravim	"	"The Spark"
Ahavah Rabah	"	"The American Jew"
Shema, 1st paragraph	"	"A Service of Jewish Giving"
Shema, 2nd paragraph	"	"The Spark"
Shema, 3rd paragraph	"	"The Spark"
Hashkivenu	"	"Noah's Sabbath"
Avot	"	"An Anticipation of Purim"
Gevurot	"	"An Anticipation of Purim"
		or "Noah's Sabbath"
Kedushah	"	"An Anticipation of Purim"
Sabbath insertion	"	"New Windows"
Concluding Benedictions	"	"New Windows"
Aleynu	"	"New Windows"

The third variety of creative services, the free-flowing "environment", is presented with several very different examples in section III, with its own introduction.

Criteria for Inclusion

We have confined ourselves in this volume to services for Shabbat evening and the minor festivals, written by students or directors in B'nai B'rith Hillel Foundations. We hope to publish texts for the major festivals and the High Holydays at a later time. Although most of these services contain material from other sources, we have included only those scripts which have integrated external material into a recognizable theme or structure, thus forming a new creation even from material written by others.

Adequacy of literary style and language was a second criterion. While unpolished language may well be acceptable in a service that is shared by one's own group, mere delight in the creativity of one's

26

friends or acquaintances is hardly an adequate criterion in a service that seeks to appeal to those outside one's own circle. Since the purpose of a prayer text is less to demonstrate the author's spirituality than to elicit spiritual feelings from the worshiper, we have tried to restrict the text to those which would perform this function. If there are prayers whose language is so elegant that it obstructs the expression of the worshiper's own feelings, we offer our apologies in the hope that he will feel encouraged to attempt the creation of his own prayer texts.

During the past few years, numerous experimental services as well as liturgical materials and supplementary readings have been published by rabbis and laymen for private circulation or public distribution. Most of these materials are readily accessible and were, therefore, not included in this collection which attempts to provide new material developed for and by the university community and generally not yet available.

Doing It Yourself

A concluding caveat. As we have indicated, there is no guarantee that a liturgy, however uplifting, created by one person, can reflect or express someone else's religious search. It is our hope that the services in this anthology will serve primarily as models for others, stimulating them to write their own liturgies, using our material if they wish, drawing on other sources if they prefer, or—most desirably—attempting to create their own prayers and settings. Blind reproduction is hardly a sign of creativity, and though each time a service is used a new experience results, it is important to develop a prayer experience that will reflect the special character of each group, however large or small, which is attempting to expand the opportunities for the expression of the religious needs of its members.

New worship opportunities can be created in a variety of ways. Contrary to popular conceptions, liturgies can be written by committees, or at least compiled by them, as those services in this book organized by Rabbi David Berner demonstrate. Guided by a knowledgeable adviser, a group of worshipers may gather to discuss the theme or the goals they wish a service to reflect, the structure of the traditional *matbea' ha-tefila,* and the problem of whether they wish the theme to follow the traditional structure or depart from it. If the former, the group might discuss how each of the parts of the service might be interpreted to carry forth the theme (though not so insistently that the meaning of the traditional prayer becomes lost and the service becomes a diatribe rather than an opportunity for worshipers to enter into the theme through prayer in their own way). Afterward, individual members of the group may be assigned to develop appropriate interpretations for the traditional sections, either through their own writing or by compiling suitable writings from elsewhere. The list of sources from which material in this volume is taken will provide the start of a useful bibliography for such a compilation.

* * * *

A group that does not wish to follow the traditional Jewish prayer structure, must of course develop its own outline for the way in which the service is to proceed. The adviser might encourage his liturgists to include some elements of a traditional service to assure that the project will have some Jewish associations, like familiar landmarks in a strange city. If the group agrees, the traditional material should not merely be inserted like unrelated foreign matter, but integrated with what has gone before and what will follow so that the Shema, for example, can help articulate the theme rather than obstruct the path of its development. Even if the traditional structure is not to be followed, some of the thematic progressions of a traditional service may be utilized, e.g., Praise (historically expressed through Kabbalat Shabbat, Shema and its Blessings), followed by Petition (Amidah), followed by a messianic vision of praise for petition granted (Aleynu); or, even more broadly, Israel's assertion of the oneness of the universe (Shema), followed by the hope for the realization of that unity which all men might bring into the universe (Aleynu). If the traditional prayers expressing such themes are not included, the service will still possess a Jewish authenticity if such traditional thematic development is followed.

Should the group determine that it does not want a fixed prayer text at all, some of the suggestions in our section on "Prayer Settings" might be utilized. Even in such a format the traditional structure can be followed if all worshipers, or a selected number, are each given a reading which relates to one of the prayers in the traditional service. The indications of these prayers can be quite specific (Barchu, Avot, Aleynu) or merely thematic (Kabbalat Shabbat, Praise, Petition), and a sensitive leader can help guide the group from one part of the traditional service to another by orally tying together the readings and initiating the singing of the responses which will identify the section of the service at which the group has arrived (L'cha Dodi, Barchu, Shema, Mi Chamocha, "May the Words of my mouth," Aleynu, Kaddish). Worshipers might be encouraged to express their feelings about each of the readings, with the leader attempting to develop the themes brought out by the group into an expression which will set the mood for the next prayer. However, if worshipers express anger or hostility toward a particular prayer, the leader must use all of his skill to enable the service to continue without rejecting the feelings of members of the group.

What is most important is a desire to try new modes, a willingness to fail and to permit others to fail, and—most important— a conviction that Jewish worship is profoundly significant, whether its garb be ancient or newly spun.

SHABBAT SERVICES

NEW WINDOWS ON AN ANCIENT DAY

THE PRAISE

MEDITATION FOR PRAISE

Our noisy day has now descended with the sun beyond our sight, and in the silence of our praying place we close the door upon the hectic joys and fears, the accomplishments and anguish, of the week that we have left behind. What was but moments ago the substance of our life has now become its memory, and what we did must now be woven into what we are. On this day we shall not do, but be: we are to walk the outer limits of our humanity, no longer ride unseeing through a world we only vaguely sense beneath our cushioned wheels. On this day heat and warmth and light must come from deep within ourselves; no longer can we tear apart the world to make our fire. On this day, but a breath away from our creation, we are to breathe in a world from which we may no longer feel apart, but as close as eye to blossom, and ear to the singing in the night. On this day we must open wide the windows behind which we have hidden from the world, and send forth hand and soul to learn where we have come, and what we have become.

BLESSING OVER LIGHTS
(responsively)

The night that settles on Shabbat is an illuminating darkness, which forces us to peer into reality and painfully make out the true shapes of our existence as they loom up from the obscurity of our uncaring lives.

The night that settles on Shabbat is followed by the night that draws the curtain on Shabbat, and to live within that darkness man must have the hopeful, healing warmth of light.

The gentle flame that gives us life knows no differences of place or color, and it burns as brightly from the simplest wick as from the most elegant taper.

The gentle flame that gives us life must struggle constantly before the winds of time, and he who would ignore its struggle consigns the flame to darkness, where each smoldering candle robs us of its warmth.

The gentle flame that gives us life is our sole beacon in our search to find the purpose of the world; out of the glaring darkness of its chaos we must struggle for the words that will bring light, that light and men might be.

בָּרוּךְ אַתָּה יְיָ אֱלֹהֵינוּ מֶלֶךְ הָעוֹלָם אֲשֶׁר קִדְּשָׁנוּ
בְּמִצְוֹתָיו וְצִוָּנוּ לְהַדְלִיק נֵר שֶׁל-שַׁבָּת:

Praised be the Lord our God, who makes us holy in the act of lighting candles, who lets us share the miracle of our people's life through light.

READER
(Alternative selections may be used where desired)

The flames that quiver on our altar
Summon now our weeklodged earthbound souls
To fly like creatures of the darkness toward their light
And kindle that sweet incense
Which will not pass from our caressing hands
Until the sun returns once more into his tent,
From which when sleep is through he does stride forth,
A bridegroom stepping from his chamber.

We know the sun,
For by the brilliance of these flames
Have we become a bridegroom
Quivering upon our evening altar
Waiting for the Sabbath who shall be our bride
To enter through the tent that is our lonely love
And wreathe us with aromas from a world just born.

Holy one with holy other,
The goblet shared which one day all will share with God,
The fragments pieced together of our shattered world,
We two shall stride forth down the light that is
This day,
And stars of goodness dancing overhead
Shall fly like creatures of the darkness
Toward our light.

SONG: LCHA DODI

לְכָה דוֹדִי לִקְרַאת כַּלָּה. פְּנֵי שַׁבָּת נְקַבְּלָה:

לִקְרַאת שַׁבָּת לְכוּ וְנֵלְכָה. כִּי הִיא מְקוֹר
הַבְּרָכָה. מֵראשׁ מִקֶּדֶם נְסוּכָה. סוֹף מַעֲשֶׂה
בְּמַחֲשָׁבָה תְּחִלָּה:

לְכָה דוֹדִי לִקְרַאת כַּלָּה. פְּנֵי שַׁבָּת נְקַבְּלָה:

הִתְעוֹרְרִי הִתְעוֹרְרִי. כִּי בָא אוֹרֵךְ קוּמִי אוֹרִי.
עוּרִי עוּרִי שִׁיר דַּבֵּרִי. כְּבוֹד יְיָ עָלַיִךְ נִגְלָה:

לְכָה דוֹדִי לִקְרַאת כַּלָּה. פְּנֵי שַׁבָּת נְקַבְּלָה:

בּוֹאִי בְשָׁלוֹם עֲטֶרֶת בַּעְלָהּ. גַּם בְּשִׂמְחָה
וּבְצָהֳלָה. תּוֹךְ אֱמוּנֵי עַם סְגֻלָּה. בּוֹאִי כַלָּה. בּוֹאִי
כַלָּה:

לְכָה דוֹדִי לִקְרַאת כַּלָּה. פְּנֵי שַׁבָּת נְקַבְּלָה:

Come my beloved to meet the bride,
Come welcome the Sabbath!

Come, let us meet the Sabbath,
The fountain of blessing, poured forth from of old,
Last act of creation, yet first in God's thought.

Come my beloved. . . .

Rise up, rise up, for your light has come,
Arise and shine!
Awake, awake, utter a song!
The glory of the Lord is revealed upon you.

Come my beloved. . . .

Enter in peace, O crown of your husband, in joy
    and exultation!
Amid the faithful of a treasured people,
Enter O bride! Enter, O bride!

Come my beloved. . . .

CONGREGATION

If our prayer were music only, we could surely sing our way into
the world we want and the heaven we desire, for each would find
his own words for the melody and from every song would pour a
hundred different prayers, each the unique creation of its author,
the prayer of the heart no different from the prayer of the lips. But
the ancient men who taught us music taught us words as well, and
while we pray their music we cannot always pray their words. The
urgent noises of our fragmented lives too often drown them out,
and a prayer which says Yes we often bury in a storm of Whys and
Hows, No Longers, and Not Yets.

READER

It was not always so. To speak the ancient words returns us to that simpler time when as children we understood that the world could be one, and that somehow it was ours. That understanding has become but a fragile hope, and yet to speak the words we used to speak is to give substance to that hope, which has remained though we and all our world have changed. Since that childhood time, other truths and many questions have found their home within our minds, but this truth we affirm tonight is the oldest we remember, and it reunites the person we are now with the person we were once long ago.

CONGREGATION
(rising)

The old words lead us all to blessing: for our lives that have emerged from the Nos and Yesses of the world; for the God who forever calls being forth from emptiness.

בָּרְכוּ אֶת־יְיָ הַמְבֹרָךְ:

Praise the Lord to Whom all praise is due.

בָּרוּךְ יְיָ הַמְבֹרָךְ לְעוֹלָם וָעֶד:

The Lord is praised; to Him all praise is due
forever and ever.

(Congregation seated)

READERS

Once we knew one truth, and it was cherished or discarded but it was one. Now we know the world can be perceived by many truths, and in the facts all men accept some men find lessons other men deny. Once we knew one kind of life, one morality, and it too we

39

adopted or we scorned, but right was clear and wrong was always wrong. Now we know that there are many rights, and what is wrong may well be what is wrong for you, but right for me. Yet we sense that some acts must be wrong for every man, and that beyond the many half-truths must be a single Truth all men may one day grasp. That clear way, that single truth, is what we seek to glimpse in coming here, to join our people who saw One, where others could see merely Now.

*   *   *   *

But we may not announce too soon that One has come. In every age have men arisen who would make their kingdom one, and unite by force all disparate beliefs and factions under their sway. Our people's lives have taught us that no man may institute the rule of One. In man's world, One has not yet come, and so there must be room for many, that the One may take root and spread abroad. The lives of many must be cultivated, lest a part of Oneness be cut off before its time has come. God is One, and some day His unity will be the sole existence for all men. Yet man is also one; the ancients tell us that the world was formed with but one man to teach us that one man's life is worth the life of the whole world, and so each man, and each unique belief, must be protected, for in each one is a breath of the ultimate One. Through the many, One may be obscured; yet only through the many may One become reality.

CONGREGATION
(rising)

The call to oneness is an affirmation and a goal, and to speak of God as One is to commit ourselves once more to our people's ancient quest:

שְׁמַע יִשְׂרָאֵל יְהֹוָה אֱלֹהֵינוּ יְהֹוָה אֶחָד:

Hear O Israel, the Lord our God, the Lord is one.

בָּרוּךְ שֵׁם כְּבוֹד מַלְכוּתוֹ לְעוֹלָם וָעֶד:

Praised be His name whose glorious kingdom is forever and ever.

CONGREGATION
(seated)

וְאָהַבְתָּ אֵת יְיָ אֱלֹהֶיךָ בְּכָל-לְבָבְךָ וּבְכָל-נַפְשְׁךָ
וּבְכָל-מְאֹדֶךָ: וְהָיוּ הַדְּבָרִים הָאֵלֶּה אֲשֶׁר אָנֹכִי
מְצַוְּךָ הַיּוֹם עַל-לְבָבֶךָ: וְשִׁנַּנְתָּם לְבָנֶיךָ וְדִבַּרְתָּ
בָּם. בְּשִׁבְתְּךָ בְּבֵיתֶךָ וּבְלֶכְתְּךָ בַדֶּרֶךְ וּבְשָׁכְבְּךָ
וּבְקוּמֶךָ: וּקְשַׁרְתָּם לְאוֹת עַל-יָדֶךָ. וְהָיוּ לְטֹטָפֹת
בֵּין עֵינֶיךָ: וּכְתַבְתָּם עַל-מְזֻזוֹת בֵּיתֶךָ וּבִשְׁעָרֶיךָ:
לְמַעַן תִּזְכְּרוּ וַעֲשִׂיתֶם אֶת-כָּל-מִצְוֹתָי וִהְיִיתֶם
קְדֹשִׁים לֵאלֹהֵיכֶם: אֲנִי יְיָ אֱלֹהֵיכֶם:

RESPONSIVE READING

You shall love the Lord your God with all your heart, with all your soul, and with all your might.

> In the eyes of the One God, there is no dichotomy of here and there, of me and them. They and I are one; here is there, and there is here. Oceans divide us; God's presence unites us.

And these words which I command you this day shall be upon your heart.

> To pray is to stake our very existence, our right to live, on the truth and on the supreme importance of that which we pray for. Prayer, then, is radical commitment, a dangerous involvement in the life of God.

You shall teach them diligently to your children, and shall speak of them when you sit in your house, when you walk on the road, when you lie down, and when you rise up.

The world is not the same since Auschwitz and Hiroshima. The decisions we make, the values we teach must be pondered not only in the halls of learning but also before the inmates in extermination camps, and in the sight of the mushroom of a nuclear explosion.

You shall bind them for a sign upon your hand, and they shall be for frontlets between your eyes.

The groan deepens, the combat burns, the wailing cry does not abate. In a free society, all are involved in what some are doing. Some are guilty, all are responsible.

You shall write them upon the doorposts of your house and upon your gates.

Some are guilty, all are responsible.

That you may remember and do all my commandments and be holy before your God.

For my people's sake I will not keep silent,
For mankind's sake I will not rest.
Until the vindication of humanity goes forth as brightness,
And peace for all men as a burning torch.

ANTIPHONAL READING
(Congregants facing right side of pulpit begin reading;
congregants facing left side respond)

Redemption will not come while senseless hatred rules the earth, and men and heaven hide their faces from each other.

Redemption will not come until love comes to rule the earth, and men reveal their faces to each other, that God may reveal His face to men.

Redemption will not come until men mourn the exile of God's presence, and yearn for its return.

Redemption will not come until men return out of their exile from each other, and Isaac and Ishmael, Jacob and Esau, can embrace upon the peaceful shores of love.

Redemption will not come until we each can pray for the wicked of the world—until we each can love the wicked as ourselves.

Redemption will not come until we search out the holy sparks of God that have gone astray in wicked men, and bring them back to their true selves.

Redemption will not come until we see the flaws in our own souls, and struggle to efface them; we shall be redeemed only insofar as we can see ourselves.

Redemption will not come until each man realizes the uniqueness of his being, and attunes his very special self to its perfection.

Redemption will not come until we renounce excessive self-concern, and allow our hearts to be moved enough by the misery of men to dare what must be dared.

Redemption will not come until a time we cannot know, when out of our turmoil and travail a new world may be born.

Praised be the Lord, Who will fulfill the time of redemption for Israel and for all mankind.

מִי־כָמֹכָה בָּאֵלִם יְיָ מִי כָּמֹכָה נֶאְדָּר בַּקֹּדֶשׁ
נוֹרָא תְהִלֹּת עֹשֵׂה פֶלֶא:
מַלְכוּתְךָ רָאוּ בָנֶיךָ בּוֹקֵעַ יָם לִפְנֵי מֹשֶׁה זֶה
אֵלִי עָנוּ וְאָמְרוּ.
יְיָ יִמְלֹךְ לְעֹלָם וָעֶד:
וְנֶאֱמַר כִּי־פָדָה יְיָ אֶת־יַעֲקֹב וּגְאָלוֹ מִיַּד חָזָק
מִמֶּנּוּ. בָּרוּךְ אַתָּה יְיָ גָּאַל יִשְׂרָאֵל:

43

(From the travail of Egyptian bondage, our forefathers emerged from their redemption by the Red Sea and sang this song of praise to God:

Who is like You, O Lord, compared to the gods men worship? Who is like You, majestic in holiness, awesome in splendor, doing wonders? The Lord will reign forever and ever.)

A SABBATH SONG

In celebration of the foretaste of redemption which is the Seventh Day

וְשָׁמְרוּ בְנֵי יִשְׂרָאֵל אֶת־הַשַּׁבָּת לַעֲשׂוֹת אֶת־הַשַּׁבָּת

לְדֹרֹתָם בְּרִית עוֹלָם: בֵּינִי וּבֵין בְּנֵי יִשְׂרָאֵל אוֹת

הִיא לְעֹלָם כִּי־שֵׁשֶׁת יָמִים עָשָׂה יְהֹוָה אֶת־הַשָּׁמַיִם

וְאֶת־הָאָרֶץ וּבַיּוֹם הַשְּׁבִיעִי שָׁבַת וַיִּנָּפַשׁ:

(Alternative selections may be used)

THE PRAYER

MEDITATION FOR PRAYER

To praise God and His Creation is to celebrate the world to which we have been born; it is to dig beneath its sorrow and injustice to find a beauty in our lives which might redeem the ugliness too easily apparent. To praise is to accept the rhythms of the life we know and seek God's presence through our workday song. And yet sometimes that song constricts His presence, and ugliness and grief drown out the strains we love. Then we long for bolder sounds, for rhythms that might break a cycle in which sorrow always follows joy and celebration of the right is incomplete without a condemnation of the wrong. Praise of the world that is can linger on our lips just so long, and then we must cry out that there are worlds which we shall not accept, that there are evils, cruelties and horrors which we shall not let our celebration drown. These, rather, we must point to, rage at and denounce before those who would insist

44

that whatever is unjust must be unreal. And so our praise is not complete until we also pray, until we take the world our Sabbath vision celebrates and make of it the text of a new song, shattering the rhythms of the life we know in a chorus of resolve to wipe out cruelty and ugliness and write an anthem which all men might sing in celebration of a world of justice, love and peace.

READER

Our fathers prayed for that world in voices much more eloquent than ours, each through his own experience of God, each through his own private name for the vision that his people shared. Abraham, who knew the fervor of morning prayer, pled the cause of cities; Isaac understood the fragility of life, and prayed in the afternoon for love; and when the sun had set Jacob offered up his night prayer as a ladder reaching into heaven, and gained the strength, in later days, to turn aside aggression with the quiet confidence of peace. To all their prayers came the response that hope would ultimately rest with those who one day would rise up to be their seed, and so their charge has thundered down to us: so act that others might find blessing through our lives.

To pray is to stake our very existence, our right to live, on the truth and on the supreme importance of that which we pray for. Prayer, then, is radical commitment, a dangerous involvement in a life that could be God's.

בָּרוּךְ אַתָּה יְיָ אֱלֹהֵינוּ וֵאלֹהֵי אֲבוֹתֵינוּ. אֱלֹהֵי
אַבְרָהָם אֱלֹהֵי יִצְחָק וֵאלֹהֵי יַעֲקֹב. הָאֵל הַגָּדוֹל
הַגִּבּוֹר וְהַנּוֹרָא. אֵל עֶלְיוֹן. גּוֹמֵל חֲסָדִים טוֹבִים.
וְקֹנֵה הַכֹּל וְזוֹכֵר חַסְדֵי אָבוֹת. וּמֵבִיא גְאֻלָּה לִבְנֵי
בְנֵיהֶם. לְמַעַן שְׁמוֹ בְּאַהֲבָה: מֶלֶךְ עוֹזֵר וּמוֹשִׁיעַ
וּמָגֵן. בָּרוּךְ אַתָּה יְיָ מָגֵן אַבְרָהָם:

Blessed be the God whose presence was our fathers' shield, whose promise is our hope.

RESPONSIVE READING

אַתָּה גִבּוֹר לְעוֹלָם אֲדֹנָי. מְחַיֶּה מֵתִים אַתָּה. רַב לְהוֹשִׁיעַ.

We pray that we might stand before the Power whose gift is life, who quickens those who have forgotten how to live on earth.

מַשִּׁיב הָרוּחַ וּמוֹרִיד הַגֶּשֶׁם:

We pray for winds that will disperse the choking air about our lives, for cleansing rains that make parched hopes flower and give un-creative lives the strength to rise up toward the sun.

מְכַלְכֵּל חַיִּים בְּחֶסֶד. מְחַיֶּה מֵתִים בְּרַחֲמִים רַבִּים.

We pray for love that will encompass us for no reason save that we are human, for love through which defeated souls may blossom into beings who have gained power over their own lives.

סוֹמֵךְ נוֹפְלִים וְרוֹפֵא חוֹלִים וּמַתִּיר אֲסוּרִים. וּמְקַיֵּם אֱמוּנָתוֹ לִישֵׁנֵי עָפָר.

We pray to stand upright, we fallen; to be healed, we sufferers of the sickness of our kind; we pray that we might break the bonds that keep us from the world of beauty and from our own authentic selves.

מִי כָמוֹךָ בַּעַל גְּבוּרוֹת וּמִי דוֹמֶה לָּךְ. מֶלֶךְ מֵמִית וּמְחַיֶּה וּמַצְמִיחַ יְשׁוּעָה.

We pray that we might walk within the garden of a life of purpose, our own powers in touch with the Power in the world, that we might find the meaning of the earth.

וְנֶאֱמָן אַתָּה לְהַחֲיוֹת מֵתִים. בָּרוּךְ אַתָּה יְיָ מְחַיֶּה הַמֵּתִים:

Blessed be the God whose gift is life, whose cleansing rains let parched souls flower toward the sun.

46

אַתָּה קָדוֹשׁ וְשִׁמְךָ קָדוֹשׁ וּקְדוֹשִׁים בְּכָל־יוֹם
יְהַלְלוּךָ סֶּלָה. בָּרוּךְ אַתָּה יְיָ הָאֵל הַקָּדוֹשׁ:

Blessed be the God whose name is uttered in the holy acts of every-
day, whose holy ground our words now seek in the blazing silence
of a prayer.

SILENT PRAYER
(or such other prayer as the heart may prompt)

אֱלֹהֵינוּ וֵאלֹהֵי אֲבוֹתֵינוּ. רְצֵה בִמְנוּחָתֵנוּ קַדְּשֵׁנוּ
בְּמִצְוֹתֶיךָ וְתֵן חֶלְקֵנוּ בְּתוֹרָתֶךָ. שַׂבְּעֵנוּ מִטּוּבֶךָ
וְשַׂמְּחֵנוּ בִּישׁוּעָתֶךָ. וְטַהֵר לִבֵּנוּ לְעָבְדְּךָ בֶּאֱמֶת.
וְהַנְחִילֵנוּ יְיָ אֱלֹהֵינוּ בְּאַהֲבָה וּבְרָצוֹן שַׁבַּת קָדְשֶׁךָ.
וְיָנוּחוּ בָהּ יִשְׂרָאֵל מְקַדְּשֵׁי שְׁמֶךָ. בָּרוּךְ אַתָּה יְיָ
מְקַדֵּשׁ הַשַּׁבָּת:

Our God and God of our fathers,
May the rest we choose for this Shabbat be pleasing.
May the mitzvot we undertake bring us near
    to holiness.
May the portion which is ours in Torah
    remain with us as a loved one's gift.
Let us sense the joy of mastering our own
    lives,
Yet know the purity of a heart which reaches
    out to serve our brothers.
Let us touch the love and holiness of this day
    as we would caress a precious heirloom,
And from its touch find rest.
God, who leads men into the holiness of Shabbat,
You are blessed.

SHARING OF PRAYER

(If you are so moved, you might wish to share your prayer with someone near you.)

יִהְיוּ לְרָצוֹן אִמְרֵי־פִי וְהֶגְיוֹן לִבִּי לְפָנֶיךָ. יְיָ צוּרִי וְגוֹאֲלִי:

May the words of my mouth and the meditations of my heart be acceptable in Your sight, O Lord, my Rock and my Redeemer. Amen.

RESPONSIVE READING

Our single prayers are thought and uttered, and the world is different, for it now contains these new yearnings we have shared. Yet none beside ourselves can feel the change, and we cannot be content to merely offer up our prayers, and not vow as well to strive for their fulfillment. There are promises and there are prayers, but there is not yet justice, and there is not yet peace.

The prophet said: "In the end of days the Lord shall judge between the nations, and they shall beat their swords into plowshares and their spears into pruninghooks." But we cannot wait until the end of days for judgment, and surely not for peace.

The rabbi said: "He who makes peace in his house is as though he had brought peace to all of Israel, indeed, even to all the world." If peace is to be more than a distant vision, we must do the work of peace ourselves; if peace is to be brought to the world, we must bring peace to our families and our communities.

The psalmist said: "Seek peace, and pursue it:" be not content merely to make peace in your own household; go forth to work for peace wherever men are struggling in its cause.

יְהוָֹה עֹז לְעַמּוֹ יִתֵּן. יְהוָֹה יְבָרֵךְ אֶת־עַמּוֹ בַשָּׁלוֹם:

May God give his people strength, that they might work for peace.

עֹשֶׂה שָׁלוֹם בִּמְרוֹמָיו. הוּא יַעֲשֶׂה שָׁלוֹם עָלֵינוּ
וְעַל כָּל־יִשְׂרָאֵל וְאִמְרוּ אָמֵן:

May God who has made peace among the stars, enable us to make peace here on earth.

יִשָּׂא יְיָ פָּנָיו אֵלֶיךָ וְיָשֵׂם לְךָ שָׁלוֹם:

May God from whom we are so often hid, reveal the brightness of His countenance to us, and place the power of peace in our outstretched, longing, yearning hands.

(A Song of Peace is sung)

TORAH SERVICE
(As the Song of Peace concludes, the ark is opened)

READER

The road to peace is a dark and twisting path, and fortunate is he whose light can guide him to its end. Our light is Torah, and our lamp mitzvot; the ways of Torah are pleasing ways, and all her paths are peace. Said the rabbis: "Students of Torah increase the peace of the world," for it is said: "When all your children are taught of the Lord, great will be the peace of your children." Through Torah we too shall become taught of the Lord, and so discover the acts which can lead us into a life of peace, that we might join with all the children of God to become builders of a single, peaceful world.

READER AND CONGREGATION
שְׁמַע יִשְׂרָאֵל יְהוָֹה אֱלֹהֵינוּ יְהוָֹה אֶחָד:

SONG

לְךָ יְיָ הַגְּדֻלָּה וְהַגְּבוּרָה וְהַתִּפְאֶרֶת וְהַנֵּצַח
וְהַהוֹד. כִּי־כֹל בַּשָּׁמַיִם וּבָאָרֶץ לְךָ יְיָ הַמַּמְלָכָה
וְהַמִּתְנַשֵּׂא לְכֹל לְרֹאשׁ. רוֹמְמוּ יְיָ אֱלֹהֵינוּ וְהִשְׁתַּחֲווּ
לַהֲדֹם רַגְלָיו קָדוֹשׁ הוּא: רוֹמְמוּ יְיָ אֱלֹהֵינוּ
וְהִשְׁתַּחֲווּ לְהַר קָדְשׁוֹ כִּי־קָדוֹשׁ יְיָ אֱלֹהֵינוּ:

BLESSINGS FOR THE READING OF THE TORAH

בָּרְכוּ אֶת־יְיָ הַמְבֹרָךְ:

בָּרוּךְ יְיָ הַמְבֹרָךְ לְעוֹלָם וָעֶד:

בָּרוּךְ אַתָּה יְיָ אֱלֹהֵינוּ מֶלֶךְ הָעוֹלָם אֲשֶׁר
בָּחַר־בָּנוּ מִכָּל־הָעַמִּים וְנָתַן־לָנוּ אֶת־תּוֹרָתוֹ. בָּרוּךְ
אַתָּה יְיָ נוֹתֵן הַתּוֹרָה:

READING AND TRANSLATION OF TORAH PORTION

בָּרוּךְ אַתָּה יְיָ אֱלֹהֵינוּ מֶלֶךְ הָעוֹלָם אֲשֶׁר
נָתַן־לָנוּ תּוֹרַת אֱמֶת וְחַיֵּי עוֹלָם נָטַע בְּתוֹכֵנוּ.
בָּרוּךְ אַתָּה יְיָ נוֹתֵן הַתּוֹרָה:

RETURNING THE SCROLL TO THE ARK

This is the covenant that I shall make with the house of Israel
after those days, says the Lord: I shall put my Torah in their inward
parts, and on their heart shall I write it, and I shall be their God
and they shall be My people. No more need a person teach his
neighbor to know the Lord, for they shall all know Me, from the
smallest of them to the greatest of them, says the Lord.

גַּדְּלוּ לַיְיָ אִתִּי וּנְרוֹמְמָה שְׁמוֹ יַחְדָּו:

הוֹדוּ עַל־אֶרֶץ וְשָׁמָיִם   וַיָּרֶם קֶרֶן לְעַמּוֹ

תְּהִלָּה לְכָל־חֲסִידָיו   לִבְנֵי יִשְׂרָאֵל עַם קְרֹבוֹ

הַלְלוּיָהּ:

50

RESPONSIVE READING

The Torah of the Lord is unblemished, restoring
the soul.
The witness of the Lord is trustworthy, making wise
the simple.
The precepts of the Lord are straightforward,
rejoicing the heart.
The verdicts of the Lord are truth, the sum of them
is justice.
I have given you good teaching, says the Lord;
forsake not My Torah.
It is a tree of life for those who hold fast to it,
and its supporters are happy.
Its ways are ways of pleasantness, and all its paths
are peace.

עֵץ־חַיִּים הִיא לַמַּחֲזִיקִים בָּהּ וְתֹמְכֶיהָ מְאֻשָּׁר:

דְּרָכֶיהָ דַרְכֵי־נֹעַם וְכָל־נְתִיבוֹתֶיהָ שָׁלוֹם:

הֲשִׁיבֵנוּ יְיָ אֵלֶיךָ וְנָשׁוּבָה חַדֵּשׁ יָמֵינוּ כְּקֶדֶם:

ARK IS CLOSED

ADORATION
(Congregation rising)

עָלֵינוּ לְשַׁבֵּחַ לַאֲדוֹן הַכֹּל לָתֵת גְּדֻלָּה לְיוֹצֵר בְּרֵאשִׁית:

READER

We have shared many words together. That we could speak them,
and hear them spoken, means that there is a place in the world for
them, that our songs of praise and prayers of hope have not gone

51

empty from our mouths, but remain in the air, waiting for other words to join them. Too often they are not joined, but lost in hopeless words, rhetoric propounded but not meant, accents without acts. If the hopes that we have shared tonight are not to have been shared in vain, we must not leave our words here in our seats, neatly folded in our books. Our words must leave with us, go streaming out the doors with us, accompany us as we walk on the road, when we sit in our houses, when we lie down and when we rise up. They must emblazon the doorposts of our house, and seal themselves into our hands and before our eyes, that the world might remember the words it has so long forgotten, and form from them a new song which all might sing in celebration of the world we all desire. Before that hope, before the God who is the substance of that hope, let us bow the head and bend the knee in the holy spaces of our yearning, praised be He.

(Congregation seated)

May the time not be distant, O God, when Your name shall be worshipped in all the earth, when despair shall disappear and error be no more. We pray that the day be not far off when all men shall find their way to calling on Your name, when corruption and evil shall give way to integrity and goodness, when the many kinds of human beings on the earth shall recognize not alone their difference but their unity, that each people may, in its unique way, work for the coming of God's single kingdom. Hear O Israel is only for the present; the day will come when all the earth will hear that the Lord is God, the Lord is One.

בַּיּוֹם הַהוּא יִהְיֶה יְיָ אֶחָד וּשְׁמוֹ אֶחָד:

KADDISH

It is hard to sing of oneness when our world is not complete, when those who once brought wholeness to our life have gone, and naught but memory can fill the emptiness their passing leaves behind. But memory can tell us only what we were, in company with those we loved; it cannot help us find what each of us, alone, must now become. Yet no one is really alone; those who live no more echo still within our thoughts and words, and what they did has become woven into what we are. He does best homage to his dead who lives his life most fully even in the shadow of his loss. For each of our lives is worth the life of the whole world; in each one is the breath of the Ultimate One. In affirming the One, we affirm the worth of each one whose life, now ended, brought us closer to the Source of Life, in whose unity no one is alone and every life finds purpose. Before that Source, the ultimate author of that purpose, let us rise in hopefulness and praise, in blessing and in trust.

(Rising)

MOURNERS' KADDISH

יִתְגַּדַּל וְיִתְקַדַּשׁ שְׁמֵהּ רַבָּא. בְּעָלְמָא דִּי־בְרָא כִרְעוּתֵהּ. וְיַמְלִיךְ מַלְכוּתֵהּ בְּחַיֵּיכוֹן וּבְיוֹמֵיכוֹן וּבְחַיֵּי דְכָל־בֵּית יִשְׂרָאֵל בַּעֲגָלָא וּבִזְמַן קָרִיב. וְאִמְרוּ אָמֵן:

יְהֵא שְׁמֵהּ רַבָּא מְבָרַךְ לְעָלַם וּלְעָלְמֵי עָלְמַיָּא:

יִתְבָּרַךְ וְיִשְׁתַּבַּח וְיִתְפָּאַר וְיִתְרֹמַם וְיִתְנַשֵּׂא וְיִתְהַדָּר וְיִתְעַלֶּה וְיִתְהַלָּל שְׁמֵהּ דְּקֻדְשָׁא. בְּרִיךְ הוּא. לְעֵלָּא (וּלְעֵלָּא) מִן־כָּל־בִּרְכָתָא וְשִׁירָתָא תֻּשְׁבְּחָתָא וְנֶחֱמָתָא דַּאֲמִירָן בְּעָלְמָא. וְאִמְרוּ אָמֵן:

יְהֵא שְׁלָמָא רַבָּא מִן־שְׁמַיָּא וְחַיִּים עָלֵינוּ וְעַל־כָּל־יִשְׂרָאֵל. וְאִמְרוּ אָמֵן:

עֹשֶׂה שָׁלוֹם בִּמְרוֹמָיו הוּא יַעֲשֶׂה שָׁלוֹם עָלֵינוּ וְעַל־כָּל־יִשְׂרָאֵל. וְאִמְרוּ אָמֵן:

53

Yis-ga-dal v'yis-ka-dash sh'may ra-bo,
B'ol-mo dee-v'ro hir u-say, v'yam-leeh mal-hu-say,
B'ha-yay-hon uv-yo-may-hon, uv-ha-yay d'hol bays yis ro ayl,
Ba-a-go-lo u-viz'man ko-reev, v'im-ru o-mayn.
Y'hay sh'may ra-bo m'vo-rah, l'o-lam ul-ol-may ol-ma-yo.
Yis-bo-rah v'yish-ta-bah, v'yis-po-ar v'yis-ro -mam,
V'yis-na-say v'yis-ha-dar, v'yis-a-leh,
    v'yis-ha-lal sh'may d'kud-sho b'rih hu;
L'ay-lo (ul'ay-lo) min kol bir-ho-so v'shee-ro-so,
Tush-b'ho-so v'ne-heh-mo-so, da-a-mee -ron b'ol-mo,
V'im-ru o-mayn.
Y'hay sh'lo-mo ra-bo min sh'ma-yo,
V'ha-yeem o-lay-nu v'al kol yis-ro-ayl v'im-ru o-mayn
O-se sho-lom bim-ro-mov hu ya-a-se sho-lom
O-lay-nu v'al kol yis-ro-ayl v'im-ru o-mayn.

(Seated)

CONCLUDING MEDITATION

I do not believe in a self-naming of God,
A self-definition of God before men,
The Word of revelation is *I am that I am.*
That which reveals is that which reveals.
The eternal voice sounds forth, and nothing more.

Men do not find God if they stay in the world.
They do not find Him if they leave the world.
He who goes out with his whole being to meet his *Thou*
And carries to it all being that is in the world,
Finds Him who cannot be sought.

I become through my relation to the *Thou.*
As I become *I,* I say *Thou.*

All real living is meeting.

BLESSING OF NEIGHBOR

(Please turn to someone sitting near you and express to him your own words of blessing for Shabbat.)

CONCLUDING SONG

אדון עולם

אֲדוֹן עוֹלָם אֲשֶׁר מָלַךְ   בְּטֶרֶם כָּל יְצִיר נִבְרָא:

לְעֵת נַעֲשָׂה בְחֶפְצוֹ כֹּל   אֲזַי מֶלֶךְ שְׁמוֹ נִקְרָא:

וְאַחֲרֵי כִּכְלוֹת הַכֹּל   לְבַדּוֹ יִמְלוֹךְ נוֹרָא:

וְהוּא הָיָה וְהוּא הֹוֶה   וְהוּא יִהְיֶה בְּתִפְאָרָה:

וְהוּא אֶחָד וְאֵין שֵׁנִי   לְהַמְשִׁיל לוֹ לְהַחְבִּירָה:

בְּלִי רֵאשִׁית בְּלִי תַכְלִית   וְלוֹ הָעֹז וְהַמִּשְׂרָה:

וְהוּא אֵלִי וְחַי גּוֹאֲלִי   וְצוּר חֶבְלִי בְּעֵת צָרָה:

וְהוּא נִסִּי וּמָנוֹס לִי   מְנָת כּוֹסִי בְּיוֹם אֶקְרָא:

בְּיָדוֹ אַפְקִיד רוּחִי   בְּעֵת אִישַׁן וְאָעִירָה:

וְעִם רוּחִי גְּוִיָּתִי   יְיָ לִי וְלֹא אִירָא:

קדוש

בָּרוּךְ אַתָּה יְיָ אֱלֹהֵינוּ מֶלֶךְ הָעוֹלָם. בּוֹרֵא פְּרִי הַגָּפֶן:

בָּרוּךְ אַתָּה יְיָ אֱלֹהֵינוּ מֶלֶךְ הָעוֹלָם. אֲשֶׁר קִדְּשָׁנוּ

בְּמִצְוֹתָיו וְרָצָה בָנוּ. וְשַׁבַּת קָדְשׁוֹ בְּאַהֲבָה וּבְרָצוֹן

הִנְחִילָנוּ זִכָּרוֹן לְמַעֲשֵׂה בְרֵאשִׁית. כִּי הוּא יוֹם תְּחִלָּה

לְמִקְרָאֵי קֹדֶשׁ זֵכֶר לִיצִיאַת מִצְרָיִם. כִּי־בָנוּ בָחַרְתָּ

וְאוֹתָנוּ קִדַּשְׁתָּ מִכָּל־הָעַמִּים וְשַׁבַּת קָדְשְׁךָ בְּאַהֲבָה

וּבְרָצוֹן הִנְחַלְתָּנוּ. בָּרוּךְ אַתָּה יְיָ. מְקַדֵּשׁ הַשַּׁבָּת:

KIDDUSH

You are blessing, Adonay
Compassionate God
Source of coherence in the world
Source of this fruit from the vine.

You are blessing, Adonay
Compassionate God
Source of coherence in the world
Source of mitzvot
   through which we rise to holiness.
In love and acceptance
You have dowered us with Your
   holy Shabbat,
   rediscovery of Creation
   recollection of our going-forth
     from Egypt,
   first among our holy days of
     gathering together.
You have singled us out among the
   holy peoples
In offering us Your holy Shabbat,
   a gift of love.
You are blessing, Adonay.
Yet set Shabbat apart
As holy time.

Baruch Atta
Adonay Eloheynu
Melech ha-olam
Borey pree ha-gafen.

Baruch Atta
Adonay Eloheynu
Melech ha-olam
Asher kidd'shanu b'mitzvotav
   v'ratza vanu
V'Shabbat Kod'sho b'ahava uv'ratzon
   hincheelanu
Zikaron l'ma-asey Bereysheet.
Kee hu yom t'cheela l'mikra-ey
   kodesh
Zeycher leetzee-at mitzrayim.
Kee vanu vacharta v'otanu kidashta
   meekol ha-amim.
V'Shabbat Kodsh'cha b'ahava
   uv'ratzon hinchaltanu.
Baruch Atta Adonay
M'kadeysh
Ha Shabbat.

THE SPARK

READER

Many centuries ago, on this day—Friday—just at the hour when the sun's rays slant and the shadows lengthen, the great mystics of the town of S'fat would dress in white robes to walk out and welcome the Sabbath Queen. Off they would go, dancing through green fields. The sun spun further and further west. From the edges of the sky, twilight mustered. The mystics of S'fat sang six psalms for the six weekdays, and with each psalm they savored once again the taste of that particular and irretrievable day.

VOICE 1

For Sunday they sang: "Let's sing to the Lord and shout to the One who saves us."

VOICE 2

For Monday they sang, "Sing God a new song. Sing to God, all the earth."

VOICE 3

For Tuesday they sang, "God is ruling. Let the earth be glad. Let the far-flung islands celebrate."

VOICE 4

For Wednesday they sang, "Sing God a new song, for He has made miracles."

VOICE 5

For Thursday they sang, "God is ruling. Let nations tremble."

VOICE 6

For Friday, Friday which melts into Shabbat, they sang King David's song, "Winds and weathers, sons of the mighty ones, say that glory and strength are God's."

READER

The sinking sun made their eyes dazzle. Faster and faster the great wheel of the week revolved for them, and as they danced, they cried out words of love for the loving God who had made the green earth and the golden Torah and the lovely Queen Shabbat who was even now walking toward them across the fields.

(The group hums L'cha Dodi)

They could see her now, as the world grew greyer. She wore a dress the color of wine and her arms were outstretched and her eyes were shining. The mystics reached out to embrace her, and they sang her the song which one of their number had composed in her honor.

(The group sings:)

L'cha dodi likrat kallah, pnei shabbat n'kablah.

Shamor v'zachor b'dibur echad	The One God told us in one command
Hishmianu el ham'yuchad	To keep and remember Shabbat.
Adonai echad u'shmo echad	The Lord is One and His name is One.
l'shem u'l'tiferet v'lit'hila.	His Oneness is His Glory.
Hitor'ri, hitor'ri	Rouse, rouse yourself.
Ki va orech kumi ori	Your light has come. Rise up and shine,
Uri, uri shir daberi	Awake, awake and sing.
K'vod Adonai alaiyich niglah.	The glory of God is revealed upon you.
Bo'i v'shalom ateret ba'lah	Come in peace, Shechina, crown of God,
Gam b'simcha u'v'tzahalah	In joy and gaiety
Toch emunai am segulah	Among the faithful of Your cherished people,
Bo'i kallah, bo'i kallah.	Come, bride; come, bride.

60

READER

Hand in hand with Queen Shabbat, the mystics of S'fat walked into the Sabbath world. Once again, it was the last day of the first week that had ever been, and with Sabbath eyes, they saw the new-minted creation. There were great black trees with crumbly bark and tender leaves. There was new grass to walk on, and the smell of soil and growing. There was a freshly forged sky set with untarnished stars. There was the first of all silences since the clatter of creation began. Far away, the Sabbath day sang to God in its deep quiet voice.

VOICE

"A song by the Sabbath day. It is good to thank God and sing His praise."

READER

And just as we do now, the mystics called one another to the world's first Sabbath prayer.

BAR'CHU ET ADONAI HAM'VORACH.

Praise God to whom praise is due.

BARUCH ADONAI HAM'VORACH L'OLAM VA'ED.

Praise God to whom praise is due forever and ever.

GROUP

(In davened non-unison)

The king of the universe
(Praised be He)
Brings on evening with a word,
Opens heaven's gates with wisdom,
Cycles time with sensitive judgment,
Switches the seasons,
And orders the orbits of a sky full of stars.

He creates each day and night afresh,
Rolls light in front of darkness
And darkness in front of light
So gently
That no moment is quite like the one before
Or after.
Second by second
You make day pass into night
And You alone know the boundary point
Dividing one from the other.
Unifier of all beings is Your name.

Timeless God,
Be King forever.
You who bring the evening in
Are praised.

With infinite love
You loved us, Lord.
You taught us for love-language

Torah,

    Mitzvot,

        Laws and judgments.

Sleeping and walking
We bear them in mind.
We shall enjoy them forever.
They are our life.
They give dimension to our days.
We form our words around them
Night and day.
Never withhold Your love from us.
Lover of Israel
You are praised.

READER

Let us prepare to affirm the Oneness of God.

ANTIPHONAL READING

His Oneness is not like human oneness, for He and His knowledge and His life are one. He knows nothing outside Himself, for outside Himself, nothing is.

He is the Place where the universe exists, but the universe is not His place.

He is the One of which there is no fraction, the only One which cannot be divided.

We are often divided. We are of two minds. Our feelings and our knowings war within us. But He is the only true One.

He is without beginning and without end and without limits; the mystics call him Ain-Sof, Endless One.

His love for man is also endless. He demands only the demand of a lover: that we return His love and act lovingly toward Him and toward His creation.

GROUP

(When saying the Shema, draw out the word "One.")

SHEMA YISRAEL ADONAI ELOHENU ADONAI ECHAD.

Listen, Israel: the Lord our God, the Lord is the only One.
(whisper)
Baruch shem k'vod malchuto l'olam va'ed.
Praised is His true name, whose meaning is Majesty, beyond all time and all worlds.

And you shall serve the Lord your God out of LOVE
with an undivided heart
with your lifeblood
with all that you own.

Take to heart
These things I am commanding you today.
Tell your children about them.
Talk about them
                    at home and on the street
                    night and morning.
Wear them on your arm and between your eyes
In t'filin—
To remind you that your hands and mind
Are dedicated to My work.
Write them on the doorpost of your house
and on the gates of your city
to tell those who enter:
These are the words this household lives by.

If you will listen to my mitzvot which I am commanding you today—to love the Lord your God and to serve Him with your whole
heart and soul—then I will provide for your physical needs so that
you can devote your mind to My Torah. But watch yourself lest
you open your heart to temptation and stray into serving gods of
greed and ego and bow down to them. For then God's anger will
be kindled against you, and He will leave you to contend with
nature like the exploiters and destroyers you imitated. And sometimes there will be no rain and the tired earth will yield no produce—you will fast disappear from the good land God gave you.

BUT EVEN THEN,
store these words of mine in your heart
and in your soul.
Still wear their token
        on your hand and between your eyes.
Still teach your children to speak of them
        at home and on the street
        night and morning.
Write them on the doorposts of your house
and on your gates.
Then your days and your children's days
In the land God swore to give your fathers
will be as long
as the days of the sky arching over earth.

God told Moses:
Tell the people of Israel to make fringes on the corners
of their garments.

And on the fringe of every corner, put a cord of blue . . .
The blue of the sky reflected in the sea.

The fringe will remind you that you are Mine.
You will look at it and think of all the mitzvot of God
and fulfill them.

And you will not simply follow your own whims, which might
lead you to be false to Me.

But you will remember and do ALL my mitzvot and be wholly
dedicated for your God.

I am the Lord your God who liberated you from the land of Egypt
in order to be your God.

READER

It was at the creation that God took some of His own light and
poured it into the vessels of the spheres of the universe. But the
lower spheres were too weak to contain a light so powerful. They
cracked, and sparks of light fell down and down until they reached
the lowest created world—the physical world. In falling the sparks
took on form and became embedded in physical things: wood and
water and living creatures, metal and stone. Ever and ever the
spark wishes to return to the source of all light. And when a mitzvah
is done with any physical thing or when God is thanked for having
created it so beautiful or strong or fragrant, the spark within is
wakened. It flames out and rises and is reunited with its source.

THE SPARK SONG

(to the tune of Joan Baez's folk song, "The Silkie.")

Plant and pebble, beast and bough,
Shells for sparks no eye can see,
You have waited up till now
For a hand to set you free.

From the forge where all was made
Down you drifted still aflame
And with form were overlaid
To wait for the awakening Name.

Plant and pebble, beast and bough
Though your shells be crude and coarse,
I have come to wake you now,
To send your flame back to its source.

With your sap I'll write my prayer,
With your stone an altar raise,
Of your meat I'll eat and share,
From your vines take cups of praise.

Plant and pebble, beast and bough,
You who, through me, serve and bless,
Turn to your creator now.
You were used in Holiness.

Page and petal, coin and cake,
Send your spark to blaze above.
Say I blessed you for His sake.
Say that you were sent with love.

GROUP

And just as we redeem the sparks and rescue them from the tyranny
of matter, so God redeems us. It is written, "The Lord has redeemed
Jacob and rescued him from a stronger power." You are praised,
Lord, Redeemer of Israel.

Lay us down in peace, Lord.
And in the morning
Let us wake up alive.
Spread peace over us
And repair us with your good advice.
Save us, since Peace
Is what Your name stands for.
Protect us and protect the world
From enemies and disease,
From war and hunger,
From anguish.
Don't let us be confronted with the temptation to destroy.
And don't let the desire to destroy steal up behind us and
    whisper in our ear.
Keep us safe under Your wing,
Since You are kind and compassionate.
Guard our comings and goings
For life and for peace
For now and forever.
Spread Your shelter of peace over us all.

You are praised, Lord,
Who spread the shelter of peace
Over all of us,
Over all Israel,
And over Jerusalem.

MEDITATION BEFORE THE AMIDAH

Lord of all worlds, I have come before You as a single Jew to pray
the great prayer of my people. It may be that no one has ever used
this paper I read to praise You. It may be that no one has ever
addressed You from the spot on which I stand. It may be that this
mouth of mine has never formed these words to speak to You. Perhaps some spark is slumbering here, waiting for me and my prayer
. . . a spark which only I can raise. Give me the strength to con-
centrate my mind, my body, my senses on this prayer, this time,
this place alone; so that no spark will oversleep its time on my
account.

AMIDAH

Lord, help me to voice my praises of You.
Praised are You, Lord,
Our God
and God of our fathers,
God of Abraham
God of Isaac
God of Jacob.
Great   powerful   and   awesome   God
Supreme God
who loves even the unworthy.
Creator   of   all.

You remember the acts of devotion which our grandfathers, Abraham, Isaac, and Jacob did for You, and
You will return their love by bringing their children's
children a Messiah and an age in which mercy and justice govern the actions of men and nations, for these
are the ideals Your name stands for.

King who helps, saves, and protects. *You are praised,
God, Protector of Abraham.*

You are infinitely powerful, Lord;
You have the power to give life to the dead;
It is You who have the power to save us.
(Between Sukkot and Pesach Add:
You make the wind blow and the rain fall.)
Lovingly
You supply the needs of all living things.
With great mercy
You grant immortal life to the dead.
You
steady the weak
heal the sick
free the enslaved.
You keep Your word to those who sleep
in the dust.

Who is like You, wielder of power?
Who resembles You, O King who gives both life and
  death
              and who makes redemption blossom?
You can be trusted to give immortal life to the dead.
You are praised, Lord,
who give immortal life to the dead.

You are beyond the worldly
        and the true meaning of Your name is beyond under-
          standing.
              Beings set apart for Your service praise You every
                day.
Praised are You, Lord, the holy God.

        It was the seventh day that You marked as dedicated
        to You, because on it You willed to end the creation
        of heaven and earth. And You blessed it beyond all days
        and You separated it from the stream of time, as it is
        written in Your Torah:

        The heavens and the earth and all their hosts were
        finished. On the seventh day God had completed His
        work which He had made, and He rested on the seventh
        day and set it apart as a holy day because on it He rested
        from all His work of creating materials for man to fashion.

Our God and God of our fathers,
              be pleased with our soul-rest.
Dedicate us
        to Your service, through Your mitzvot, and
grant us
        our share in the understanding of Your Torah.
Satiate us
        with Your goodness.
Gladden us
        with Your help.

Purify our motives,
           so that we can serve You sincerely.
As a sign of love, Lord our God,
grant
           that we keep Your holy Sabbath as a heritage;
let the Jewish people,
           who consecrate their actions to Your name,
take their soul-rest on this day.
You are praised, Lord, who set apart the Shabbat.

Be pleased with Your people Israel, Lord our God, and with their prayer. Restore the service to Your holy temple in Jerusalem and lovingly accept Israel's offerings and prayers. May the worship of Your people Israel always be pleasing to You.
May we see Your merciful return to Zion with our own eyes.
You are praised, Lord, who will return Your presence to Zion.

           For all these things we praise You:
Because You are the Lord our God and God of our fathers,
      the one our lives depend on,
      the one who shields and rescues us.
In every generation we will thank You and retell Your praise
      for our lives which You hold in Your hand
      and for our souls which You direct
      and for Your miracles which we see every day
      and for Your wonders and the favors You do us
           at all times—
                 Evening, morning, afternoon.
Because You are the good God
the compassionate One
      whose miracles never run out;
      whose kindnesses never stop.
You have always been our hope.

And for all these things, our King, may Your name be blessed and gain esteem in men's eyes forever and ever.

Every living thing will truly thank You and sincerely praise Your name, O God who rescues and helps us. *You are praised, Lord, who stand for kindness; it is only fitting to praise You.*

Spread great and lasting peace over Your people Israel, You who are king and lord of all peace. May it please You to bless Your people Israel at all seasons and all times with Your peace. *You are praised, Lord, who bless Your people Israel with peace.*

Lord, keep my tongue from evil
and my lips from flattery and deceit.
To those who defame me, let my soul keep silent.
Teach my soul true humility
so that I may learn even from those who hate me.
Open my heart to Your Torah
and let my soul search out Your mitzvot.
As for all who think to harm me,
frustrate their plans and their purposes.
Do it because truthfulness and peace are Your signature.
Do it to show that You have the power to protect.
Do it for the sake of Your holiness and Your Torah.
Preserve those who try to live by Your teachings.
Save me with Your power, Lord, and answer me.
May the words in my mouth and the thoughts in my heart
be equally acceptable to You, Lord,
my rescuer, on whom I can depend.

ALEYNU

We Jews must praise the Ruler of all. For He brought our nation into being in a way no other nation was born, and He set us apart from the families of the earth. Our lot and our destiny are forever distinct, for He revealed Himself to us and so we must renounce men's idols. He gave us His Torah and so we can accept no lesser law of life.

We bow down before Him and affirm that He, the Holy One, is the King of all Kings.

He stretches out these skies and founds this earth, but His essence is beyond the furthest heavens, out of time and mind. He alone is our God. He is our true King. We have none beside Him.

As the Torah says, "This day you shall know and take to heart that the Lord alone is God, both in heaven above and on earth below. There is no one else."

May it be Your will, that before it is too late all men may have a revelation of You. Then they will sweep away the idols of ego and pride and do away with the false gods of greed and cruelty. They will repair the world and live by Your rule of peace. All mankind will call on Your name and the lovers of destruction will turn to You and learn to create. Then Your oneness will be complete, for Your law of peace in heaven will be one with the law of peace on earth. And that peace will never end. As it says in the Torah, "The Lord shall reign forever and ever." And the Prophet adds, "The Lord will become King over all the earth. And on that day the Lord shall be one, and His name shall be One."

READER

Let us rise in support of the mourners among us as they recite Kaddish.

Yisgadal v'yiskadash shmey raboh
B'olmoh dee-v'roh chir-usey
V'yamlich malchussey b'cha-yeychon uvyo-meychon,
Uvchayey d'chol beys yis-roel
Ba-agoloh uvizman koreev v'imru omeyn.
Y'hey shmey raboh mevorach l'olam ul'olmey olmayoh,

Yisborach v'yishtabach v'yis-po-ar v'yisromam v'yisnassey
V'yis-haddar v'yis-alleh v'yishallal
Shmey d'kudshoh, brich hu,
L'eyloh min kol birchosoh v'shirosoh
Tush-b'chosoh v'nechemosoh
Da-ameeron b'olmoh; v'imru omeyn.

72

Y'hey shlomoh raboh min sh'mayoh, v'chayeem
Oleynu v'al kol yisroel; v'imru omeyn.

O-seh shalom bimromov hu ya-aseh sholom
Oleynu v'al kol yisroel; v'imru omeyn.

READER

We are all inside the Shabbat now. It is singing to us the same
song it has sung to Jews ever since there were Jews to hear it. We
can join in the singing—to welcome Shabbat angels of peace and
to toast the Shabbat with friendship and good wine.

*(All sing "Shalom Aleichem Malachei Ha-Sharet" and reassemble
for Kiddush.)*

THE SABBATH BRIDGE

Reader A: What is the purpose of the Sabbath, the day of rest? It is a renewal, an affirmation of our bond with God. A separation from the other days of the week, a time to realize our obligation in the way we live our lives during the rest of the week.

Can just rest do this? Can praise of God alone do it? Will standing and sitting, singing and reading make us better, more compassionate human beings? or even better Jews?

I doubt it. Let us make this Sabbath service a building experience. Let's not rest; let's strain toward building the kind of life that God commands us over and over again to live all of the time. The Sabbath is different, yes, but to claim that its *spirit* should not be carried through the rest of the week is a perversion of Jewish teaching. Let us bridge the gap. The two themes stressed in the Sabbath ritual, those elements that seem to make the day different from the rest of the week, are a proclaiming of our unity with God and a reminder of our obligations to each other. These two themes also constitute the bridge between Jews and all of mankind and between the Sabbath and the rest of the week. The ritual portrays the unity of all men and the obligations of righteous behavior toward all, through the week. Join with us now in an effort to make this Sabbath ritual a bridge . . .

Reader B: In our construction of a bridge we must begin with the proper foundations. Both our minds and hearts must be open to this building process. We must be ready to look at the Sabbath in a new way, not afraid of a different order in the service, not absorbed in our own private thoughts of the day. We must open our hearts to God and to our fellowmen by raising our voices in song.

(After song—perhaps "Blowing in the Wind" —Reader B takes two of the cement cinder- blocks and places them on chalk marks.)

Reader C: I saw an ad in the subway the other day in Chicago. It read: YOU HAVE 24 HOURS TO LIVE, Today that is. So what are you doing with your time? Are you helping another human being towards the dignity you want for yourself? Are you doing one thing to overcome the hate in this world—with love? These 24 hours can be a great time to be alive— If you live right. BREAK THE HATE HABIT; LOVE THY NEIGHBOR.

Lay the rest of the foundations of our bridge with your thoughts. Think about your last 24 hours; think about what the next 24 will be like. Think about it . . .

(After about 5 minutes meditation, Reader C takes the other two cinderblocks and puts them on the appropriate chalk marks.)

Reader A: We are now ready to erect the main pillars of our bridge. The first one seems to be a familiar one. The Shema says: Hear O Israel, the Lord Our God, the Lord is One. The basis of monotheism, you might say. Yes, but the basis of unity as well. For if the Lord is One, then aren't all of his creatures One? If he is the only Creator, then is He not the father of us all? Are we not truly brother and sister, though we be black and white, Jew and Gentile? The Shema says, *Hear* O Israel . . . Heed the message—stand and joyously affirm our unity and that of our Creator.

(After the Shema is sung and recited in Hebrew and English, Reader A places one of the 5'1" x 3" planks in one of the cinderblocks.)

78

Reader B: What is the source of our ethical values about which we talk endlessly on the Sabbath but which we seem to forget during the rest of the week? It is the Ten Commandments. Though we spend much time defining our relationship to God, only three of the Commandments deal with this relationship. The rest are devoted to our dealings with our fellow man. By reading them now we will firmly erect the second pillar of our bridge. Please repeat each commandment after I read it.

(After the responsive reading, Reader B places another one of the planks in another cinder-block.)

Reader C: Very often we become wrapped up in our own world of concerns, insensitive to the strivings of other men. Judging from our individual standards we see no meaning in others' lives. William James once spoke of a poet who, when riding in the country, stopped before a cleared field, stripped of its trees and checked with rows of dirt and fences. The poet mourned the scene, saw in it only ugliness and death. He was joined on the country road by a farmer who admired the same scene because he saw the beauty of hard work and celebrated the miracle of farming which would provide food for a community from the rows of soil.

We are often blind to the holiness of others' ways of life. Yet in the Sabbath service the sanctification reminds us that the *whole world* is full of God's holiness, that we have only to look beyond our meager portion to see another's worth. This is the third pillar supporting the bridge. Please rise for the Sanctification.

(After the Sanctification has been sung in Hebrew, Reader C takes the plank and places it in another cinderblock.)

79

Reader A: I stand before the Ark today, head bowed in re-
             verence, but mind racing, searching for the light
             that has illumined so many hearts before me. Here
             is the wisdom and the history of my people. I know
             their world is not mine and their answers are not
             mine, yet the knowledge of their struggles and re-
             solutions can help me in the tasks that confront me.
             If we are to be a light unto the nations, then what
             better place to look for the last pillar of the bridge
             than here in the Torah?

             *(After Torah ceremony, Reader A takes
             last plank and puts in last cinderblock.)*

Reader B: In constructing a ramp that leads us from our unique
             and separate position as Jews on the Sabbath to a
             week-long empathy with all men, we must first rid
             ourselves of vanity and conceit. When we credit
             one group of people with more intelligence, more
             sensitivity, more talent, or even more holiness we
             create artificial barriers between men. We must
             realize that we, by ourselves, are nothing. We owe
             everything to our Creator. The ramp onto our bridge
             is the *Barchu,* for it directs all praise to the Lord.
             Please rise for the *Barchu.*

             *(After the Barchu is sung and recited in both
             Hebrew and English, Reader B should take the
             entrance plank and place it.)*

Reader A: What makes up the platform of our bridge, the
             symbol of the underlying spirit and understanding
             that links the Sabbath ritual with the rest of the
             week? Perhaps it is just the understanding that our
             heritage and tradition instill in us. The paradox of
             life is that we are all individuals and alone in the
             world. Yet at the same time we are at one with the
             rest of creation, part of nature. As a family is bound

together, so too are the Jews bound together. As Jews are bound, so is all of mankind. As mankind is bound together, so are all of God's works. Please stand now and affirm this bond, laying the floorboards of our bridge. Join hands with the persons next to you. Now that our bodies are linked, tie the separate floorboards together to gain strength from this union. Direct your minds to the image of the Eternal Light which hangs from every Ark. The hand which you touch on the right and the hand which touches you on the left signify the chain of unending generations which have gazed at the light and sought its mystery. We are all links in the chain; the flesh you touch is a part of you. True peace will come when all men can join hands and recognize that they are touching part of themselves. This union of mind and body is meaningless unless it is translated into action. Let us raise our voices to God, proclaiming our unity.

(Reader A leads in the singing of Hinei Ma Tov *and then, assisted by another reader, places the large plywood floorboard of the bridge on the cinderblocks.)*

Reader C: Our bridge is almost finished, but it is not yet joined to the rest of the week; it lacks the ramp to involvement in our brothers' lives. Involvement is not just smooth words but also hard action. Such empathy is only symbolized by sharing another's grief. Much more is needed if we are truly to link the spirit of the Sabbath to the rest of the week. Today, as is the custom, the mourners will rise to recite the Kaddish. Let us take the first small step towards involvement with others. Today let us all stand together when the Kaddish is recited. Let us lay the ramp off our bridge as we all recite the words of this prayer, for as the poet said, "Any man's death diminishes me because I am involved in mankind . . ."

> *(After the Kaddish is recited, Reader C takes ramp off bridge and places it on edge of the cinderblock.)*

Reader A: Now that our bridge is complete we must not sit idly by and admire it. Rather let us use it as it was meant to be used. We must cross that bridge, glad and straight into a new world.

> *(Reader A crosses the bridge followed by Reader B, followed by Reader C. Each turns once they have crossed the bridge and embraces the person following them. The congregation follows.)*

ROUGH DRAWINGS FOR BRIDGE

Materials: 4 cinderblock (12" x 6")
1 piece of ¼" plywood (5' x 2½')
2 pieces of ¼" plywood (4 x 2½")
4 1" x 3" 5' long planks
2 cement blocks (any type)

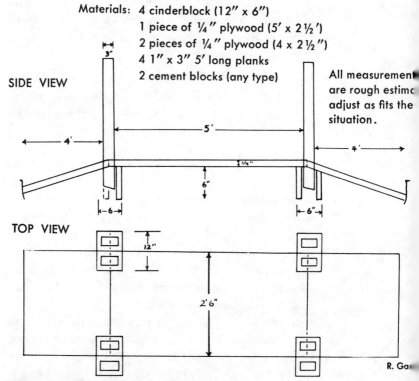

All measurement are rough estim adjust as fits the situation.

SIDE VIEW

TOP VIEW

R. Ga

SPECIAL THANKS TO: Joan Goodman for help in writing, designing, and producing the service.

82

SILENCE

Reader 1:   Throbs the night with mystic silence,
Hushed the weary world and still;
And the ever-flowing brooklet
Murmurs 'neath the resting mill.

Darker grows the night and darker,
Shadows upon shadows creep;
One bright star and yet another
Falls into the darkness deep.

All the world is wrapped in silence,
As I sit here pensively;
One world have I—yea, no other
Than the world which lives in me.

All: I seek silence. I need it sometimes. Sometimes I
wish that people would just go away and let me be.

Solo 1:   *(to "Sounds of Silence")*
I want to scream, I want to laugh,
I want to run, I want to sing
But people all around are watching me
And I dare not think of being free
And I'm trapped inside a wall of fear to be
The person that's hidden deep inside of me.

All: Many times I want to be left alone to go to my room
and be all alone. So I escape, and I listen. I learn
about myself. I find the self I hide from others. I
hide it so much that it seems hidden from me.

Solo 2:   *(to "Sounds of Silence")*
I sat and listened to myself
And I heard a searching voice
Revealing strength that I didn't know before
And once I had it there I wanted more
And I looked around and sought the world about
I reached out
And kept on growing inwardly.

All:	I never found the companion that was so companionable as solitude.
Reader 2:	To be alone with Silence Is to be alone with God.
Reader 3:	I need not shout my faith. Thrice eloquent Are quiet trees and green listening sod; Hushed are the stars, whose power is never spent; The hills are mute; yet how they speak of God!
Reader 4:	In silence I review my past. I seek my inner self. Sometimes it's peaceful, sometimes it cries out desperately. You can listen to silence and learn from it. It has a quality and a dimension of its own. It talks to me sometimes. I feel myself alive in it. It talks. And I can hear it. You have to want to listen to it, and then you can hear it. It has a strange, beautiful texture. It doesn't always talk. Sometimes, sometimes it cries, and you can hear the pain of the world in it. It hurts to listen to it then. But you have to.
All:	There are silences in love that destroy us. We must learn to talk about people who are far from us and people who are gone from us, in order to ease the ache of being without them. We may not be silent. We must not be silent. We must learn to talk about things that are difficult to even think about, for only then will we reach the depth of life that we seek in order to find ourselves.
Reader 5:	I hear my love speaking to me In the wondrous crystals on my window the vivid silver of the earth the clear morning air the fascination of water cooled till time suspends it in the rain on my cheeks my smile welcoming the warmth of the sun

                    fiery red colors
                    brilliant golden leaves
          in the sweet sorrow of the death of autumn leaves
          the gentle caress of wind through my hair
          the tender flow of waves down a brook
          the sacred streaks of sunlight among the trees
          the sparkling emeralds glittering in the forest
                    and in the warm pain of my tears.
          Yes, my love, you speak to me most, then.
          If I can tell others
          My love for you
          through this poem
          Then I will have taken the first step
          Towards breaking my silence.
          If I can convey my love for you
          Through words to them
          Then they too shall know how much you meant to
          me.
          If I am silent, they may never understand.
          It is silence which isolates.

Reader 2:   And there was peace
              Of a sort.
              But God was lonely.
              He looked all around,
              Through the timeless reaches of His domain,
              Round the corner of infinity,
              And saw nothing.
              So He made the light, and the world,
              And then He smiled,
              And made man.

Reader 3:   And God was pleased.
              And in the course of a day
              He watched his man grope
              Through the darkness of centuries
              Toward the little bit of God
              Which was his Soul.

Reader 1:	Then, God grew puzzled,
	For man saw the light,
	But shunned it.
	Man had found something better.

All:	Why love when it was so easy to hate?
	Why create when it was so easy to destroy?
	Why have peace, when it was so easy to have war?

Reader 3:	So man hated,
	Man killed,
	Man threw rocks at his brother,
	And then shot spears,
	And then fired guns,
	And then exploded bombs,
	And called it progress.

Reader 2:	And God was angry.
	And in a matter of minutes
	God saw His man
	Open his eyes to the Hell
	That he had made of God's Eden.
	And man grew afraid of the destruction
	That he, himself, had created.
	So man made organizations
	And tried to talk
	Instead of fight.
	But his words were hypocrisy
	And even he didn't believe them.

All:	And God was afraid.
	And in the space of seconds
	God watched, as in desperation
	His man turned to Him.

Reader 5:	And God tried to help,
	But man couldn't hear,
	Or maybe wouldn't.
	And then . . . in one instant,
	The mushrooms flowered,

And the missiles flew,
And the burning, blackened sphere was still.

All: And there was peace
Of a sort.
Except for the sound
of God,
Weeping.

Solo 1: Just outside my wisdom are words that would answer everything.

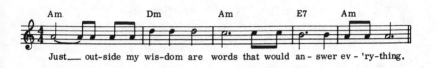

Just__ out-side my wis-dom are words that would an - swer ev - 'ry-thing.

Reader 1: Dear Mom and Dad,
The war is over now. My tasks at last are done. But Mom, there is something I must ask of you. I have a friend, oh, such a friend, that has no home you see; so Mom, I would like to know if he could come home with me.

Reader 2: Dear Son,
Of course we don't mind if he comes home with you. I'm sure that he could stay with you for a day of two.

Reader 1: Dear Mom,
But Mother, you don't understand. What I'm trying to say is I want him to live with us, for as long as he wants to stay. But Mom, I must tell you something. Please don't be alarmed. My friend in battle happened to lose an arm.

Reader 2: Dear Son,
Don't be afraid to bring him home with you. He can stay even for a week or two.

Reader 1:   Dear Mom,
              But Mother, he's quite a friend. He's like a
              brother to me. That's why I would like him to live
              with us. And be a son to you. But before you give
              your answer, there's something I must say. My friend
              in battle happened to lose a leg.

Reader 2:   Dear Son,
              It hurts me to say this, but my answer is "No."
              Your father and I could not manage with a boy who
              is crippled so.

Reader 3:   Some months later a letter came saying that their
              son had died. When they looked for the cause of
              death, the note said, "Suicide."

Reader 4:   And when the casket came,
              Draped with the country's flag
              They saw their son lying,
              Without an arm or leg.

Reader 5:   I see you every day
              In the seat beside me,
              On the street,
              Always by me as I work
              As I speak
              As I walk
              You're always there
              Yet people claim you are gone.
              How foolish they speak
              Can they not see you beside me?
              Why, you can't be gone
              Not if I can still touch you
              And I can hear you and see you.
              What fools!
              What fools!
              Oh, God, God,
              Don't let me believe them.

All sing: Just outside my wisdom are words that would answer
              everything.

90

All:	I am surrounded by a wall of silence. I try to get out, but I can't. I can only get out if everyone realizes what's happening inside of me. If they only knew how restrained I felt in front of them, how incapable of expressing myself I am! I am afraid, and so I am silent. Surrounded by a wall of silence. They could tear down the wall, if they would take the time to do so. But nowadays, nobody has time for me. They each say that they would love to talk to me, if they only had the time to do so. But they must study. I am not even as important as a book— a collection of words on paper. Me. Silence.
Reader 4:	Before I built a wall I'd ask to know What I was walling in or walling out, And to whom I was likely to give offense. Something there is that doesn't love a wall, That wants it down. . . .
All:	I run from silence. Maybe some day, someone will stop me in my path, catch me, hold on to me. Then my wall will crumble, right there in their hands.
Solo 1:	Just outside my wisdom are words that would answer everything.
All:	We must not commit the error of silence. We must have silence when we need it, but we must speak when necessary.
Reader 1:	In Russia, Elie Wiesel was confronted by an old man, glutted with fear, who had finally decided, no matter what the consequences, to break his silence. He told of the horrors that he had seen in his life, though he said little. He had learned that what he had to say could be said. He had learned to control silence.
All:	Silence must not control us, we must control it. We must find a special love for it.

Reader 2:	Behold this and
	Always love it!
	It is very sacred
	And you must
	Treat it as such.

Reader 5: Silence is sacred when words would only distort your feelings. Danny, living with his Hasidic father, learned this lesson. He related his story to his friend.

Reader 3: "Father taught me with silence. He taught me to look into myself, to find my own strength, to walk around inside myself in company with my soul.

"Words are cruel, words play tricks, they distort what is in the heart, they conceal the heart. The heart speaks through silence. One learns of the pain of others by suffering one's own pain—by turning inside oneself, by finding one's own soul. And it is important to know of pain. It destroys our self-pride, our arrogance, our indifference toward others. Upon seeing an old man, I once commented to my father that the old man was an ignoramus. My father replied wisely. 'Look into his soul', he said. 'Stand inside his soul and see the world through his eyes. You will know the pain he feels because of his ignorance, and you will not laugh.' "

Reader 5: Then his friend sat and listened to Danny cry. He held his face in his hands, and his sobs tore apart the silence of the room and racked his body.

Yes, silence hurts, but it teaches. Growth often comes out of pain. It can also come out of happiness.

All: Silence is feeling life. Sometimes I'm the observer of mankind. I sit and watch and learn from the examples people set. I learn from them without words.

Reader 2: Silence is feeling love. When I look at people's eyes, I understand their love for me, for eyes are the silent tongues of love.

Reader 4: Shall I say my love
    in one word
        one breath
            one whisper
Shall I paint
    in one picture
Shall I sing
    in one song
Or shall I cry
    in one tear.
No, I shall only hold you.

Reader 5: I didn't tell him I loved him. Some things are just too good to tell.

All: Words deceive. We speak in superfluities, for being real means to make ourselves vulnerable to mocking, and we are not willing to do so. If we weren't mocked for expressing ourselves, then our words would be beautiful indeed. But we are forced to keep our feelings hidden in the vastness of silence. If we could only be honest in front of others, we would emerge from that dark corner of silence, in which we cannot grow. We are like flowers—we need light to grow. Oh, that we might be honest once again in our lives. Then we would have silence only for loving—there would be no hate in it—no death, no walls—only friendship, love and peace of mind.

Solo 1: Just outside my wisdom are words that would answer everything.

All sing: Just outside my wisdom are words that would answer everything.

NOAH'S SABBATH

And God saw the earth, and behold, it was destroying itself;
All flesh had destroyed its way upon the earth;
And God said to Noah: the end of all flesh has come before me,
For the earth is filled with violence because of them,
And so I am now destroying them along with the earth. . . .

(Gen. 6:11-13)

MEDITATIONS ON A DESTROYING EARTH

Another day has gone for keeps
Into the bottomless pit of time.
Again it has wounded a man, held captive by his brethren.
After dusk, he longs for bandages.
For soft hands to shield the eyes
From all the horrors that stare by day.
But in the ghetto, darkness too is kind
To weary eyes which all day long
Have had to watch.

That bit of filth in dirty walls,
And all around barbed wire,
And 30,000 souls who sleep
Who once will wake
And once will see
Their own blood spilled.
I was once a little child,
Three years ago.

97

That child who longed for other worlds.
But now I am no more a child
For I have learned to hate.
I am a grown-up person now,
I have known fear.

These 30,000 souls who sleep
Among the trees will wake,
Open an eye
And because they see
A lot

They'll fall asleep again . . .

*   *   *   *

Everything leans, like tottering, hunched old women.

Every eye shines with fixed waiting
And for the word, "when"?

Here there are few soldiers.
Only the shot-down birds tell of war.

You believe every bit of news you hear.

The buildings now are fuller,
Body smelling close to body,
And the garrets scream with light for long, long hours.

This evening I walked along the street of death.
On one wagon, they were taking the dead away.

Why so many marches have been drummed here?
Why so many soldiers?

Then
A week after the end,
Everything will be empty here.

A hungry dove will peck for bread.
In the middle of the street will stand
An empty, dirty
Hearse.

* * * *

Listen!
The boat whistle has sounded now
And we must sail
Out toward an unknown port.

We'll sail a long, long way
And dreams will turn to truth.
Oh, how sweet the name Morocco!
      Listen!
Now it's time.

The wind sings songs of far away,
Just look up to heaven
And think about the violets.

Listen!
Now it's time.

SONG

God gave Noah the rainbow sign,
No more water—the fire next time.
Pharaoh's army got drownded,
Oh, oh, don't you weep.

Oh, oh, don't you weep, don't you mourn,
Oh, oh, don't you weep, don't you mourn,
Pharaoh's army got drownded,
Oh, oh, don't you weep.

If I could I surely would
Stand on the rock where Moses stood;
Pharaoh's army got drownded,
Oh, oh, don't you weep.

99

One of these days around twelve o'clock,
This old world's gonna reel and rock
Pharaoh's army got drownded,
Oh, oh, don't you weep.

Oh, oh, don't you weep, don't you mourn,
Oh, oh, don't you weep, don't you mourn,
Pharaoh's army got drownded,
Oh, oh, don't you weep.

God gave Noah the rainbow sign:
No more water—the fire next time. . . .

READER

From heaven and the eyes of men water threatens to inundate us, as with the blackness of this Sabbath eve we would smother the sounds of man's oppression before they reached our ears. The black on white of morning's pages mutely screams the violence that so bleeds our earth, as war and poverty, fear, exploitation, hatred and the very air's disease cavort before our daily sleep-numbed eyes too far out of reach to seize and stop, too near our vision to blink away. The evils we did not create we cannot ignore—but shall we live among them like the men of Noah's time or with Noah escape, and in living risk infection, and in escape, destruction for those we leave behind? In such a world no man may make a faultless choice; in such a world, no man is innocent. That world is ours—and it was Noah's, a one-eyed man in a city of the blind. We are the men of the city Noah left behind; yet we are also with him in his escape. What sort of man was Noah, who were the men he dwelt among? We need but turn each to the other, and find out.

(Worshipers turn and introduce themselves to those sitting near them)

RESPONSIVE READING

There are not two kinds of man, but two poles of humanity:

The *person* becomes conscious of himself as sharing in being;

Individuality becomes conscious of itself as being such-and-such and nothing else.

No man is pure person and no man pure individuality; every man lives in the twofold I.

The aim of relation is relation's own being. The aim of relation is the contact with the Thou.

Through contact with every Thou we are stirred with a breath of the Thou.

Through contact with every Thou we are stirred with a breath of eternal life.

(rising)

בָּרְכוּ אֶת־יְיָ הַמְבֹרָךְ:

(Praise the Eternal to whom all praise is due.)

בָּרוּךְ יְיָ הַמְבֹרָךְ לְעוֹלָם וָעֶד:

(Praised be the Eternal to whom all praise is due forever and ever.)

READER

There are lost men and frightened men, selfish men and saving men, yet the world is an ark that might embrace them all. Make yourself an ark, said God to Noah; make *yourself* an ark, He says to us. Let each man become the world that Adam was, who encompassed the whole world: let each man build rooms into his soul as refuge to contain the changing needs, desires, fears, and hopes of men; let each man cement the corners of his soul with love, and kindle there a light which all the race might see and thereto find their way. Let man build himself into the image after which we were created, and so in unity with ourselves, in unity each man with each other, we may listen for the Oneness which would embrace the world.

101

שְׁמַע יִשְׂרָאֵל יְהֹוָה אֱלֹהֵינוּ יְהֹוָה אֶחָד:

(Listen, Israel: the Lord our God, the Lord is One.)

בָּרוּךְ שֵׁם כְּבוֹד מַלְכוּתוֹ לְעוֹלָם וָעֶד:

(Praised be His Name whose glorious kingdom is forever and ever.)

(seated)

RESPONSIVE READING

You shall love the Lord your God with all your heart, with all your soul, and with all your might.

> In the eyes of the One God, there is no dichotomy of here and there, of me and them. They and I are one: here is there, and there is here. Oceans divide us; God's presence unites us.

And these words which I command you this day shall be upon your heart.

> To pray is to stake our very existence, our right to live, on the truth and on the supreme importance of that which we pray for. Prayer, then, is radical commitment, a dangerous involvement in the life of God.

You shall teach them diligently to your children, and shall speak of them when you walk on the road, when you lie down, and when you rise up.

> The world is not the same since Auschwitz and Hiroshima. The decisions we make, the values we teach must be pondered not only in the halls of learning but also before the inmates in extermination camps, and in the sight of the mushroom of a nuclear explosion.

You shall bind them for a sign upon your hand, and they shall be for frontlets between your eyes.

> The groan deepens, the combat burns, the wailing cry does not abate. In a free society, all are involved in what some are doing. Some are guilty, all are responsible.

You shall write them upon the doorposts of your house and upon your gates.

> Some are guilty, all are responsible.

That you may remember and do all my commandments and be holy before your God.

> For my people's sake I will not keep silent,
> For mankind's sake I will not rest.
> Until the vindication of humanity goes forth as brightness,
> And peace for all men as a burning torch.

מִי־כָמְכָה בָּאֵלִם יְיָ מִי כָּמְכָה
נֶאְדָּר בַּקֹּדֶשׁ נוֹרָא תְהִלֹּת עֹשֵׂה
פֶלֶא:
מַלְכוּתְךָ רָאוּ בָנֶיךָ בּוֹקֵעַ יָם
לִפְנֵי מֹשֶׁה. זֶה אֵלִי עָנוּ וְאָמְרוּ.
יְיָ יִמְלֹךְ לְעֹלָם וָעֶד:
וְנֶאֱמַר כִּי־פָדָה יְיָ אֶת־יַעֲקֹב
וּגְאָלוֹ מִיַּד חָזָק מִמֶּנּוּ. בָּרוּךְ אַתָּה יְיָ
גָּאַל יִשְׂרָאֵל:

(As our forefathers sang on the shores of the divided Red Sea: Who is like you, O Lord, compared to the gods men worship? Who is like you, majestic in holiness, awesome in splendor, doing wonders? The Lord shall reign forever and ever.)

And the Lord said to Noah: Go into the ark, you and all your household, for I have seen that you are righteous enough for this generation and for My presence.

(Gen. 7:1)

Let us make our bed here, Lord our God, in peace.

And when there shall again be life, O King,
Raise us up beneath a covering of peace
That will perfect Your righteousness
Through the counsel of Your presence.
Liberate us from the place we are
That we might effect Your name.

Lead us in our journey
Far away from enmity
From slaughter

103

From hunger of the body and the soul
From unexpected sorrow
Fom those who would accuse us
Of being merely men.

Bring us into shelter
In the soft, long evening shadows
Of Your truth,
For in Your harbor lie protection and safekeeping
And in Your presence is acceptance and gentle love.

Watch over us as we go forth.
Prepare for us as we return
A peaceful welcome
Life
A future
And a now.

Spread over us a covering of peace
And over all we love
And over the peaceful city whither we shall take
Our final journey.

Go with us.

*And on the seventh day the waters of the flood were beginning
on the earth.* (Gen. 7:10)

SONG (*What Have They Done to the Rain?*)

Just a little rain, falling all around,
The grass lifts its head to the heavenly sound;
Just a little rain, just a little rain,
What have they done to the rain?

Just a little breeze out of the sky,
The leaves nod their heads as the breeze blows by.
Just a little breeze with some smoke in its eye.
What have they done to the rain?

Just a little boy, standing in the rain,
The gentle rain that falls for years;
And the grass is gone, the boy disappears,
And the rain keeps falling like helpless tears,
And what have they done to the rain?
And what have they done to the rain?

RESPONSIVE READING

I called to the Lord in my distress, and He answered me;
> Out of the belly of the nether world I cried, and You listened to my voice.

For You cast me into the deep, into the heart of the seas, and the flood was roundabout me:
> All the waves and billows passed over me.

And I said: I am cast out from before Your eyes; but I shall look again upon Your holy temple.
> The waters encompassed me, even to the soul; the deep was roundabout me; the weeds were wrapped about my head.

I went down to the bottom of the mountains; the earth with her bars closed upon me forever.
> Yet You have brought up my life from the pit, O Lord my God.

> (Jonah 2)

אַתָּה גִבּוֹר לְעוֹלָם אֲדֹנָי. מְחַיֵּה מֵתִים אַתָּה. רַב לְהוֹשִׁיעַ.

We yearn to stand before the Power whose gift is life, who quickens men who have forgotten how to live on earth.

מַשִּׁיב הָרוּחַ וּמוֹרִיד הַגָּשֶׁם:

We yearn for winds that will disperse the choking air about our lives, for cleansing rains that make parched hopes flower and give our uncreative lives the strength to clamber toward the sun.

105

מְכַלְכֵּל חַיִּים בְּחֶסֶד. מְחַיֶּה מֵתִים בְּרַחֲמִים רַבִּים.

We yearn for love that will encompass us for no reason save that we are human, for love through which defeated souls may blossom into men who can determine their own lives.

סוֹמֵךְ נוֹפְלִים וְרוֹפֵא חוֹלִים וּמַתִּיר אֲסוּרִים. וּמְקַיֵּם אֱמוּנָתוֹ לִישֵׁנֵי עָפָר.

We yearn to stand upright, we fallen; to be healed, we sufferers of the sickness of our kind; we yearn to break the bonds that keep us from ourselves and from the world beyond the flood.

מִי כָמוֹךְ בַּעַל גְּבוּרוֹת וּמִי דוֹמֶה לָךְ. מֶלֶךְ מֵמִית וּמְחַיֶּה וּמַצְמִיחַ יְשׁוּעָה.

We yearn to walk within the garden of a life of purpose, our own powers in touch with the Power in the world, that we might find the meaning of the earth.

וְנֶאֱמָן אַתָּה לְהַחֲיוֹת מֵתִים. בָּרוּךְ אַתָּה יְיָ מְחַיֶּה הַמֵּתִים:

Blessed be the God whose gift is life, whose cleansing rains let parched men flower toward the sun.

SILENT PRAYER

SONG (*I Think It's Going to Rain Today*)

Broken windows, empty hallways . . . pale dead moon in a sky streaked with grey, Human kindness overflowing, and I think it's going to rain today.

Scarecrows dressed in the latest styles with frozen smiles to keep love away; Human kindness is overflowing, and I think it's going to rain today.

Bright before me the signs implore me: help the needy
and show them the way; Human kindness overflowing, and
I think it's going to rain today.

*And everything existing on the face of the ground was blotted
out, man and beast and bird and insect, leaving only Noah and
his family and the animals with him in the ark, while the waters
kept increasing on the earth, one hundred and fifty days.*
(Gen. 7:23-24)

SONG (*Brilliant Man/Music on p. 115*)

The rabbit is a stupid thing, he loves to socialize;
He spends his time at making love and how he multiplies.

> But man, man, brilliant man,
> By his great brain he is guided;
> He's learned to walk on just two feet
> But still he stands divided.

The beaver is a stupid thing, he builds dams in the water;
To make a snug and cozy home for his son and daughter.

> But man, man, brilliant man,
> He runs around helter skelter,
> He's invented steel and concrete
> To build a fallout shelter.

The peacock is a stupid thing, with his gorgeous feathers;
He loves to mix their colors up, they go so well together.

> But man, man, brilliant man,
> His laws are so sublime
> He cannot mix his colors up
> To do so is a crime.

> Yes man, man, brilliant man
> Your memory is so long;
> You're listening to me attentively,

But you won't recall this song.
You won't recall this song.
You won't recall this song.

READER

And the seventh month brought the ark to rest, as the seventh day brings rest to us. What was the substance of life becomes its memory, and what we did must now somehow be woven into what we are. On this day we shall not do but be; we are to walk the outer limits of our humanity, no longer ride unseeing through the world we only vaguely feel beneath our vessel. On this day heat and warmth and light must come from deep within ourselves, no longer may we tear apart the world to make our fire. On this day, but a breath away from our creation, we are to breathe the world from which we may no longer feel apart. On this day we open wide the windows behind which we have hidden from the world, and send forth to learn where we have come, and what we have become.

THE MESSENGERS OF BLACK AND WHITE

And it came to pass at the end of forty days that Noah opened the window of the ark, and sent forth a raven which went to and fro, until the waters were dried up from off the earth.

(Gen. 8:6)

We are the same in our despair
Who now disturb your peace with riot—
The dark oppressed of yesteryear
Who swallowed grief and bled in quiet.

You dumped tea in Boston Harbor.
We dumped junk in New York streets.
Now you're the law and we're the robber.
Strange how history repeats.
We couldn't get no government funds,
But we got guns.

108

We couldn't get no chance to climb no higher,
But we got fire.
I was surprised
When I looked into the eyes
Of my old army pal.
It broke down my morale
The way he held that bayonet
Against my chest, and pressed;
The way his eyes were set—
Like there had never been that other war,
Like he had never seen my face before
And somehow times-gone-by had lied
That had us friends and fighting side by side;
Like I had never been within the law.
But I was black and in the street
And he was armed and there to meet
Me—like a blind date someone planned;
And being late, I smiled and raised my hand.

Those people live too far
From where we are.
They think because
They have no wish to know,
My suffering should not show
To break their narrow laws.
They think because they judge life good,
I should.
But none of them would choose to be
In their world and black like me.

And he sent forth a dove from him, to see if the waters were
abated, but the dove found no rest for the sole of her foot.
                                                    (Gen. 8:8-9)

I am one of those who could tell every word the pin went
through. Page after page I could imagine the scar in a
thousand crowned letters. . . .

There was a promise to me from a rainbow, there was a covenant with me after a flood drowned all my friends, inundated every field: the ones we had planted with food and the ones we had left untilled. . . .

Soldiers in close formation. Paratroops in a white Tel Aviv street. Who dares disdain an answer to the ovens? Any answer.

I did not like to see the young men stunted in the Polish ghetto. Their curved backs were not beautiful. Forgive me, it gives me no pleasure to see them in uniform. I do not thrill to the sight of Jewish battalions.

But there is only one choice between ghettos and battalions, between whips and the weariest patriotic arrogance. . . .

It is painful to recall a past intensity, to estimate your distance from the Belsen heap, to make your peace with numbers. Just to get up each morning is to make a kind of peace.

It is something to have fled several cities. I am glad that I could run, that I could learn twelve languages, that I escaped conscription with a trick, that borders were only stones in an empty road, that I kept my journal.

Let me refuse solutions, refuse to be comforted.

After seven days he again sent forth the dove out of the ark, and perhaps some Shabbat near the fall of evening the dove and the raven shall return, bearing in their mouths an olive leaf freshly plucked from a fertile earth at peace.

Everything now, we must assume, is in our hands; we have no right to assume otherwise. We relatively conscious whites and we relatively conscious blacks must, like lovers, insist on or create the consciousness of the others. If we do not falter in our duty now, we may be able, handful that we are, to achieve our country, and change the history of the world. If we do not now dare everything, the fulfillment of that prophecy, recreated from the Bible in song by a slave, is upon us: God gave Noah the rainbow sign: no more water, the fire next time.

ADORATION

For this is like the waters of Noah to Me: as I have sworn that the waters of Noah shall never again go over the earth, though the mountains may depart and the hills be removed My kindness shall not depart from you, nor shall my covenant of peace be removed. Everyone that thirsts, come ye for water, and he that has no money, come, and eat: for all your children shall be taught of the Lord, and great shall be the peace of your children.

(rising)

עָלֵינוּ לְשַׁבֵּחַ לַאֲדוֹן הַכֹּל לָתֵת גְּדֻלָּה לְיוֹצֵר בְּרֵאשִׁית שֶׁלֹּא עָשָׂנוּ כְּגוֹיֵי הָאֲרָצוֹת וְלֹא שָׂמָנוּ כְּמִשְׁפְּחוֹת הָאֲדָמָה שֶׁלֹּא שָׂם חֶלְקֵנוּ כָּהֶם וְגֹרָלֵנוּ כְּכָל הֲמוֹנָם:

וַאֲנַחְנוּ כּוֹרְעִים וּמִשְׁתַּחֲוִים וּמוֹדִים לִפְנֵי מֶלֶךְ מַלְכֵי הַמְּלָכִים הַקָּדוֹשׁ בָּרוּךְ הוּא.

(It is incumbent upon us to praise the Lord of all, to attribute greatness to the molder of Creation, for He did not make our lot like the nations, nor like the other families of the earth: for we bow down in reverence and thanksgiving before the king of kings, the holy one, praised be He.)

(sitting)

111

READER

And God said: This is the sign of the covenant which I am
placing between Me and you and every living creature with you
throughout all generations for all time: I have placed My bow
in the cloud, that it may be a sign of the covenant between Me
and all Creation. For when I see the bow in the cloud I shall
remember the eternal covenant between God and every creature
that has ever lived upon the earth.

MOURNERS' KADDISH

יִתְגַּדַּל וְיִתְקַדַּשׁ שְׁמֵהּ רַבָּא. בְּעָלְמָא דִי־בְרָא כִרְעוּתֵהּ.
וְיַמְלִיךְ מַלְכוּתֵהּ בְּחַיֵּיכוֹן וּבְיוֹמֵיכוֹן וּבְחַיֵּי דְכָל־בֵּית יִשְׂרָאֵל
בַּעֲגָלָא וּבִזְמַן קָרִיב. וְאִמְרוּ אָמֵן:

יְהֵא שְׁמֵהּ רַבָּא מְבָרַךְ לְעָלַם וּלְעָלְמֵי עָלְמַיָּא:

יִתְבָּרַךְ וְיִשְׁתַּבַּח וְיִתְפָּאַר וְיִתְרֹמַם וְיִתְנַשֵּׂא וְיִתְהַדָּר וְיִתְעַלֶּה
וְיִתְהַלָּל שְׁמֵהּ דְּקֻדְשָׁא. בְּרִיךְ הוּא. לְעֵלָּא (וּלְעֵלָּא) מִן־כָּל־
בִּרְכָתָא וְשִׁירָתָא תֻּשְׁבְּחָתָא וְנֶחֱמָתָא דַּאֲמִירָן בְּעָלְמָא. וְאִמְרוּ
אָמֵן:

יְהֵא שְׁלָמָא רַבָּא מִן־שְׁמַיָּא וְחַיִּים עָלֵינוּ וְעַל־כָּל־יִשְׂרָאֵל.
וְאִמְרוּ אָמֵן:

עֹשֶׂה שָׁלוֹם בִּמְרוֹמָיו הוּא יַעֲשֶׂה שָׁלוֹם עָלֵינוּ וְעַל־כָּל־יִשְׂרָאֵל.
וְאִמְרוּ אָמֵן:

CONCLUSION

Make yourself an ark, God says to us.
Let us build rooms into our soul
As refuge for the fears and hopes of men.
Let us kindle there a light which all the race might see
And thereto find their way.
Let us build ourselves into the image
After which we were created.
Let us embark upon a journey which might one day embrace
The world, God's glory, and all the children of the Lord.

SONG

The Lord said to Noah:
There's gonna be a floody, floody
The Lord said to Noah:
There's gonna be a floody, floody
Get your children out of the muddy, muddy
Children of the Lord.

Rise and shine
And give God your glory, glory
Rise and shine
And give God your glory, glory
Rise and shine and
Give God your glory, glory,
Children of the Lord.

So Noah he built him,
He built him an arky, arky
So Noah he built him,
He built him an arky, arky
Made it out of hickry barky barky
Children of the Lord.

Rise and shine . . .

The animals they came in,
They came in by twosy twosy
The animals they came in,
They came in by twosy twosy
Elephants and kangaroozy-roozy
Children of the Lord.

Rise and shine . . .

It rained and poured
For forty daysy daysy
It rained and poured
For forty daysy daysy
Drove those animals nearly crazy crazy
Children of the Lord.

Rise and shine . . .

The sun came out
And dried up the landy landy
The sun came out
And dried up the landy landy
Everything was fine and dandy dandy
Children of the Lord.

Rise and shine. . . .

BRILLIANT MAN

JAIMIE KANNER
TINA & JACK NIDES

1. The rab - bit is a stu - pid thing he loves to so - cial - ize he spends his time at ma - king love and how he mul - ti - plies.
2. The bea - ver is a stu - pid thing he builds dams in the wa - ter to make a snug and co - zy home for his son and daugh - ter.
3. The pea - cock is a stu - pid thing with his gor - geous fea - thers he loves to mix their col - ors up they go so well to - geth - er,

Chorus

But man man bril - liant man by his great brain he is guid - ed he's learned to walk on just two feet but still he stands di - vi - ded.

But man man bril - liant man he runs a - round helter skelter he's in - vent - ed steel and con - crete to build a fall - out shel - ter.

But man man bril - liant man his laws are so sub - lime he can - not mix his col - ors up To do so is a crime.

(Coda-Chorus) Yes man, man brilliant man
Your memory is so long;
You're listening to me attentively,
But you won't recall this song.
You won't recall this song.
You won't recall this song.

A VISIT TO SODOM:
A Torah Reading in Mixed Media

CANTOR

(Hebrew text of Genesis 18: 20-22)

וַיֹּאמֶר יְהֹוָה זַעֲקַת סְדֹם וַעֲמֹרָה כִּי־רָבָּה

וְחַטָּאתָם כִּי כָבְדָה מְאֹד: אֵרֲדָה־נָּא וְאֶרְאֶה

הַכְּצַעֲקָתָהּ הַבָּאָה אֵלַי עָשׂוּ כָּלָה וְאִם־לֹא אֵדָעָה:

וַיִּפְנוּ מִשָּׁם הָאֲנָשִׁים וַיֵּלְכוּ סְדֹמָה וְאַבְרָהָם עוֹדֶנּוּ

עֹמֵד לִפְנֵי יְהֹוָה:

RABBI

"And the Lord said: the cry of Sodom—it is great; and their sin—it is very weighty; I shall go down and see whether they have acted completely according to the cry which has come to me, and if not, I shall know. And (the messengers of God) turned and went to Sodom. . . ."

(lights dim)

CANTOR

(Hebrew text of Gen. 19:1, as MESSENGER enters)

וַיָּבֹאוּ שְׁנֵי הַמַּלְאָכִים סְדֹמָה בָּעֶרֶב וְלוֹט יֹשֵׁב בְּשַׁעַר־סְדֹם

וַיַּרְא־לוֹט וַיָּקָם לִקְרָאתָם וַיִּשְׁתַּחוּ אַפַּיִם אָרְצָה:

RABBI

And the two messengers entered into Sodom in the evening, while Lot was sitting at the Sodom gate; and when Lot saw them, he arose and urged them to lodge with him till morning.

MESSENGER

(bowing, to congregation)

You are very kind, but we come not to seek for lodging
But for the meaning of this city—
Who live here, how do they build their lives,
What are their loves and hates?
What do they think about when sundown ends their day?
You are Lot, we understand, and you dwell in Sodom, on the plain.

119

CHORUS

We are Lot, we who have come tonight to pray, and we dwell in
   Sodom, on the plain.
Sodom is our world—it is all men's world—the world as it is now;
Yet we do not dwell at ease—for we know Sodom, and its sins;
You have heard the cry of Sodom—we have felt its cry:
Greed, and great frustration; distrust and fear and hatred;
Violence, and the threat of violence—justice for the few and
   poverty for the many—
Justice for us—kind smiles for us; but cruelty for others,
   debasement for those not our color or our caste.
We hear the cry of Sodom, and we know its sin—yet we stay, and
   try to speak some light into the darkness.

CANTOR

(chants Gen. 19:4-5 in English)

"No sooner had the messengers come to Lot's house, and shared
his food,

(knocking heard at door, increasing)

than the men of the city—both young and old—surrounded the
house, and threatened to break down the doors, demanding that
Lot bring the messengers out to them."

WOMAN

(from congregation)

See now—look for yourselves upon Sodom, and hear its cry.

(lights go down)

Look into the darkness and see what we must live among!
   *(knocking continues as lights go out, film comes on showing
   war scenes, police beating citizens, whites and blacks, riot loot-
   ings, plane crashes, unpleasant headlines—all the while a rock
   song, critical of society, is playing)*

CHORUS

This is Sodom—but we are Lot, and innocent.
To be innocent in a guilty city—that is our guilt,
To be innocent in a guilty world—that is our burden and our anguish;
For we share the evil of the world,

And to end that evil we would have to act—
But to act is in itself to risk committing evil;
> *(each member of the chorus takes a line)*

We are not violent men—and we cannot break even an unjust law;
We are not warriors—nor can we easily be militant for peace;
We are not racists—nor can we relate to black men's racism;
We are peaceful men, and it was peaceful once, but now for us
    there is no peace—
In the burning air . . .
In the burning heart . . .
In the burning city . . .
In the burning jungle . . .
> *(whole CHORUS begins to chant. "burning" after "In the burning city" as CANTOR chants Gen. 19 12-13)*

Burning . . . burning . . . burning . . . burning . . .

CANTOR

"And the men said to Lot: Take your wife and your daughters and
their husbands out of this place, for we are about to destroy it—"

MESSENGER

The Lord has sent us to destroy it!

TWO YOUNG MEN
(Husbands of Lot's Daughters)

(laughing)

We have heard that many times, we have heard that threat so many
    times. . . .
We built shelters once, to hide us from destruction,
And now the weeds grow over them and spiders spin upon the
    beams;
From our morning doorstep great black letters roar,
But our eyes are now accustomed to their sound.
Destruction! and Destruction! will not scare us anymore.
We shall stay here and sniff the blossoms when the air is clear. . . .

CANTOR

"And the warning was a joke to the husbands of Lot's daughters."

MESSENGER

But the air is clouded now with ozone, tear gas, pesticides, and
    napalm,
And the burning eye blocks off the nose from scent;
You breathe destruction—and you will not see?
You are not violent men—yet you support a law that breeds
    violence from those it only carelessly protects;
You are not warriors—nor will you fight for peace, demand it,
    suffer for it, batter at the stubborn ears of those who think it is
    not possible;
You are not racists—but you do not understand how oppressed men
    suffer, how impotent is legislation, how hollow good will;
Where the law and the heart fail, a man must use his fist or he will
    die. . . .

CHORUS

But we are peaceful men, and it was peaceful once!

MESSENGER

But now there is no peace for you,
As there has been no peace for other men their whole lives—
Now your sons are taken to a war they do not want,
Or go to jail rather than pervert their conscience;
Now your neighborhoods, your stores, the color of your skin is
    threatened,
And yet you shake your heads and say: Awful, awful,
But nothing can be done;
You cluck your tongues amidst this city but you do not change
    your lives—
No change is possible, you say—

CHORUS

For us no change is necessary:
                    (one line per member)
The government must change its policy,
Protesters must change their tactics,
Blacks must change their frame of mind—

122

MESSENGER

And only you continue in your present course!
Only you stay here in comfort on the plain,
Shielded by the sheltering mountains from the ugliness beyond—
While the mountains hide you, you will mourn the unseen misery
    far off,
But mourning will not move you from your sheltered ghetto to open
    up the fettered ghetto on the other side. . . .

WOMAN

What can we do?

CHORUS

What can we do?

WOMAN

When we lived in ghettos, it was pleasant there,
Just us—no outsiders, and we could live the life we chose;
Study kept us in, but let us out when we desired—
For us the ghetto was a window looking out—
            (slide of prison bars with Jew behind)

MESSENGER

But the black man's ghetto is a prison hemming in!
            (Jew changes to black man)

WOMAN

I look back at what we did in our ghetto—
Let Negroes do it too: let them go back to study,
Study and hard work saved us and it will them. . . .
I look back at Sodom, even as I heed your cry to leave.
For only some men there are evil, not the town,
Not the structure, not the schools, the factories, the government,
    the law—
What has held the past together holds yet today—
There is no need to change the basic things—just people's hearts—
    just a few people's hardened hearts. . . .
            (she remains standing—a spotlight shines on her)

123

CANTOR

And Lot's wife looked back, and remained—a pillar of salt.

DAUGHTERS

Our mother cannot move, the present has captured her—
How things should be, she understands,
But how things are she cannot escape.
But we see the evils lurking under present life,
The naked filth beneath the silken gown—
Not the structure, not the schools can stay—
Not factories, not government, not law as they are now
Will cleanse our city's leprous skin,
But only some abrasive white-hot soap
Will burn away the hatred, ignorance, despair, that live here now.
We shall go away with you, our father,
And free ourselves from this society that binds us down,
And there together found a new town—with songs of free beings on
    the air—
Songs of those without restraints, without fetters, without concern
    for color or belief—
With naught to cloud their souls but love,
Love that accepts all people, love that lets each man act only as he
    wishes—
    each man his own guide, deaf to all who would direct or alter
    what he wants to do—
A free society, where each may live his way: thither we shall fly
    with you, and create from ruin room for life.
    *(At "ruin" sights flash on the wall of a city in flames. Phrases
    from a recording of "A Hard Rain's Gonna Fall," [by Bob
    Dylan] alternate with the chanting of the Torah portion.)*

CANTOR

"And the Lord rained on Sodom and Gomorra brimstone and fire
from heaven, and He overthrew these cities, and all the plain, and
all who dwelt in the cities, and every little shoot from the ground
. . . and the town went up like a smoking furance . . . and while
God was destroying the cities of the plain, He sent for Lot from the

124

midst of the overthrown cities, and he dwelt in a cave with his two daughters . . ."

MESSENGER

They did not believe us, but the deed is done . . .
This angry city, this bitter land, has fallen down about the heads
Of those who could no longer listen to the cries beyond the
    mountain.
And so, each man screaming at the silence, lit his torch that others
    might see his anguish if they would not hear,
And from those myriad torches lit up all the mountains in one
    great consuming flame,
Which crashed and screamed into the silence blind so long to
    others' agonies . . .

CHORUS

What can we do?

DAUGHTERS

These fires roar with vibrant life,
Blowing up great winds of change,
Burning up the dross of cynical oppression,
To leave behind the pure new metal of a new society—
From the fires will come forth a city forged in freedom,
Where no man fetters any man, where no man says, "You cannot!"
    or "You ought not!"
We must sing within the flames of Sodom, for they have burnt away
    oppression and restriction and control.
No more oppression! or restriction!

CHORUS

Or control!

MESSENGER

What worlds you dream of from this blackened cave!
The fires have not helped your sight, but in your world will burn
    more fiercely even than these which have consumed Sodom;

Men need laws to be free—the poor need laws to give them ease,
    the world needs laws to give it peace;
In your world every man would be each other's enemy—if each
    man defines freedom only by what he desires!
The structures of Sodom were corrupted, but in your city there
    would be no structures, no man would be protected,
You would impose heaven on what is not yet even earth!

CHORUS

What can we do?
(on screen: What Can We Do?)

RABBI

A man stood once beside a bush consumed with flames which yet
    was not consumed,
He paused there, listening to the flames and to the cry within—
A cry of anguish from his people far away beyond the mountains,
And he drew off his shoes, for by their cry he knew he stood on holy
    ground . . .

MESSENGER

Draw off your shoes—that fleetly you may run and heed that cry,
To comfort, challenge, and demand in all the realms your life may
    touch:

CHORUS

(a line for each member)
There are letters to be written,
Petitions to be signed,
Children to be tutored,
Men to be elected,
Men to be defeated,
Speeches to be made,
Marches to be taken,
Books to be read,
Facts to be shared,
Schools to be opened,
Brothers to be freed,

Sisters to be freed,
Money to be given,
Money to be raised,
Souls to save—

CHORUS

A world to save!

(pause)

A world to save!

CANTOR

"And the Lord said: . . . Behold, the cry of the children of Israel has come to me . . . and now go: I shall send you to bring my people forth. . . ."

CONGREGATION

(Underneath this speech, CHORUS repeats the chant "There are letters . . ." with "A world to save" said three times.)
We can no longer stay in comfort on the plain,
Shielded by the sheltering mountains from the ugliness beyond,
For the mountains hide us from the unseen misery far off,
There is a world to save, crying to us on the other side. . . .
Together with all people we must cross the wilderness of pain,
    quickened as we go by the bread of understanding;
That we might arrive together at the mountain, and forge from all
    the tongues of men a new law,
Whose statutes may guide us as a pillar of consuming fire to the
    Promised Land.

RABBI

There is a world to save—crying to us on the other side.

CANTOR

(concluding Torah blessing)

(at end of Torah blessing, Torah is silently raised up and re-placed in the ark)

HAVDALAH

(The lights are dimmed or turned off. The group gathers closely about the leader(s). The Havdalah candle is lit. A song such as "Hiney Ma Tov" may be sung. The leader concentrates upon the light.)

LEADER

Havdalah means "separation." It marks the separation of Shabbat from the other days of our week. We take leave of Shabbat with light, just as we welcomed it with light. The days of our week sorely need the last rays of our departing Shabbat, and in this light we seek to read the warmth that fills Shabbat that we might translate it into the days that are before us.

Shabbat is a moment from another time. It is a glimpse into an ideal world where peace and love have a reality often lacking in our real world. We seek to infuse the real with the ideal that we might be strengthened to pursue our goals with renewed strength and hope.

Tradition tells us that God's first creative act was the creation of light, and the light of this Havdalah candle participates in that first light. In this Havdalah flame we could kindle a deeper kind of light within us all. We would share for this moment the hope that is part of a greater light that someday will dispel the darkness that is hate, war, poverty, and distrust.

(The leader lifts a cup of wine and turns the focus from the candle to that symbol.)

Wine, too, is a precious symbol which at the conclusion of our service we shall share. It is sometimes strange to share its sweetness when so much of our life is caught up in moments not so sweet. And yet to share it is to know that sweetness is possible, that in reaching out for one another we can discover common bonds that make a future possible. As we say a blessing that looks toward the time when together we shall taste the sweetness of the wine, we ourselves become symbols of the future for which we live. We sing together:

בָּרוּךְ אַתָּה, יְיָ אֱלֹהֵינוּ, מֶלֶךְ הָעוֹלָם, בּוֹרֵא פְּרִי הַגָּפֶן.

(The wine cup is set down, its fruit to be shared after the blessing over the candle later on.)

131

The third symbol which we share at this moment of separation—at this moment of ending and beginning—is spice. A legend of our tradition tells us that on Shabbat each Jew is granted an extra soul —a soul to perceive more clearly that which is dimmed during the other days of our week—and at the moment when Shabbat takes her leave, our extra soul flees as well. And so the legend tells us that we sniff sweet spice to refresh our own soul, that we might better face the week that is to be. So we share the scent together and join in blessing:

בָּרוּךְ אַתָּה, יְיָ אֱלֹהֵינוּ, מֶלֶךְ הָעוֹלָם, בּוֹרֵא מִינֵי בְשָׂמִים.

(The spice box is passed around.)

On Shabbat our vision of a greater world unfolds and with that vision come other longings from our past. The yearnings of generations from their darkness toward the messianic have been given shape through the awaited presence of an ancient prophet called Elijah. We sing of him now, casting our dreams together with those of our people, making an ancient hope again, letting it live through us.

Song: Eliyahu ha-navi

בִּמְהֵרָה בְיָמֵינוּ   אֵלִיָּהוּ הַנָּבִיא,

יָבֹא אֵלֵינוּ,   אֵלִיָּהוּ הַתִּשְׁבִּי,

עִם מָשִׁיחַ בֶּן דָּוִד.   אֵלִיָּהוּ הַגִּלְעָדִי,

(The song is sung several times and hummed. During the song the candle may be passed around the group, during which time it may be appropriate to share a story, or legend, or feeling either from past or present tradition. One such legend follows.)

THE BAAL SHEM'S DREAM

Into the darkness of 18th Century Eastern European Jewish life came a light that spoke of joy, ecstasy, and hope. He was called the Baal Shem Tov—the Master of the Good Name. He was a simple man who served with a soul that touched other lives with beauty and peace.

132

One night the Baal Shem returned home after a long day of helping others and lay down for a much needed rest. He fell deeply asleep and yet was suddenly awakened by an angel who shook him and said, "Baal Shem, Baal Shem, wake up!" The tired Rabbi opened his eyes, saw the angel and said, "What is it you want?" But the angel took his arm and simply said, "Come, come with me." They walked through darkness and mist and finally the Baal Shem said, "Where are we going?" And the angel said, "You will see." And suddenly they came upon a clearing and the Baal Shem saw a man walking slowly on a narrow circular path, his eyes seeing only the path beneath his feet. But the Baal Shem saw that on the inside of the circular ridge was a raging sea of blood—a sea of the most intense passions, loves, and fears. And on the outside of the ridge was the cold blackness of nothing, the absence of the human. The Baal Shem tried to call out to the man, to warn him of where he stood and where he walked, but the angel sealed the Rabbi's lips so that he could not speak.

Suddenly the scene was lit up by an almost blinding flash of light and the eyes of the man who slowly walked his path were opened. He saw for the first time the raging sea of blood on the one side and the empty nothingness on the other, and his face twisted in horror. He began to totter. The sea of blood licked up at his heels, pulling him into its midst, and icy gnarled hands reached to pull him from his path into the darkness. He was losing his balance, almost falling into the sea, almost being sucked into the emptiness.

But then the Baal Shem's lips were freed and he screamed out to the man, "Fly! You can fly!"

And the man flew.

(Whether any interpretation of this story is necessary is a matter of personal choice and the particular situation. Some moments of silence can follow it effectively as well as another song. After the story, the leader turns again to the candle, which by now should have returned to him.)

This candle we have held together is but a symbol of ourselves, of all men, and of life itself. Like life it is kindled, it burns, it glows, it gives off beauty and rays of warmth, and then before the winds of time it flickers and is no more. As the many wicks of this Havdalah light blend into one soaring flame, so may we recall that like this candle we are one, that we are fragile, that we each possess the power for warmth and deep humanity. The blessing of its lights is a blessing for our different lives, and our single life.

(All cup hands toward the light, that light might appear through their fingernails and shadows on their palms, demonstrating the distinction between light and darkness of the Hamavdil blessing.)

בָּרוּךְ אַתָּה, יְיָ אֱלֹהֵינוּ, מֶלֶךְ הָעוֹלָם, בּוֹרֵא מְאוֹרֵי הָאֵשׁ.

We have shared this light, the wine, and the spices. We have shared blessing and song. We have become part of this moment through sight, taste, smell, sound, touch and speech. And this moment lives in us. This light of Havdalah must now go out, but it can live in each of us. We can carry its warmth out of the special Shabbat into the more ordinary days that come, and like a candle we can bring our special warmth to others. May this be the nature of the week to come. May it be the direction we travel toward our next Shabbat. Together we bless the moments we have shared, and the moments that still await us.

בָּרוּךְ אַתָּה, יְיָ אֱלֹהֵינוּ, מֶלֶךְ הָעוֹלָם, הַמַּבְדִּיל
בֵּין קֹדֶשׁ לְחֹל, בֵּין אוֹר לְחֹשֶׁךְ, בֵּין יִשְׂרָאֵל
לָעַמִּים, בֵּין יוֹם הַשְּׁבִיעִי לְשֵׁשֶׁת יְמֵי הַמַּעֲשֶׂה.
בָּרוּךְ אַתָּה, יְיָ, הַמַּבְדִּיל בֵּין קֹדֶשׁ לְחֹל.

(Following the blessing, the wine is shared, and the flame is extinguished with the remaining wine. The Havdalah service can be concluded with the singing of "Shavuah Tov". If the group has not yet come together physically, this might be done now simply by the leader extending his arms to those near him. If the service is concluded with a benediction, people might be encouraged to share their blessings for each other and then to say in unison, "Amen.")

SERVICES ON SPECIAL THEMES

A SERVICE FOR ISRAEL

READER

My Heart Is In The East

In the East, in the East is my heart,
And I dwell at the end of the West;
How shall I join in your feasting,
How shall I share in your jest;
How shall my offering be paid,
My vows with performance be crowned,
While Zion pines in Edom's thrall,
And I am pent in the Arab's bound!
All the beauties and treasures of Spain
Are worthless as dust, in my eyes;
But the dust of the Lord's ruined house
Is the most precious treasure I prize.

RESPONSIVE READING (by Stanza)

Israel

When I think of the liberation of Palestine,
When my eye conceives the great black English line
Spanning the world news of two thousand years,
My heart leaps forward like a hungry dog,
My heart is thrown back on its tangled chain,
My soul is hangdog in a Western chair.

When I think of the battle for Zion I hear
The drops of chains, the starting forth of feet,
And I remain chained in a Western chair.
My blood beats like a bird against a wall,
I feel the weight of prisons in my skull
Falling away; my forebears stare through stone.

When I see the name of Israel high in print
The fences crumble in my flesh; I sink
Deep in a Western chair and rest my soul.
I look the stranger clear to the blue depths
Of his unclouded eye. I say the name
Aloud for the first time unconsciously.

Speak of the tillage of a million heads
No more. Speak of the evil myth no more
Of one who harried Jesus on his way
Saying, *Go faster*. Speak no more
Of the yellow badge, *secta nefaria*.
Speak the name only of the living land.

A FEMALE VOICE, UNSEEN

The relationship of the Jewish people to the land of Israel is itself
living history. Just as ardent love between human beings can be
real and powerful even though they don't dwell together on one spot
in space, the love of the Jewish people for the land is an ongoing,
powerful being together even when living at a distance, a real link,
a being at home spiritually, an embrace that never tires, a hope that
never ceases.

SILENT MEDITATION

(musical background: Yerushalayim— *From Mt. Scopus)*

We are a people in whom the past endures, in whom the present
is inconceivable without moments gone by. The vision of the prophets lasted a moment, a moment enduring forever. What happened
once upon a time happens all the time.

Genuine history occurs when the events of the present disclose the
meaning of the past and offer an anticipation of the promise of the
future.

History is encounter of the eternal and temporal.

READER

Born under the Egyptian lash, this people painfully won its redemption. They were bound by a common vision, a hope for liberation that was self-fulfilling.

As one timeless moment gave way to another, in that somewhere called Sinai, ancestral bodies bent by servitude were raised up by a dream and promise.

Enriched now as a community in covenant, the people discovered its land. Vision became reality as Israel confirmed the dignity of her promise. Land and people were rooted in ideal as well as stone.

In affirming their identity as a people of common strivings, solemnly our ancestors were consecrated to the quest for salvation and human redemption.

With that quest came a spirit of antagonism to ignorance, to superstition, to tyranny.

This quest and this spirit ennobled Israel in her encounter with time.

CONGREGATION

Ours was a unique light shining in antiquity. The first Jewish Commonwealth was not unlike other nation-states of the time; it knew political intrigue, it knew corruption. Yet the spirit of a consecrated people could not be broken. Rooted in the soil of the promised land, Israel and Judah discovered a prophetic zeal. With sublime passion the Jewish prophets challenged their strife-ridden people with demands yet unheard in the annals of man.

VOICE

I hate, I despise your feasts,
And I will take no delight in your solemn assemblies.

Yes, though you offer Me burnt-offering and your meal offerings,
I will not accept them;
Neither will I regard the peace-offering of your fat beasts.
Take away from Me the noise of your songs;
And let Me not hear the melody of your psalteries.
But let justice well up as waters,
And righteousness as a mighty stream.

ANTIPHONAL READING

This was our charge.
> It remained our constant challenge.

To respond was to give quality to our essential being.
> We learned to respond.

It was understood that the act of each Jew reflects the character of all Israel.
> We welcomed that responsibility.

Pursuit of ideals often demanded personal sacrifice.
> We offered that sacifice.

Ethical commitments could not be compromised.
> We found the courage for that loyalty.

Even in exile the meaning of Jewish existence demanded strong conviction in our worth as Jews and in our moral sense of universal responsibility.
> Challenged by our suffering we bore witness together. By the rivers of Babylon, as in all places thereafter, Israel proclaimed its unity of purpose and vision.

READER

(with musical accompaniment)

By the rivers of Babylon,
There we sat down, yes, we wept,
When we remembered Zion.
Upon the willows in the midst thereof
We hanged up our harps.
For there they that led us captive asked of us words of song,
And our tormentors asked of us mirth:
"Sing us one of the songs of Zion."

How shall we sing the Lord's song
In a foreign land?
If I forget you, O Jerusalem,
Let my right hand forget her cunning.
Let my tongue cleave to the roof of my mouth,
If I remember you not;
If I set not Jerusalem
Above my chiefest joy.

READER

Exiled once and then again, the Jew became history's perennial
victim. For two millenia the nations reconsecrated us with blood and
fire, with crusade and inquisition and pogrom.

CONGREGATION

We have been victim and witness to the depths of human depravity.
But while our flesh was torn, we preserved our spirit.

VOICE

It is written: Exile can become a source of redemption if the Jew
feels its pain in all his being.

READER

Though defeated by destiny and dispersed among the nations, we
wrought in exile a saga of spiritual resistance. Determined to endure, we transformed, through Torah, our superhuman suffering
into inspired and fervent loyalty to our ravaged land and people.
Thus enriched by heritage, wisdom became the baggage of our
dispersion; genius, the substance of our survival.

VOICE

Masada

The chain has not been broken
The chain continues still
From fathers to sons
From bonfires to bonfires
The chain continues . . .

The chain has not been broken
The chain continues still
From nights of rejoicing in the Torah
To nights of rejoicing on Masada
The chain continues . . .

So our forefathers danced
One arm around a comrade
The other holding a Torah scroll
Carrying the nation's suffering with love
So our forefathers danced . . .

So will we dance too
One arm around a comrade
The other embracing a generation's suffering . . .
So will we dance too

When our forefathers danced
They closed their eyes tight
And thus opened wellsprings of ectasy
Their feet were light
When their eyes were closed
So our forefathers danced . . .

They knew, our forefathers did
That they were dancing on an abyss
And if they opened their eyes
The wellsprings of ecstasy would close
And the chain would crumble to nothing.
They knew, our forefathers knew.

So will we dance too
Our eyes closed
So will we continue the chain . . .

SILENT MEDITATION

Despoiled and dispersed, abased and harassed, we knew we were not estranged forever. We mourned you, we never wept you away. Hope was hatched in the nests of agony.

The love of this land was due to an imperative, not to an instinct, not to a sentiment. There is a covenant, an engagement of the people to the land. We live by covenants. We could not betray our pledge or discard the promise.

When Israel was driven into exile, the pledge became a prayer; the prayer a dream; the dream a passion, a duty, a dedication.

Intimate attachment to the land, waiting for the renewal of Jewish life in the land of Israel, is part of our integrity, an existential fact. Unique, *sui generis,* it lives in our hopes, it abides in our hearts. It is a commitment we must not betray. Three thousand years of faithfulness cannot be wiped off.

READER

Exile from the land was conceived as an interruption, as a prelude to return, never as an abandonment or detachment. Bonds of hope tied us to the land. To abandon these bonds was to deny our identity.

CONGREGATION

In our own time, too, darkness engulfed the Jewish people. The life of our fathers was turned into one long night of death. In the nocturnal silence which descended upon Israel the only sound heard was the roar of the oven. When the crematories turned Jewish flesh to smoke, neither God nor man cried out. These things are to be remembered.

VOICE

Never shall I forget that night . . . which has turned my life into one long night, seven times cursed and seven times sealed. Never shall I forget that smoke. Never shall I forget the little faces of the children, whose bodies I saw turned into wreaths of smoke beneath a silent blue sky . . . Never shall I forget these things, even if I am condemned to live as long as God Himself. Never.

145

Tizkor v'al tishkach!   Remember.   Remember.

CONGREGATION

Let us remember the life and death of our people. Let us speak of
our slaughtered, of their despair, of their hope.
May we the living remember our dead, and let us not rest until our
lives are worthy of their memory.

READER

Rise then and let us honor the dead martyrs of our people.

KADDISH

ANI MAAMIN
("I Believe")

ANI MAAMIN

("I Believe")

A-ni ma-a-min be-e-mu-no sh'le-mo
B'vi-as ha-mo-shi-ah, v'af al pi
She-yis-ma-mey-ah, im kol ze a-ni ma-a-min.

READER

Time's endless pattern is repeated. The flame is dimmed and snuffed out. Yet even the darkness reveals new life. In the ashes of the holocaust future strivings were made present. The survivors brought forth a new generation. Together, they and we have taken up the age-old dream, struggled with it and triumphed. Israel, land and people, lives!

VOICE

I believe that a wondrous generation of Jews will spring into existence. The Maccabeans will rise again. Let me repeat . . . The Jews who wish it will have their State. We shall live at last as free men on our own soil, and die peacefully in our own homes.

ANTIPHONAL READING

We have gathered up human remnants and bound them into the fruitful nucleus of a nation reborn.

In the desolate spaces of a ruined and abandoned Homeland we have built villages and towns, planted gardens and established factories.

We have breathed new life into our muted ancient language.

This country made us a people; our people made this country.

That little land of revelation which, like some precious jewelled clasp, draws three continents together on the shore of the Western Sea.

147

A message of hope and good cheer issues from this place, from this sacred city, to all oppressed people and to all who struggle for freedom and equality.

We, a people of orphans, have entered the walls to greet the widow, Jerusalem, and the widow is a bride again. She has taken hold of us, and we find ourselves again at the feet of the prophets. We are the harp, and David is playing.

Israel has restored to the people living in its midst their wholeness as Jews and human beings.

Our lives have once again become . . . a complete unity of existence and experience, which embraces in a Jewish framework all the contents of the life of man and people.

READER

But as Chaim Weitzman once reminded us: "A nation does not receive a state on a silver platter."

VOICE

(*with musical background*)

The Silver Platter

There is peace in the land.
A red sky slowly dims
Over smoldering frontiers.
And a nation is gathered
Scarred but alive . . .
To welcome the miracle
To which none is compared . . .

She prepares for the ceremony.
Arising under the moon
She stands before day-break
Wrapped in festivity and awe.

Then a lad and a maiden
Approach from afar
And they march in slow cadence
And confront the nation.
In their work-clothes and full gear
Heavy shoes on their feet
Up the path they
Silently march.
Their garb has not been changed
Nor has water erased
The traces of the day's hard toil
And the night's heavy fire.
Exhausted beyond measure
Having forsworn repose
And dripping the dew-drops
of Hebrew youth
Speechlessly the two step forward
and stand motionless
And there is no sign if they are living or slain.

The nation then asks
Bathed in tears and in wonder
"Who are you?"
And the two reply:
"We are the silver platter

Upon which the Jewish State was served to you."
Thus they speak
And they fall at her feet
Shrouded in shadows.

The rest will be told in Israel's chronicles.

SOLO: *Rachel of Kinneret*

149

CONGREGATION

Let the Jewish people remember the best of her sons
The strong of heart and pure of vision
The first strength in the Homeland
The last embers from the diaspora
Who took arms to defend
The honor and independence of Israel
Who died defending its borders . . .
Let the Jewish people remember
All those who fell
In the struggles for Israel's redemption
For in their Death,
They bequeathed life to us.

SILENT MEDITATION

(Hatikvah *played as background music*)

The Jewish people has risen once again in the Land of Israel . . .
Therefore, have we, Members of the People's Council, representatives of the Yishuv and the Zionist Movement, foregathered, on the day of the conclusion of the British Mandate for Palestine, and by virtue of our natural and historic right, and on the basis of the Resolution of the United Nations Assembly, we proclaim the establishment of a Jewish State in Eretz Israel, the State of Israel.

The State of Israel will be open to Jewish immigration and to the ingathering of the exiles. It will endeavor to develop the country for the benefit of all inhabitants and be founded upon the principles of freedom, justice and peace, in the spirit of the vision of the prophets of Israel . . .

We stretch forth our hands in peace and good neighborliness to all neighboring States and nations, and call upon them to cooperate in a spirit of mutual assistance with the independent Jewish people in its own country. The State of Israel is prepared to make its contribution in the united effort for the development of the entire Middle East.

We call upon the Jewish people in all lands of its dispersion to rally round the Yishuv, in immigration and construction, and to assist it in the great struggle for the realization of the aspirations of generations for the redemption of Israel.

Hatikvah

Kol od baleyvav p'neema
Nefesh yehudee homee-ah
Ul'fa-atey mizrach kadeemah
Ayin l'tzee-on tzofee-ah.

כָּל עוֹד בַּלֵּבָב פְּנִימָה
נֶפֶשׁ יְהוּדִי הוֹמִיָּה
וּלְפַאֲתֵי מִזְרָח קָדִימָה
עַיִן לְצִיּוֹן צוֹפִיָּה.

Od lo avdah tikvateynoo
Hatikva shnat alpayim
Lihyot am Chofshee b'artzeynoo
Be'retz tzee-on veerooshalayim.

עוֹד לֹא אָבְדָה תִקְוָתֵנוּ
הַתִּקְוָה שְׁנַת אַלְפַּיִם
לִהְיוֹת עַם חָפְשִׁי בְּאַרְצֵנוּ
בְּאֶרֶץ צִיּוֹן וִירוּשָׁלָיִם.

READER

1948 . . . . 1956 . . . . 1967 . . . It is as if each generation must be annointed for struggle. Each is somehow called to walk forward into the valley of the past It is as if each generation must rediscover for itself and its children the quarry of Jewish experience with which to build Israel's future.

VOICE

Then he said to me, 'Son of man, these bones are the whole house of Israel. Behold, they say, Our bones are dried up, our hope is lost; we are clean cut off. Therefore prophesy, and say to them, Thus says the Lord God: Behold I will open your graves, and raise you from your graves, O my people; and I will bring you home into the land of Israel . . . And I will put my Spirit within you, and you shall live, and I will place you in your own land. . . . says the Lord.'

CONGREGATION

Our national renaissance is not mere national freedom or rejuvenation; our national revival is like a resurrection of the dead, an event that has no parallel.

READER

When I go to Israel every stone and every tree is a reminder of hard labor and glory, of prophets and psalmists, of loyalty and holiness. The Jews go to Israel not only for physical security for themselves and their children; they go to Israel for renewal, for the experience of resurrection.

SILENT MEDITATION

*(musical background, "Jerusalem of Gold"
continue to conclusion of service)*

It was before the outbreak of the Six Day War. The battalion was stationed in the Negev along the old border. It was terribly hot, and water was rationed, so we were all covered with dust and filthy dirty from the manoeuvres. We were only waiting to be given a chance to lie down and doze off in our pup-tents. I shared my tent with a reservist, a man older than most of us, who had nevertheless stood up well to the tough conditions. As evening fell, he amazed me by pulling out of his rucksack two sheets, laundered and ironed. I couldn't help smiling as I watched him spread them out, but then he started speaking quietly and sadly: "Everywhere I've been for years now I've taken these sheets with me—ever since the Second World War. I worked in a laundry then, washing sheets for German soldiers—but there weren't any sheets in our ghetto . . . yet every day we washed sheets for them . . . I swore an oath then that if I got out of it all alive, I'd always sleep on a clean sheet." And so saying, he lay down between the sheets and fell asleep.

READER

If I were to be asked what symbolizes this war, then I wouldn't choose the great conquests, I'd choose something that appears to be much more modest but is, perhaps, much greater than it seems at first sight, much more all-embracing—for me, what symbolizes this war is the paratrooper who stood facing the Western Wall and could find no outlet for his emotion other than tears. It's symbolic too because that same paratrooper wasn't just facing the Western Wall—he was also facing two thousand years of exile, the whole history of the Jewish people.

CONGREGATION

Yes, he was facing the history of the Jewish people—and perhaps it was the first time that he was doing so in such a concrete manner. And perhaps there's some educational value in the whole thing—here we are standing in the places which have been sacred to our nation since its earliest history, here we are face to face with the whole of Jewish history. Not every generation has such an opportunity.

VOICE

(like a small child speaking)

Outside, the shells are falling. In the shelter the children are asleep.

In between the bombshells you can hear the rhythmic breathing of the children.

Only one little girl keeps turning restlessly from side to side.
I go over to her. She sits up and whispers:

"I can't sleep. Maybe you can phone the Arabs and tell them to stop shooting?"

153

READER

Our attitude to the land is complex, one of longing and attachment, starting with the dreams of our childhood and involving a deep desire to take root, a desire which is sometimes the expression of a fear of being torn away. This desire also embraces the people in the country . . . Once Jewish sovereignty was gained, once it became clear that this was the home of the whole Jewish people, that it was their shelter, the home of their dreams, their creative spirit—then we were left with another great dream, one no less fantastic, perhaps, than the vision of the establishment of the State: that we should be able to take root not only on the mountains, in the soil, but also in the human scene—among the Arabs.

VOICE

(like a small child speaking)

If all the countries would make peace—what fun:
Israel, Jordan, Egypt, Syria, Lebanon.
No more scary wars that kill
Not to run to shelters during meals.
Peace all over hand in hand,
and no one bombing any land,
Let Israel be for the Jews
And all the people friends and true.
War is not worthwhile,
Let's have peace—that's all.

READER

Pray for the peace of Jerusalem.

CONGREGATION
(sings)

Jerusalem of Gold

154

JERUSALEM OF GOLD

ירושלים של זהב

Verse (♩=90)

1. A - vir ha-rim tsa-lul ka-ya-in Ve-re-ach o - ra - nim Ni - sa be-ru-ach ha - ar - ba - im Im kol pa - a - mo - nim.

tar - de-mat i-lan va - e - ven Shvu - ya ba-cha-lo - ma Ha - ir a - sher - ba-dad yo - she - vet U - ve-li - ba cho - ma. Uv - Ye - ru - sha -

Refrain

la - im Shel Za-hav Ve-shel ne - cho-shet ve-shel or Ha-lo le - chol shi - ra-ich A - ni ki-nor. Ye - ru-sha - nor. Ye - ru-sha - 2. (Ei-)

(Last time to Coda) *D.S. al Coda*

⊕ **Coda**

nor. Ye - ru-sha - la - im Shel Za-hav Ve-shel ne cho-shet ve-shel or Ha-lo le - chol - shi - ra-ich A - ni ki - nor, ki - nor.

2. Eicha yavshu borot hama'im
   Kikar hashuk reika
   Ve'ein poked et har haba'it
   Ba'ir ha'atika
   Uvam'arot asher basela
   Meyalelot ruchot
   Ve'ein yored el Yam Hamelach
   bederech Yericho.

3. Ach bevo'i hayom lashir lach
   Velach likshor ktarim
   Katonti mitse'ir bana'ich
   Ume'achron hamshorerim
   Ki shmech tsorev et hasfata'im
   Kineshikat saraf
   Im eshkachech Yerushala'im
   Asher kula zahav.

Added Verse: Chazarnu el borot hama'im
   Lashuk velakikar
   Shofar kore Behar Haba'it
   Ba'ir ha'atika
   Uvam'arot asher basela
   Alfei shmashot zorchot
   Nashuv nered el Yam Hamelach
   bederech Yericho.

Refrain: Yerushala'im Shel Zahav
   Veshel nechoshet veshel or
   Halo lechol shira'ich
   Ani kinor, kinor.

155

ירושלים של זהב

אַךְ בְּבוֹאִי הַיּוֹם לָשִׁיר לָךְ	אֲוִיר־הָרִים צָלוּל כַּיַּיִן
וְלָךְ לִקְשֹׁר כְּתָרִים	וְרֵיחַ אֳרָנִים
קָטֹנְתִּי מִצְּעִיר בָּנַיִךְ	נִשָּׂא בְּרוּחַ הָעַרְבַּיִם
וּמֵאַחֲרוֹן הַמְשׁוֹרְרִים	עִם קוֹל פַּעֲמוֹנִים
כִּי שְׁמֵךְ צוֹרֵב אֶת הַשְּׂפָתַיִם	וּבְתַרְדֵּמַת אִילָן וָאֶבֶן
כִּנְשִׁיקַת־שָׂרָף	שְׁבוּיָה בַּחֲלוֹמָהּ
אִם אֶשְׁכָּחֵךְ יְרוּשָׁלַיִם	הָעִיר אֲשֶׁר בָּדָד יוֹשֶׁבֶת
אֲשֶׁר כֻּלָּהּ זָהָב . . .	וּבְלִבָּהּ חוֹמָה
יְרוּשָׁלַיִם שֶׁל זָהָב וְשֶׁל נְחֹשֶׁת וְשֶׁל אוֹר	יְרוּשָׁלַיִם שֶׁל זָהָב וְשֶׁל נְחֹשֶׁת וְשֶׁל אוֹר
הֲלֹא לְכָל שִׁירַיִךְ אֲנִי כִּנּוֹר	הֲלֹא לְכָל שִׁירַיִךְ אֲנִי כִּנּוֹר
חָזַרְנוּ אֶל בּוֹרוֹת־הַמַּיִם	אֵיכָה יָבְשׁוּ בּוֹרוֹת־הַמַּיִם
לַשּׁוּק וְלַכִּכָּר	כִּכַּר־הַשּׁוּק רֵיקָה
שׁוֹפָר קוֹרֵא בְּהַר־הַבַּיִת	וְאֵין פּוֹקֵד אֶת הַר־הַבַּיִת
בָּעִיר הָעַתִּיקָה	בָּעִיר הָעַתִּיקָה
וּבַמְּעָרוֹת אֲשֶׁר בַּסֶּלַע	וּבַמְּעָרוֹת אֲשֶׁר בַּסֶּלַע
אַלְפֵי שְׁמָשׁוֹת זוֹרְחוֹת —	מְיַלְּלוֹת רוּחוֹת
נָשׁוּב נֵרֵד אֶל יָם הַמֶּלַח	וְאֵין יוֹרֵד אֶל יַם־הַמֶּלַח
בְּדֶרֶךְ יְרִיחוֹ !	בְּדֶרֶךְ יְרִיחוֹ
יְרוּשָׁלַיִם שֶׁל זָהָב וְשֶׁל נְחֹשֶׁת וְשֶׁל אוֹר	יְרוּשָׁלַיִם שֶׁל זָהָב וְשֶׁל נְחֹשֶׁת וְשֶׁל אוֹר
הֲלֹא לְכָל שִׁירַיִךְ אֲנִי כִּנּוֹר	הֲלֹא לְכָל שִׁירַיִךְ אֲנִי כִּנּוֹר

THE AMERICAN JEW

CONGREGATION
(Singing)

Heenay ma tov uma-nayeem,
Shevet acheem gam yachad.

(How good and how pleasant it is for
brethren to dwell together in peace.)

READER

"Listen, you asses, brutes, drunken sots! Listen, you hooligans,
you murderers! We have to thank you for having reached this
haven, this refuge, this great and blessed land, the land of the free.
If not for you who persecuted us with your evil edicts and your
pogroms, to this very day we wouldn't get to know Columbus, and
Columbus wouldn't get to know us. You'll have to wait a long,
long time till we return to you. Do you ever expect to see your
own ears? That's when you'll see us again. Some day you'll wake
to the fact that you have lost a treasure—the people of Israel. The
treasure was once yours, and you let it slip through your fingers.
Yours will be the fate of Spain. Some day you'll wake up and start
howling for us. You'll start searching for a Jew in all the corners
of your land, but you won't find a single one. You'll start begging
us to return. You'll plead—but nobody will be there to reply, and
nobody will come to your call . . ."

Who knows how far Pinney's fine phrases would have carried
him, if Jonah the biscuit man hadn't put his hand on his shoulder
and said, "Pinney, in God's name! Whom are you lecturing to?
The waves? Come, or we'll miss the ferry. Or do you want to
spend the night on Ellis Island?"

We pick up our bundles and start for the ferry.

159

INDIVIDUAL READING

(A line for each member of the congregation)

Sing a new song to the Lord;
sing to the Lord, all men on earth.

Sing to the Lord and bless his name,
proclaim his triumph day by day.

Declare his glory among the nations,
his marvelous deeds among all people.

Great is the Lord and worthy of all praise;
he is more to be feared than all gods.

For the gods of the nations are idols every one;
but the Lord made the heavens.

Majesty and splendour attend him,
might and beauty are in his sanctuary.

Ascribe to the Lord, you families of nations,
ascribe to the Lord glory and might.

Ascribe to the Lord the glory due to His name,
bring a gift and come into His courts.

Bow down to the Lord in the splendor of holiness,
and dance in His honor, all men on earth.

Declare among the nations, 'The Lord is king.
He has fixed the earth firm, immovable;
He will judge the peoples justly.'

Let the heavens rejoice and the earth exult,
let the sea roar and all the creatures in it,
let the fields exult and all that is in them.

Then let all the trees of the forest shout for joy
before the Lord when He comes to judge the earth.

He will judge the earth with righteousness
and the peoples in good faith.

ANTIPHONAL READING

On ash-grey covered-wagon caravans
Across the Sierras to you we did not wend.
When we prayed to the God of Abraham, Isaac and Jacob
Our heads over loaded rifles we did not bend.

Not our tents your redskin warriors set fire to,
So that they burned under the steel-blue, night-cold sky
Of your black-bodied prairies,
Like red-dripping wounds raw and new.

Not our arms bronzed by the sun
Washed in your streams your gold-dust,
Our blood did not flow when your scalping knives
Into human heads were thrust.

Not we with bowed heads and silent tongues
Buried in the desert our pioneer dead,
Not our flocks and herds in famine and drought
Your vultures and your carrion crows fed.

We did not have to break in
Your wild bucking broncos,
Nor with the lasso ride to stop a wild rush
Of your infuriated buffaloes.

Not our feet over your highlands
Trod the first pathways,
Not our hands in your plains began
The first towns to raise.

How can broken backs
That carry dust-grey pedlars' sacks
Move to that swing?
The wanderer s staff along the exile roads everywhere,
Bronze arm and steel fist
Ever expect to resist?

We waited and waited and waited
Till our ears heard the song of the railroad,
The rush of the iron steed
We were intoxicated
By his wind-swift speed.
The poison of the metal had poisoned our blood.

We heard that your gold-dust had been
Washed and cleansed and now was clean,
We heard your every prairie lies stretched out now
Like a fat well-pastured cow,
We heard that your forests and gardens and fields
Are with eternal summer blessed,
That each hill yields
Riches from a flowing mother-breast.

We heard that the tomahawk, the bow and arrow and the
          scalping knife have come
To be exhibits in the museum,
That the buffalo is now kept on view
With gay-plumaged peacocks in the local zoo,
And your rolling fields and plains
Are now full of roads, arteries and veins.

Villages and towns shoot up from under your skin
Like mushrooms in a field after warm rain.
Over the dark hills on the rim of the western horizon
Crosses a shadowy phantom covered-wagon.
The prairie fires lit by your redskins have burned low,
Only in the hearts of your many-coloured multitude of peoples
     they still darkly glow.

We too in the whirlwind of city streets will be driven,
We too in the vortex of your swift-coming generations will be riven,
Yet over your ash-grey mountains in the sunrise,
Like the phoenix from its own fire-death in place of your dead
    generations will rise
With gay coloured wings outspread,
Our new generation too, young, swift, with fresh eager tread.

READER

The smaller boys are not allowed to work in the mornings. There is a law in America that little boys have to go to school. Otherwise their parents are punished. In America, parents get punished for their children's mischief. On the other hand, children are taught in school free of charge. Besides, they get books and writing implements free. When our friend Pinney learned of this, he almost fainted with astonishment. He recalled that in the old country, Jewish children were kept from going to school—while here in America they're actually dragged to school by their forelocks. And if they should refuse to go, they get punished. Only for this, says Pinney, Russia can bury itself in the earth for shame.

SILENT READING

Never again should one complain of buttons hanging by a thread, for tiny, tortured fingers have doubtless done their little ineffectual best. And for his lifting of burdens, this giving of youth and strength, this sacrifice of all that should make childhood radiant, a child may add to the family purse from 50 cents to $1.50 a week. In the rush times of the year, preparing for the changes of seasons or for the great "white sales", there are no idle fingers in the sweatshops. A little child of "seven times one" can be very useful in threading needles, in cutting the loose threads at the ends of seams, and in pulling out bastings. To be sure, the sewer is docked for any threads left on or for any stitch broken by the little bungling fingers. The light is not good, but baby eyes must "look sharp."

Besides work at sewing, there is another industry for little girls in the grim tenements. The mother must be busy at her sewing, or, perhaps, she is away from dark to dark at office cleaning. A little daughter, therefore, must assume the work and care of the family. She becomes the "little mother," washing, scrubbing, cooking. In New York City alone, 60,000 children are shut up in the home sweatshops. This is a conservative estimate, based upon a recent investigation of the Lower East Side of Manhattan Island, south of 14th Street and east of the Bowery. Many of this immense host will never sit on a school bench. Is it not a cruel civilization that allows little hearts and little shoulders to strain under these grown-up responsibilities, while in the same city a pet cur is jeweled and pampered and aired on a fine lady's velvet lap on the beautiful boulevards?

CONGREGATION

"Shame on you, you barbarous, ignorant, unenlightened people! I see that the stamp of your exile in darkest Russia has burned deep into you. It is keeping you down to the earth and does not permit you to rise, to stand upright, to lift your heads. You've forgotten that you are in America, the country of freedom and equality—and not in Russia, the land of swine. You forget that all American millionaires and billionaires have worked in their youth by the sweat of their brows and have made their fortunes at menial tasks. They sat in shops and sewed trousers; they sold their humble wares from pushcarts. Ask Rockefeller or Carnegic, ask Morgan or Vanderbilt—ask any of them what they used to do in their youth. Didn't they sweep the streets? Didn't they sell newspapers? Or maybe they shined shoes for a nickel? Or take the king of the automobiles, Mr. Ford—ask him whether he wasn't once a taxi-driver. Or look at the great people of this country—Washington, for instance, or Lincoln, or Roosevelt—were they all born great? Were they all presidents from birth? Or take our present president, Mr. Wilson himself. What did he used to be? Begging your pardon, nothing but a teacher!"

READER

"Look at me," he said. "Twenty years in America, and poorer than when I came. A suspender shop I had, and it was stolen from me by a villian. A house painter foreman I became, and fell off a scaffold. Now bananas I sell and even at that I am a failure. It is all luck." He sighed and puffed at his pipe.

"Ach, Gott, what a rich country America is! What an easy place to make one's fortune! Look at all the rich Jews! Why has it been so easy for them, so hard for me? I am just a poor little Jew without money."

"Poppa, lots of Jews have no money," I said to comfort him.

"I know it, my son," he said, "but don't be one of them. It's better to be dead in this country than not to have money. Promise me you'll be rich when you grow up, Mikey!"

"Yes, poppa."

"Ach," he said fondly, "this is my one hope now. This is all that makes me happy! I am a greenhorn, but you are an American! You will have it easier than I; you will have luck in America!"

"Yes, poppa," I said, trying to smile with him. But I felt older than he; I could not share his native optimism; my heart sank as I remembered the past and thought of the future.

SONG: *What now, Mr. Madison?* (*Music on p. 179*)

In the land of Long Ago
Once upon a dream
Within a distant kingdom dwelt a distant king
Who courted no one's friendship
So no one came to court
A tower sculpt of ivory
Guards the silent fort.

Chorus: America come hear
I need a friend to keep me hanging on
I'd give my eyes if I could only see
your purple mountains' majesty
Above the fruited plain
I'll help you if you help me up again.

All the dreams of ages lost
Stripped of painted pride

A castle stood in ashes sympathy denied
Waiting for a miracle
And when the rainbow came
Lo—the kingly sunken eyes
Could only see the rain.

Chorus: repeat

READERS

On Foreign Soil

I sowed on foreign soil
Plant and grain and tree.
And when the earth bore
My heart danced with glee.

I did not boast my ancestry,
Only the fruit of my hand.
Number the trees, inhale the smell.
I wasted no time in this land.

Timber, oil, fur and wool
I prepared for the wintertide.
I dreamed that one day in this place
My name would ring out wide.

But then the farmer who owns the land
Took what to him belongs,
The fruit and plant and grain he took
And I was left with my songs.

Wednesday and Sabbath Day

Across the distant land of dream,
On the other side of the purple fence
That is carved out of dream-crystal,
Lies the land of my Wednesday and my Sabbath day.
        There I wander about

By the shores of the sea,
And it is always Wednesday.
Someone has stolen my Sabbath day.
My dress is the same on Wednesday and on Sabbath day.
I eat hastily on the Sabbath as on the Wednesday.
Who juggles with my seven days,
With my seven suns?

CONGREGATION

How difficult for me is Hebrew: even the Hebrew for *mother*, for *bread*, for *sun* is foreign. How far have I been exiled, Zion.

SONG: L'CHA DODI

לְכָה דוֹדִי

לְכָה דוֹדִי לִקְרַאת כַּלָּה. פְּנֵי שַׁבָּת נְקַבְּלָה:

שָׁמוֹר וְזָכוֹר בְּדִבּוּר אֶחָד. הִשְׁמִיעָנוּ אֵל הַמְיֻחָד.

יְיָ אֶחָד וּשְׁמוֹ אֶחָד. לְשֵׁם וּלְתִפְאֶרֶת וְלִתְהִלָּה:

לִקְרַאת שַׁבָּת לְכוּ וְנֵלְכָה. כִּי הִיא מְקוֹר הַבְּרָכָה.

מֵרֹאשׁ מִקֶּדֶם נְסוּכָה. סוֹף מַעֲשֶׂה בְּמַחֲשָׁבָה
תְּחִלָּה:

בּוֹאִי בְשָׁלוֹם עֲטֶרֶת בַּעְלָהּ. גַּם בְּשִׂמְחָה וּבְצָהֳלָה.

תּוֹךְ אֱמוּנֵי עַם סְגֻלָּה. בּוֹאִי כַלָּה בּוֹאִי כַלָּה:

בָּרְכוּ אֶת־יְיָ הַמְבֹרָךְ:

CONGREGATION AND READER

בָּרוּךְ יְיָ הַמְבֹרָךְ לְעוֹלָם וָעֶד:

167

בָּרוּךְ אַתָּה יְיָ אֱלֹהֵינוּ מֶלֶךְ הָעוֹלָם אֲשֶׁר
בִּדְבָרוֹ מַעֲרִיב עֲרָבִים בְּחָכְמָה פּוֹתֵחַ שְׁעָרִים
וּבִתְבוּנָה מְשַׁנֶּה עִתִּים וּמַחֲלִיף אֶת־הַזְּמַנִּים וּמְסַדֵּר
אֶת־הַכּוֹכָבִים בְּמִשְׁמְרוֹתֵיהֶם בָּרָקִיעַ כִּרְצוֹנוֹ. בּוֹרֵא
יוֹם וָלַיְלָה גּוֹלֵל אוֹר מִפְּנֵי חֹשֶׁךְ וְחֹשֶׁךְ מִפְּנֵי אוֹר.
וּמַעֲבִיר יוֹם וּמֵבִיא לָיְלָה וּמַבְדִּיל בֵּין יוֹם וּבֵין
לָיְלָה. יְיָ צְבָאוֹת שְׁמוֹ. אֵל חַי וְקַיָּם תָּמִיד יִמְלוֹךְ
עָלֵינוּ לְעוֹלָם וָעֶד. בָּרוּךְ אַתָּה יְיָ הַמַּעֲרִיב עֲרָבִים:

ANTIPHONAL READING

You were God
And we were Israel,
Your shy, untutored lover
Long ago.

You loved us a great love
And you taught us
How to respond to You

Through Torah
Mitzvot
Statutes
Judgments
We go to sleep with them
And with them we awake

We shall enjoy them forever.

They give us life
They prolong our days
We form our words around them
At nighttime,
In daytime.

Now,
Long after long ago,
Do not withdraw Your love from us.

Lover of Israel,
You are praised.

שְׁמַע יִשְׂרָאֵל יְהֹוָה אֱלֹהֵינוּ יְהֹוָה אֶחָד:

בָּרוּךְ שֵׁם כְּבוֹד מַלְכוּתוֹ לְעוֹלָם וָעֶד:

וְאָהַבְתָּ אֵת יְיָ אֱלֹהֶיךָ בְּכָל־לְבָבְךָ וּבְכָל־נַפְשְׁךָ
וּבְכָל־מְאֹדֶךָ: וְהָיוּ הַדְּבָרִים הָאֵלֶּה אֲשֶׁר אָנֹכִי
מְצַוְּךָ הַיּוֹם עַל־לְבָבֶךָ: וְשִׁנַּנְתָּם לְבָנֶיךָ וְדִבַּרְתָּ
בָּם. בְּשִׁבְתְּךָ בְּבֵיתֶךָ וּבְלֶכְתְּךָ בַדֶּרֶךְ וּבְשָׁכְבְּךָ
וּבְקוּמֶךָ: וּקְשַׁרְתָּם לְאוֹת עַל־יָדֶךָ. וְהָיוּ לְטֹטָפֹת
בֵּין עֵינֶיךָ: וּכְתַבְתָּם עַל־מְזֻזוֹת בֵּיתֶךָ וּבִשְׁעָרֶיךָ:
לְמַעַן תִּזְכְּרוּ וַעֲשִׂיתֶם אֶת־כָּל־מִצְוֹתָי וִהְיִיתֶם
קְדוֹשִׁים לֵאלֹהֵיכֶם: אֲנִי יְיָ אֱלֹהֵיכֶם:

SILENT READING

If you will pay attention to My commandments which I command
you today, I will free you from worry about physical sustenance so
that you can devote your mind to Torah and your body to right
action. I will give rain in its season for your harvest, and good
pasture for your cattle. But if you open to temptations and serve
other sorts of gods, I will close the heavens and there will be no
rain, nor will earth yield its produce, and you shall fast disappear
from the good land which God has given you.

The Lord spoke to Moses saying: Speak to the people of Israel and
tell them to make fringes on the corners of their garments throughout their generations and to put a cord of blue on the fringe of each

169

corner. The fringe will be a symbol of your commitment: When you see it, you will be reminded of all of the commandments of the Lord and you will fulfill them, and you will not simply follow your own impulses and desires which might lead you to be false to Me. In this way you will remember and do all My commandments and you will be wholly dedicated for your God. I am the Lord your God who brought you out of the land of Egypt in order to be your God. I am the Lord your God.

SONG

מִי־כָמֹכָה בָּאֵלִם יְיָ מִי כָּמֹכָה נֶאְדָּר בַּקֹּדֶשׁ
נוֹרָא תְהִלֹּת עֹשֵׂה פֶלֶא:
מַלְכוּתְךָ רָאוּ בָנֶיךָ בּוֹקֵעַ יָם לִפְנֵי מֹשֶׁה זֶה
אֵלִי עָנוּ וְאָמְרוּ.
יְיָ יִמְלֹךְ לְעֹלָם וָעֶד:
וְנֶאֱמַר כִּי־פָדָה יְיָ אֶת־יַעֲקֹב וּגְאָלוֹ מִיַּד חָזָק
מִמֶּנּוּ. בָּרוּךְ אַתָּה יְיָ גָּאַל יִשְׂרָאֵל:

READER

Let us lie down in peace, Lord, and in the morning awaken to life. Spread peace over us like the leafy roof of a Sukkah and guide us with good counsel. Protect us and remove from the world every enemy, disease, war, famine and grief. Keep us safe under Your wing because You are a gracious and merciful King. Guard our comings and goings for life and peace. Spread Your Sukkah of peace over us. Praised are You, Lord, who spread the Sukkah of peace over us, over Israel and Jerusalem.

AMIDAH

(*silent reading*)

Dogs still bark for the American Jew. And his fears are no different from those of his ancestors in Poland, Russia, and other parts of the Old World. They are often shielded from easy view, covered over by the sophistications of a contrived modernism, and the conceits of a nonpartisan universalism. But they are there. And being there, they account for the undiminished sense of estrangement, the unabated feelings of otherness that still pervade the life and thought of the American Jew. Yet this American Jew *is* different: different not only from the non-Jew in America, but also from his own ancestors. At least his ancestors knew very well that they were living as aliens on the margins of cultures other than their own. "You know the heart of the stranger, for you were strangers in the land of Egypt"; they read these Scriptural words as a reminder of their own perennial condition. But much of the ambivalence of the American Jew toward himself stems from his pathetic confusion: he knows that in many non-Jewish hearts he is regarded as a stranger, while in his own heart he stubbornly refuses to be one. But a stranger who would not be a stranger cannot easily "know the heart of the stranger."

The Jew says: "As a citizen of my country I participate in its civic and political life; but as a member of the Jewish nationality I have, in addition, my own national needs, and in this sphere I must be independent to the same degree that any other national minority is autonomous in the state. I have the right to speak my language, to use it in all my social institutions, to make it the language of instruction in my schools, to order my internal life in my communities, and to create institutions serving a variety of national purposes; to join in the common activities with my bretheren not only in this country but in all countries of the world and to participate in all the organizations which serve to further the needs of the Jewish nationality and to defend them everywhere."

> A hundred generations, yes, a hundred and twenty-five,
> had the strength each day
> not to eat this and that (unclean!),
> not to say this and that,
> not to do this and that (unjust!),
> and with all this and all that
> to go about

as men and Jews
among their enemies
(these are the Pharisees you mocked at, Jesus).
Whatever my grandfathers did or said
for all of their brief lives
still was theirs,
as all of its drops at a moment make the fountain
and all of its leaves a palm.
Each word they spoke and every thought
was heard, each step and every gesture seen, God;
their past was still the present and the present
dread future's.
but I am private as an animal.

I have eaten whatever I liked,
I have slept as long as I wished,
I have left the highway like a dog
to run into every alley;
now I must learn to fast and to watch.
I shall walk better in these heavy boots
than barefoot.

I will fast for you, Judah,
and be silent for you
and wake in the night because of you;
I will speak for you
in psalms,
and feast because of you
on unleavened bread and herbs.

One last chance remains, for Jews who decide to remain in America, to fulfill the Reformers' mission of bringing on the world we all desire. To undertake it means to explore the depths to which our ancient heritage has been ground up by American culture into the bland pap which sickens our children and amuses our middle-aged. To undertake it means to overcome the conviction of so many of our people that Jewishness is not to be taken seriously, either because it is inferior to American culture, or because it is too narrow for a man of human concerns. To undertake it means to introduce our people to their heritage in ways we have not tried before, or in ways that have lain forgotten for millennia. To undertake it means to help each other build new structures through which our differing conceptions of Jewishness can be expressed. Thus revitalized, we may join with other peoples to overthrow the tyranny of what we have too long been taught is the true "American" culture, and together establish a society in which the cultures of all its peoples, Jews and WASPS, blacks and yellows, may live whole, profound, concerned lives beneath the sun which nourished all of them, exploiting none, hating none; with reverence for all.

EZEKIEL XXXVII

The hand of the Lord was upon me, and the Lord carried me out in a spirit, and set me down in the midst of the valley, and it was full of bones; and He caused me to pass by them round about, and, behold, there were very many in the open valley; and, lo, they were very dry. And He said unto me: 'Son of man, can these bones live?' And I answered: 'O Lord God, Thou knowest.' Then he said unto me: 'Prophesy over these bones, and say unto them: O ye dry bones, hear the word of the Lord: Thus saith the Lord God unto these bones: Behold, I will cause breath to enter into you, and ye shall live. And I will lay sinews upon you, and will bring up flesh upon you, and cover you with skin, and put breath in you, and ye shall live; and ye shall know that I am the Lord.'

CONGREGATION

We see ourselves as more than children of our times; we see ourselves as children of timelessness. We see ourselves as Jews who know that when one has an urgent matter to bring to the attention of the community, even the reading of the Torah in the synagogue may be disrupted. We see ourselves as your children, the children of Jews who with great dedication concern themselves with the needs of the community, the children of Jews who bring comfort to the afflicted, give aid to the poor, who have built mammoth philanthropic organizations, who have aided the remnants of the Holocaust, who have given unfalteringly to the building of Israel, who give more per capita to charity than any other group in America. We are your children and affirm this, but, to paraphrase the Rabbinic aphorism, we want to be not only children—*banim*—but also builders—*bonim*. We want to participate with you in the building of a vision of a great Jewish community. It is when we think of this that we become dismayed with the reality of American Jewish life which we cannot reconcile with what you have taught us to cherish.

The heavens and the earth and all thereon were completed. And on the seventh day God finished His work of creation and on the seventh day He rested from all His work. And God blessed the seventh day, making it holy, because He rested on that day from all His work which He had completed.

READER

Upon Israel and upon the rabbis
and upon the disciples and upon all the disciples of their disciples
and upon all who study the Torah in this place and in every place,
to them and to you
peace;

upon Israel and upon all who meet with unfriendly glances, sticks
        and stones and names—
on posters, in newspapers, or in books to last,
chalked on asphalt or in acid on glass,
shouted from a thousand thousand windows by radio;
who are pushed out of class-rooms and rushing trains,
whom the hundred hands of a mob strike,
and whom jailers strike with bunches of keys, with revolver butts;
to them and to you
in this place and in every place
safety;

upon Israel and upon all who live
as the sparrows of the streets
under the cornices of the houses of others,

and as rabbits
in the fields of strangers
on the grace of the seasons
and what the gleaners leave in the corners;
you children of the wind—
birds
that feed on the tree of knowledge
in this place and in every place,
to them and to you
a living;

upon Israel
and upon their children and upon all the children of their children
in this place and in every place
to them and to you
life.

ALEYNU

עָלֵינוּ לְשַׁבֵּחַ לַאֲדוֹן הַכֹּל לָתֵת גְּדֻלָה לְיוֹצֵר בְּרֵאשִׁית שֶׁלֹּא

עָשָׂנוּ כְּגוֹיֵי הָאֲרָצוֹת וְלֹא שָׂמָנוּ כְּמִשְׁפְּחוֹת הָאֲדָמָה שֶׁלֹּא שָׂם

חֶלְקֵנוּ כָּהֶם וְגֹרָלֵנוּ כְּכָל הֲמוֹנָם:

וַאֲנַחְנוּ כּוֹרְעִים וּמִשְׁתַּחֲוִים וּמוֹדִים

לִפְנֵי מֶלֶךְ מַלְכֵי הַמְּלָכִים הַקָּדוֹשׁ בָּרוּךְ הוּא.

שֶׁהוּא נוֹטֶה שָׁמַיִם וְיוֹסֵד אָרֶץ וּמוֹשַׁב יְקָרוֹ בַּשָּׁמַיִם

מִמַּעַל וּשְׁכִינַת עֻזּוֹ בְּגָבְהֵי מְרוֹמִים: הוּא אֱלֹהֵינוּ

אֵין עוֹד. אֱמֶת מַלְכֵּנוּ אֶפֶס זוּלָתוֹ כַּכָּתוּב בְּתוֹרָתוֹ

וְיָדַעְתָּ הַיּוֹם וַהֲשֵׁבֹתָ אֶל לְבָבֶךָ כִּי יְיָ הוּא הָאֱלֹהִים

בַּשָּׁמַיִם מִמַּעַל וְעַל־הָאָרֶץ מִתָּחַת. אֵין עוֹד:

וְנֶאֱמַר

וְהָיָה יְיָ לְמֶלֶךְ עַל־כָּל־הָאָרֶץ בַּיּוֹם הַהוּא יִהְיֶה

יְיָ אֶחָד וּשְׁמוֹ אֶחָד:

KADDISH

יִתְגַּדַּל וְיִתְקַדַּשׁ שְׁמֵהּ רַבָּא. בְּעָלְמָא דִּי־בְרָא כִרְעוּתֵהּ.
וְיַמְלִיךְ מַלְכוּתֵהּ בְּחַיֵּיכוֹן וּבְיוֹמֵיכוֹן וּבְחַיֵּי דְכָל־בֵּית יִשְׂרָאֵל
בַּעֲגָלָא וּבִזְמַן קָרִיב. וְאִמְרוּ אָמֵן:

יְהֵא שְׁמֵהּ רַבָּא מְבָרַךְ לְעָלַם וּלְעָלְמֵי עָלְמַיָּא:

יִתְבָּרַךְ וְיִשְׁתַּבַּח וְיִתְפָּאַר וְיִתְרוֹמַם וְיִתְנַשֵּׂא וְיִתְהַדָּר וְיִתְעַלֶּה
וְיִתְהַלָּל שְׁמֵהּ דְּקֻדְשָׁא. בְּרִיךְ הוּא. לְעֵלָּא (וּלְעֵלָּא) מִן־כָּל־
בִּרְכָתָא וְשִׁירָתָא תֻּשְׁבְּחָתָא וְנֶחֱמָתָא דַּאֲמִירָן בְּעָלְמָא. וְאִמְרוּ
אָמֵן:

יְהֵא שְׁלָמָא רַבָּא מִן־שְׁמַיָּא וְחַיִּים עָלֵינוּ וְעַל־כָּל־יִשְׂרָאֵל.
וְאִמְרוּ אָמֵן:

עֹשֶׂה שָׁלוֹם בִּמְרוֹמָיו הוּא יַעֲשֶׂה שָׁלוֹם עָלֵינוּ וְעַל־כָּל־יִשְׂרָאֵל.
וְאִמְרוּ אָמֵן:

SONG

Out of the Land of Bondage (for Leonard Cohen)
(*Music on p. 180*)

I am a Jew
The American Jew
A face in a crowd
Where my numbers are few.
Know why I've limped
Through tunnels of time
And you'll know for certain
The secret of how I've survived.

I am a saint
This known to a few

I have my friends
But no one to talk to.
A shadow hurled through
The warmth of the night,
I seal the wisdom, the
Clue which keeps me alive.

Refrain: Di di di di di di di

In Israel
I stand at the line
Gun in hand
Mission defined
I'm bullet-holed
With words such as "peace"
Our song of freedom must live
Then we shall be free.

Chorus: Our freedom song
        Of white and blue
        It will be sung
        Loud and true
        Our Songs of Songs
        Rings in our ears
        Our Prayer of Prayers
        Lies near.

In the Land of the Free
We "saints" now must give
To help our family
In troubled lands live
To tell the world
Though our numbers are few
We're strong and happy
And proud to be called "Jew."

Refrain: Di di di di di di di

A face in a crowd
Of a numberless few.
I'm bullet-holed
With words such as "peace"
Our song of freedom must live
And we shall be free.

Our freedom song
Of white and blue
It will be sung
Loud and true
Our Song of Songs
Rings in our ears
Our Prayer of Prayers
Lies near.

(Repeat above verse)

Refrain: Di di di di di di di

אדון עולם

אֲדוֹן עוֹלָם אֲשֶׁר מָלַךְ   בְּטֶרֶם כָּל יְצִיר נִבְרָא:

לְעֵת נַעֲשָׂה בְחֶפְצוֹ כֹּל   אֲזַי מֶלֶךְ שְׁמוֹ נִקְרָא:

וְאַחֲרֵי כִּכְלוֹת הַכֹּל   לְבַדּוֹ יִמְלוֹךְ נוֹרָא:

וְהוּא הָיָה וְהוּא הֹוֶה   וְהוּא יִהְיֶה בְּתִפְאָרָה:

וְהוּא אֶחָד וְאֵין שֵׁנִי   לְהַמְשִׁיל לוֹ לְהַחְבִּירָה:

בְּלִי רֵאשִׁית בְּלִי תַכְלִית   וְלוֹ הָעֹז וְהַמִּשְׂרָה:

וְהוּא אֵלִי וְחַי גּוֹאֲלִי   וְצוּר חֶבְלִי בְּעֵת צָרָה:

וְהוּא נִסִּי וּמָנוֹס לִי   מְנָת כּוֹסִי בְּיוֹם אֶקְרָא:

בְּיָדוֹ אַפְקִיד רוּחִי   בְּעֵת אִישַׁן וְאָעִירָה:

וְעִם רוּחִי גְּוִיָּתִי   יְיָ לִי וְלֹא אִירָא:

178

WHAT NOW, MR. MADISON?

(A Parable)

Words and Music by
MITCH CORBER

Verse 1:

In the land of long a- go, Once up-on a dream With-in a dis - tant king- dom Dwelt a dis - tant king Who court - ed no one's friend - ship, So no one came to court. A tow - er sculpt of i - v'ry, Guards the si - lent fort.____

Chorus

A- mer - i - ca come hear_ I need a friend to keep me hang - in' on. I'd give my eyes if I could on - ly see Your pur - ple moun-tains' ma - jes - ty.____ {1. Has cloaked} {2. A - bove} the fruit - ed plain. And I'll help__ you if you'll help__ me up a - gain.

Verse 2:

All the dreams of ages lost,
Stripped of painted pride
A castle stood in ashes
Sympathy denied
Waiting for a miracle
And when the rainbow came
Lo, the kingly sunken eyes
Could only see the rain.

(Repeat Chorus)

© 1972 by Mitch Corber

179

Out Of The Land Of Bondage
(For Leonard Cohen)

Words and Music by
SUZANNE WEISS
and MITCH CORBER

Verse 1

I am a Jew, the A-mer-i-can Jew,— a face in a
crowd where my num-bers are few. Know why I've limped through tun-nels of
time and you'll know for cer-tain the sec-ret of how I've sur - vived.

Verse 2

I am — a saint, this known to a few,
I have my friends, but no one_____ to talk to,
a shad-ow hurled through the warmth of the night, I
seal the wis - dom, the clue which keeps me a - live.

Refrain

Di di di di di di di di di di di di di
di di di di di di di di di di di di di di di
di di di di di di di di di di di di di di.

Verse 3

In Is - ra - el I stand at the line, gun in hand,__ mis - sion de - fined. I'm bul - let - holed__ with words such as "peace", our song of free - dom must live, then we shall be free.

Chorus

Our free - dom song of white and blue, it will be sung loud and true __ Our Song of Songs rings in our ears, our Prayer of Prayers lies near.

Verse 4

In the Land of the Free
We "saints" now must give
To help our family
In troubled lands live
To tell the world
Though our numbers are few
We're strong and happy
And proud to be called "Jew."

Refrain

Out Of-2

Verse 5

I am a Jew
The American Jew
A face in a crowd
Of a numberless few
I'm bullet-holed
With words such as "peace"
Our song of freedom must live
Then we shall be free.

Chorus (twice)

Refrain

A DAY OF WITNESS: A SERVICE
FOR SOVIET JEWS

MEMBERS OF THE CONGREGATION

VOICE 1

Elderly Jewish man who refuses to give up on establishing a meaningful basis for relating to God within traditional forms. He is a searching, yearning individual who is deeply in need of the immediacy of God's presence.

VOICE 2

He is also somewhat of a believer but is terribly bitter and cynical. He sees too much evil in the world and too little of God. He has given up hope but really in his heart of hearts is also groping for God. In the end he is dramatically won over.

CHIEF JUDGE

The judge is an objective, honest person who has a commanding presence on stage and in the long run loses his cool, detached attitude and becomes involved in the quest.

FIRST WITNESS

Yakob Goldberg—He has experienced all of Jewish history. He has nothing good to say about God and he still wishes to maintain a relationship with Him.

SECOND WITNESS

Malka Cohen—She is young, has never had a meaningful relationship with God but like everyone else desires one. She is looking for help. She is very much the modern assimilated Russian Jew.

PROSECUTOR

The Prosecutor is not looking for anything in terms of a relationship with God. He is simply convinced of His guilt and is here to prove it. He demands a fair judgment.

NOTE

Voices I and II become the other two judges.

*　　*　　*　　*

PRAYER OF A LOST JEW

Slowly, with feeling

1. Sun is set - ting, my soul is go - ing; in the depths I am
tossed like the sea   I am des - tined to lose the bat - tle
of the flesh and of the blood. 2. My days are pass - ing,
my days are end - ing with - out giv - ing, with - out tak - ing.
If to this you have called life,
tell me my God, what then is death? then is death?

3. Have mercy my God, for I know not
   How I can continue to be;
   Should I forget all and be happy
   Or remember all and cry?

4. Give me life until tomorrow;
   Maybe I will understand the dream.
   Sun is setting
   Clouds are coming,
   Night arises from the deep.

184

NARRATOR

From time immemorial Jewish people have been involved in a
dialogue with God, a dialogue in which Abraham points an accusing finger and says, "Will not the judge of all the world do justice?"
A relationship in which Jacob wrestles with the Almighty himself,
and a Job who asks the eternal, as yet unanswered, question, "Why
am I suffering?" It is not unheard of to call God to task for what
he has done to the Jewish people. To this very day Jews have been
involved in this. We are here to continue the ancient dialogue. We
are here to find out why, to compel Him to answer us. Please let
us all pray now.

*(Voice I enters stage right, crosses to center stage, covers head with
Talit and lifts his eyes to heaven).*

VOICE 1 *Song*

Sun is setting,
My soul is going
In the depths I am tossed like the sea
I am destined to lose the battle
Of the flesh and of the blood

My days are passing
My days are ending
Without giving
Without taking
If to this you have called life,
Tell me, my God,
What then is death? *(Repeat last three lines)*

*(Voice II enters stage left, stands, listens and stares
with a mixture of disgust and amazement)*

Have mercy my God,
For I know not
How I can continue to be,
Should I forget all and be happy,
Or remember all and cry?

185

Give me life until tomorrow;
Maybe I will understand the dream
Sun is setting, clouds are coming,
Night arises from the deep. *(Repeat last two lines)*

(Voice II enters stage left, stands, listens and stares with a mixture of disgust and amazement).

VOICE 2

What are you doing here? I thought you gave this kind of thing up a long time ago.

VOICE 1

Well maybe, just maybe, He will hear, and He will listen, and He will answer. You know how He used to do that quite often in the past.

VOICE 2

Yes, yes, I too have heard people talk of those times, but you know —now things are different. It is up to us to answer Him and we really don't know how. He left us at Babi Yar, and like Elijah the prophet, He ascended to heaven on a fiery chariot that billowed up from the smoke stacks of Auschwitz.

VOICE 1

We can answer Him with our loyalty, our praise.

(Voice I is hard and desperate)

VOICE 2

No, they tried that, and He killed 6 million of them.

VOICE 1

We can't give up. There must be a way, if we lose faith in Him—in our ability to relate to Him—then we will lose faith in man—and if that happens, if that happens . . . there must be, there has to be— a new approach.

VOICE 2

A new approach! ! ! What do you mean? I have given up. He has given up. There is no bridge left. What can you mean?

VOICE 1

I am not sure, but I have heard people talk about it late at night, only in groups of twos and threes. It has been done before, there are some who remember it. Not many, but I have heard of it.

VOICE 2

Well, tell me, what was done?

VOICE 1

You see, they, too, were tired of being just supplicants and amen sayers. They were still lovers of God and believers in Him but they wanted to relate to Him on an equal plane. Yes, He may indeed be Melech ha-Olam, master of the cosmos, but He is also Eloheinu, our personal God, who must be, who has to be near to us.

VOICE 2

Well, what did they do? Prayer is the only bridge, and to pray as we have always done is to be an amen sayer.

VOICE 1

They prayed in a different way. They prayed at Him, and not to Him, with Him and not for Him, in spite of Him and not because of Him.

VOICE 2

What do you mean?

VOICE 1

They called Him to a Din Torah—a judgment before a rabbinic tribunal. This is how they related to Him.

VOICE 2

Why?

VOICE 1

Previously, when we were well off, our relation to God was as to one who granted us a favor for nothing and we were eternally obliged to Him for it. Now our relations to God are as to one who owes us something, who owes us much, and since we feel so I believe that we have the right to demand it of Him. But I don't say, like Job did, that God should point out my sin with His finger so that I may know why I deserve this; for greater and saintlier men than I are firmly convinced that it is not a question of punishing sinners: something entirely different is taking place in the world. More exactly, it is a time when God has veiled His countenance from the world, sacrificing mankind to its wild instincts. In a situation like this we have but one choice: to try Him and shame Him into action.

VOICE 2

(*in desperation, a quick staccato voice*) Let's not wait, let's do it now. From this point on He will have no rest. He will have to answer, otherwise He will be denying His existence, and He could not bear that. (*Lights dim*).

SCENE II

(*Voices I and II remain on stage. Chief Judge enters stage left. They don Talitim and remain standing while Prosecutor and witnesses enter. Judges and witnesses sit down, Prosecutor remains standing*).

CHIEF JUDGE

We are here to try God for crimes against the Jews of Russia. Prosecutor, read the indictment.

PROSECUTOR

We the representatives of the children of Israel charge God with failure to uphold the covenant entered into by Him of His own free will, with one Moses as representative of the people of Israel. It is written in the record of the covenant, the Torah (Ex. 15:26): "If you will diligently harken to the voice of the Lord your God and will do that which is right in His eyes, and will give ear to His commandments and keep all His statutes, I will put none of the plagues upon you which I have put upon the Egyptians." We, the people of Israel, charge: the plague of darkness was placed on the Egyptians; you have plagued the Jews of Russia with an all-consuming and total darkness—a darkness which hides to this day your face; a darkness which blackens justice and freedom. It is further written (Gen. 15:18): "That day God concluded a covenant with Abraham saying: 'to your children I give this land.'" We charge this land of Israel has not been given to the children of Abraham who dwell in the Soviet Union. Finally, you have commanded us to pray to you—yet our prayer books have been taken away. You have commanded us to congregate in your house—yet you have taken away our synagogues and our places of learning. You have said that our life would be a good one; yes we, the representatives of the children of Israel, charge you with making it a living hell.

CHIEF JUDGE

Prosecutor, call your first witness.

PROSECUTOR

The prosecution calls to the stand Yakob Goldberg. Tell us your tale.

GOLDBERG

I am old, older than history itself. My tale has been told so many times, by so many different people, in so many different places, that I fear it will fall on deaf ears. *(Pointing an accusing finger)* God, I am sick unto death of having my life bear witness unto you. I am now bearing witness against you. I survived your hell of Hitler, for what? To what end? To be deprived once more of all that is Jewish, of all that is human. I have no more to say.

CHIEF JUDGE

Do you have any more witnesses?

PROSECUTOR

Yes, I call Malka Cohen. Do you have a tale to tell?

COHEN

Not really, but what I have to say is new; it has not been said before. I am young—a student—born in 1950—no Jewish background. Were it not for the vilifications and lies of my government against the Jewish people I would not be here today. Only once a year I am not afraid to be a Jew. On that day we dance in the streets and sing the songs of our people. But where are our people? I know they are out there but they, like God, have abandoned us. I want to come back to Him, and He won't let me.

PROSECUTOR

The prosecution rests.

CHIEF JUDGE

Is there anyone here on behalf of the defense? *(No one appears— silence for 10 seconds. He repeats his question and all look in wonderment).* It is quite clear then that there is no possible defense. The judge will now consult as to the verdict. *(10 seconds of muffled discussion).*

CHIEF JUDGE

We have reached our decision *(7 seconds pause).* We declare a mistrial. You don't even deserve to be declared guilty.

GOLDBERG

Wait. Don't dismiss the case. You can't leave me without an answer. There must be something we can do.

CHIEF JUDGE

(Pointing to audience) It is up to them. If we pray to them, maybe they will pray, and maybe they will act, and in acting shame Him into action. This is our prayer, this is my prayer. Yes, we will pray to you in the hope that there still is some remnant of the image of God left in you. If we can reach that which is godly in you then God himself will have been reached. You cannot forget the Jews of Russia, for if you do you will be forgetting yourselves. Their future is our future—our future is their future. May we all live to see a day when He and His name will be one on heaven and earth. Amen.

GOLDBERG

Wait, I have also got a prayer. *(Cries out)* "Don't forget me". *(Stage is darkened)*.

A SERVICE OF REMEMBRANCE FOR THE SIX MILLION

Partizaner Lid (Song of the Jewish Partisans)

(Song of the Jewish Partisans)

1 Shtil, di nacht iz oysgeshternt,
   Un der frost hot shtark gebrent.
   Tsi gedenkstu vi ich hob dich gelernt
   Haltn a shpayer in di hent?

   Silence, and a starry night
   Frost crackling, fine as sand.
   Remember how I taught you
   To hold a gun in your hand?

2 A moyd, a peltsl un a beret,
   Un halt in hant fest a nagan.
   A moyd mit a sametenem ponim,
   Hit op dem soyne's karavan.

   In fur jacket and beret,
   Clutching a hand grenade,
   A girl whose skin is velvet
   Ambushes a cavalcade.

3 Getsilt, geshosn un getrofn!
   Hot ir kleyninker pistoyl.
   An oto, a fulinkn mit vofn
   Farhaltn hot zi mit eyn koyl!

   Aim, fire, shoot—and hit!
   She, with her pistol small,
   Halts an autoful,
   Arms and all!

4 Fartog, fun vald aroysgekrochn,
   Mit shney girlandn oyf di hor.
   Gemutikt fun kleyninkn nitsochn
   Far undzer nayem, frayen dor!

195

Morning, emerging from the wood,
In her hair, a snow carnation.
Proud of her small victory
For the new, free generation!

Voices to Remember

Voice 1. (After five days of fighting, the Jews of the Warsaw
Ghetto turned to their Christian countrymen . . . .)

Voice 2. "This is a fight for your freedom as well as ours. Poles,
citizens, soldiers of freedom! Above the din of German
cannon . . . machine guns . . . through the smoke of the
burning ghetto . . . we, the slaves of the ghetto, convey
heartfelt greetings to you. We are aware that you have
been witnessing our ordeal with horror and compassion
. . . Every doorstep in the ghetto . . . shall remain a for-
tress until the end. All of us will perish in the fight but
we will never surrender . . . This is a fight for your freedom as well as ours, for your dignity and honor, as well
as ours. We shall avenge Oswiecim (Auschwitz), Treb-
linka, Belzec and Majdanek!
"Long live freedom!
"Death to the hangmen and murderers!
"Our struggle against the enemy must go on until the
end."

Voice 3. (Samuel Zygielbojm was a Polish labor leader. After the
murder of his wife and two children, he escaped to London. As a member of the Polish National Council in
London, he sought in vain to get Allied assistance for the
ghetto fighters. Realizing the futility of his efforts, on
May 12, 1943, he took his own life, leaving a farewell
note to the President and Prime Minister of the Polish
Government-in-Exile . . . . .)

Voice 4. "I cannot be silent. I cannot live while the remnants of the Jewish population of Poland, of whom I am a representative, are perishing. My friends in the Warsaw ghetto died with weapons in their hands in the last heroic battle. It was not my destiny to die together with them but I belong to them and in their mass graves.

"By my death I wish to make my final protest against the passivity with which the world is looking on and permitting the extermination of the Jewish people.

"I know how little human life is worth today, but as I was unable to do anything during my life, perhaps by my death I shall contribute to breaking down the indifference of those who may now at the last moment rescue the few.

Polish Jews still alive . . . I bid farewell to everybody and to everything that was dear to me and that I have loved."

THE SABBATH CANDLES

Come, let us welcome the Sabbath. May its radiance illumine our hearts as we kindle these tapers.

Light is the symbol of the divine. The Lord is my light and my salvation.

Light is the symbol of the divine in man. The spirit of man is the light of the Lord.

Light is the symbol of the divine law. For the commandment is a lamp and the law is a light.

Light is the symbol of Israel's mission. I, the Lord, have set thee for a covenant of the people, for a light unto the nations.

Therefore, in the spirit of our ancient tradition that hallows and unites Israel in all lands and all ages, do we now kindle the Sabbath lights.

בָּרוּךְ אַתָּה יְיָ אֱלֹהֵינוּ מֶלֶךְ הָעוֹלָם אֲשֶׁר קִדְּשָׁנוּ
בְּמִצְוֹתָיו וְצִוָּנוּ לְהַדְלִיק נֵר שֶׁל־שַׁבָּת:

Blessed art Thou, O Lord our God, King of the universe, who hast sanctified us by Thy laws and commanded us to kindle the Sabbath light.

May the Lord bless us with Sabbath joy.

May the Lord bless us with Sabbath holiness.

May the Lord bless us with Sabbath peace.

Amen.

O The Chimneys   A Voice

(There are flames other than those of candles which have meaning in Jewish life. "O The Chimneys" is the title Poem in the first English anthology of the works of Nelly Sachs, Nobel Laureate in Literature in 1966.)

"O THE CHIMNEYS"

(And though after my skin worms destroy this body, yet in my flesh shall I see God.—JOB 19:26)

O the chimneys
On the ingeniously devised habitations of death
When Israel's body drifted as smoke
Through the air—
Was welcomed by a star, a chimney sweep,
A star that turned black
Or was it a ray of sun?

O the chimneys!
Freedom way for Jeremiah and Job's dust—
Who devised you and laid stone upon stone
The road for refugees of smoke?

O the habitations of death,
Invitingly appointed
For the host who used to be a guest—
O you fingers
Laying the threshold
Like a knife between life and death—

O you chimneys
O you fingers
And Israel's body as smoke through the air!

THE CALL TO WORSHIP

(Congregation rises)

READER

בָּרְכוּ אֶת־יְיָ הַמְבֹרָךְ.

Praise ye the Lord, to whom all praise is due.

CHOIR AND CONGREGATION·

בָּרוּךְ יְיָ הַמְבֹרָךְ לְעוֹלָם וָעֶד.

Praised be the Lord to whom all praise is due forever and ever

(Congregation is seated)

READER

בָּרוּךְ אַתָּה יְיָ אֱלֹהֵינוּ מֶלֶךְ הָעוֹלָם אֲשֶׁר
בִּדְבָרוֹ מַעֲרִיב עֲרָבִים בְּחָכְמָה פּוֹתֵחַ שְׁעָרִים
וּבִתְבוּנָה מְשַׁנֶּה עִתִּים וּמַחֲלִיף אֶת־הַזְּמַנִּים וּמְסַדֵּר
אֶת־הַכּוֹכָבִים בְּמִשְׁמְרֹתֵיהֶם בָּרָקִיעַ כִּרְצוֹנוֹ. בּוֹרֵא
יוֹם וָלַיְלָה גּוֹלֵל אוֹר מִפְּנֵי חֹשֶׁךְ וְחֹשֶׁךְ מִפְּנֵי אוֹר.
וּמַעֲבִיר יוֹם וּמֵבִיא לַיְלָה וּמַבְדִּיל בֵּין יוֹם וּבֵין
לָיְלָה. יְיָ צְבָאוֹת שְׁמוֹ. אֵל חַי וְקַיָּם תָּמִיד יִמְלוֹךְ
עָלֵינוּ לְעוֹלָם וָעֶד. בָּרוּךְ אַתָּה יְיָ הַמַּעֲרִיב עֲרָבִים:

CONGREGATION AND READER

Praised be Thou, O Lord our God, ruler of the world, by whos
law the shadows of evening fall and the gates of morn are openec
In wisdom Thou hast established the changes of times and season
and ordered the ways of the stars in their heavenly course. Creato
of heaven and earth, O living God, rule Thou over us forevei
Praised be Thou, O Lord, for the day and its work and for th
night and its rest.

Infinite as is Thy power, even so is Thy love. Thou didst manifest it through Israel, Thy people. By laws and commandments, by statutes and ordinances hast Thou led us in the way of righteousness and brought us to the light of truth. Therefore at our lying down and our rising up, we will meditate on Thy teachings and find in Thy laws true life and length of days. O that Thy love may never depart from our hearts. Praised be Thou, O Lord, who hast revealed Thy love through Israel.

RABBI

How do we praise God? The words trip easily off the tongue. How do we praise God? The tongue stammers, and the words choke in our throat when we praise God from Hell, if we try to sing His praises in Auschwitz.

CONGREGATION

So did the Chasidic Rabbi argue with his disciples. The master declared: "You know, there's a possibility that the "ribbono shel olam"—the Master of the Universe—is a liar." The disciple asked: "How can that be possible?" "Because," answered the Rebbe, "if the ribbono shel olam should open His window now and look down here and see Auschwitz, He would close the window again, and say, 'I did not do this.' And that would have been a lie."

From the Depths of Hell   Silent Meditation

> (Yitzchak Katzenelson perished in a crematorium. His poetry is the most powerful lamentation of the plight of the Jewish children.)
>
> The first ones to be destroyed were the children
> little orphans, abandoned upon the face of the earth
> they who were the best in the world
> the acme of grace on the dark earth!
> Oh, tender orphans!
> From them, the bereaved of the world
> in a house of shelter we drew consolation;

From the mournful faces, mute and dark,
we said the light of day will yet break upon us!

* * * * * *

They, the children of Israel, were the first in doom and dis-
    aster,
most of them without father and mother,
were consumed by frost, starvation and lice;
holy messiahs sanctified in pain . . . .
Say then, how have these lambs sinned?
Why in days of doom are they the first victims of wickedness,
the first in the trap of evil are they!

The first were they detained for death;
the first into the wagons of slaughter,
they were thrown into the wagons, the huge wagons,
like heaps of refuse, like the ashes of the earth—
killed them,
and they transported them,
exterminated them
without remnant or remembrance . . . .
The best of my children were all wiped out!
Oh woe unto me—
Doom and Desolation!

"But Who Emptied Your Shoes of Sand"   (*by Nelly Sachs*)
    Rabbi: But who emptied your shoes of sand
            When you had to get up, to die?
    Cong.: The sand which Israel gathered,
            Its nomad sand?
    Rabbi: Burning Sinai sand,
            Mingled with throats of nightingales,
            Mingled with wings of butterflies,
            Mingled with the hungry dust of serpents;
    Cong.: Mingled with all that fell from the wisdom of Sol-
            omon.
            Mingled with what is bitter in the mystery of worm-
            wood.

Rabbi:	O you fingers
	That emptied the deathly shoes of sand.
Cong.:	Tomorrow you will be dust
	In the shoes of those to come.

THE GHETTO   A Voice

(Emmanuel Ringelblum was one of the chief chroniclers of the Warsaw Ghetto. None captured its mood as did he.)

"Most of the populace is set on resistance. It seems to me that people will no longer go to the slaughter like lambs. They want the enemy to pay dearly for their lives. They'll fling themselves at them with knives, staves, coal gas. They'll permit no more blockades. They'll not allow themselves to be seized in the street, for they know that work camp means death these days. They want to die at home, not in a strange place . . . Whomever you talk to, you hear the same cry: The resettlement should never have been permitted . . We should have run out into the street, have set fire to everything in sight, have torn down the walls, and escaped to the Other Side. The Germans would have taken their revenge. It would have cost tens of thousands of lives, but not 300,000. Now we are ashamed of ourselves, disgraced in our own eyes, and in the eyes of the world, where our docility earned us nothing. This must not be repeated now. We must put up a resistance, defend ourselves against the enemy, man and child."

AFFIRMATION

Rabbi:	Yet Emmanuel Ringelblum would not despair.
Cong.:	"I do not know who of our group will survive, who will be deemed worthy to work through our collected material. But one thing is clear to all of us. Our toils and tribulations, our devotion and constant terror, have not been in vain."
Rabbi:	Nor was the counsel of another eyewitness, the vision of Chaim Kaplan, one of surrender.

Cong.: "A nation that can live in such terrible circumstances as these without losing its mind, without committing suicide—and which can still laugh—is sure of survival. Which will disappear first, Nazism or Judaism? I am willing to bet! Nazism will go first!"

A LETTER TO GOD FROM A 16 YEAR OLD GIRL
POLAND, 1944

God,
The Sun
    rose
this morning. In England the people are eating their breakfasts.
In Germany the soldiers are changing the watches.
In Bergen-Belsen my mother died . . . . .
Shma Yisrael, chant the people
                  shuffling . . .
    into boxcars to meet their
               Death.
Shma Yisrael Adonay Elohaynu Adonay Echad.
    Hear, O Israel, the Lord Our God, the Lord is One.
Fools, those
             Fools,
                 There is no God.
    A God wouldn't let this happen
    A God wouldn't look down and let this
suffering
             exist.
                        There is no
   Mercy
                        There is no
   Hope.
   There is no God.
   There is no reason to live.
    Today, I weighed in at 83 pounds, Yet, every time they hit me, I resist . . . . .
Fight back,
    Live . . . . .

Don't let these animals beat you.
Don't let them win.
But it is so hard . . . . . so difficult.
And if there were a God,
a God who   loves and cares
        for His people . . . .

                        We wouldn't be here
                        My mother wouldn't have died
                        Four million
                                wouldn't be dead.

And if there is a God, I hate Him
                        because He allowed this to
happen . . . .
The sun
        rose
this morning. In England the people are eating their breakfasts.
In Germany the soldiers are changing the watches.
In Bergen-Belsen my mother
        died . . . . .
    God,   go to hell.

(*Some silent moments, then congregation rises*)

שְׁמַע יִשְׂרָאֵל יְהֹוָה אֱלֹהֵינוּ יְהֹוָה אֶחָד:

בָּרוּךְ שֵׁם כְּבוֹד מַלְכוּתוֹ לְעוֹלָם וָעֶד:

(*Congregation is seated*)

READER

וְאָהַבְתָּ אֵת יְיָ אֱלֹהֶיךָ בְּכָל־לְבָבְךָ וּבְכָל־נַפְשְׁךָ
וּבְכָל־מְאֹדֶךָ: וְהָיוּ הַדְּבָרִים הָאֵלֶּה אֲשֶׁר אָנֹכִי
מְצַוְּךָ הַיּוֹם עַל־לְבָבֶךָ: וְשִׁנַּנְתָּם לְבָנֶיךָ וְדִבַּרְתָּ
בָּם. בְּשִׁבְתְּךָ בְּבֵיתֶךָ וּבְלֶכְתְּךָ בַדֶּרֶךְ וּבְשָׁכְבְּךָ
וּבְקוּמֶךָ: וּקְשַׁרְתָּם לְאוֹת עַל־יָדֶךָ. וְהָיוּ לְטֹטָפֹת
בֵּין עֵינֶיךָ: וּכְתַבְתָּם עַל־מְזֻזוֹת בֵּיתֶךָ וּבִשְׁעָרֶיךָ:

204

CONGREGATION AND READER

Thou shalt love the Lord, they God, with all thy heart, with all thy soul, and with all thy might. And these words, which I command thee this day, shall be upon thy heart. Thou shalt teach them diligently unto thy children, and shalt speak of them when thou sittest in thy house, when thou walkest by the way, when thou liest down, and when thou risest up. Thou shalt bind them for a sign upon thy hand, and they shall be for frontlets between thine eyes. Thou shalt write them upon the doorposts of thy house and upon thy gates: That ye may remember and do all My commandments and be holy unto your God.

From "NIGHT"   Rabbi or Voice

> (Elie Wiesel is, beyond any doubt, the prosecution's most telling witness in the trial of the justice of God. "NIGHT" is his personal record of his adolescent years in the concentration camps.)

"My father's voice drew me from my thoughts: . . . . .

"My forehead was bathed in cold sweat. But I told him that I did not believe that they could burn people in our age, that humanity would never tolerate it . . . .

"Humanity? Humanity is not concerned with us. Today anything is allowed. Anything is possible, even these crematories . . . ."

His voice was choking.

"Father," I said, "if that is so, I don't want to wait here. I'm going to run to the electric wire. That would be better than slow agony in the flames."

He did not answer. He was weeping. His body was shaken convulsively. Around us, everyone was weeping. Someone began to recite the Kaddish, the prayer for the dead. I do not know if it has ever happened before, in the long history of the Jews, that people have ever recited the prayer for the dead for themselves.

"Yitgadal veyitkadash shmei raba . . . May His Name be blessed and magnified . . ." whispered my father.

For the first time, I felt revolt rise up in me. Why should I bless His name? The Eternal, Lord of the Universe, the All-Powerful and Terrible, was silent. What had I to thank Him for?"

The Voice of Children

CONGREGATION

"I Sit With My Dolls"

I sit with my dolls by the stove and dream
I dream that my father came back
I dream that my father is still alive
How good it is to have a father
I do not know where my father is.

"I Never Saw Another Butterfly"

For seven weeks I've lived in here,
Penned up inside this ghetto
But I have found my people here,
The dandelions call to me
And the white chestnut candles in the court
Only I never saw another butterfly.
That butterfly was the last one.
Butterflies don't live in here
    in the ghetto.

Chorus of the Orphans   A Voice

We orphans
We lament to the world:
Our branch has been cut down
And thrown in the fire—
Kindling was made of our protectors—
We orphans lie stretched out on the fields of loneliness.
We orphans

We lament to the world:
At night our parents play hide and seek—
From behind the black folds of night
The faces gaze at us.
Their mouths speak:
Kindling we were in a woodcutter's hand—
But our eyes have become angel eyes
And regard you.
Through the black folds of night
They penetrate—
We orphans
We lament to the world:
Stones have become our playthings,
Stones have faces, father and mother faces
They wilt not like flowers, nor bite like beasts—
and burn not like tinder when tossed into the ovens—
We orphans we lament to the world:
World, why have you taken our soft mothers from us
And the fathers who say: My child, you are like me!
We orphans are like no one in this world any more!
O world
We accuse you!

From "NIGHT"   Voice or Rabbi

Never shall I forget that night, the first night in camp, which has turned my life into one long night, seven times cursed and seven times sealed. Never shall I forget that smoke. Never shall I forget the little faces of the children, whose bodies I saw turned into wreaths of smoke beneath a silent blue sky.

Never shall I forget those flames which consumed my faith forever.

Never shall I forget that nocturnal silence which deprived me, for all eternity, of the desire to live. Never shall I forget those moments which murdered my God and my soul and turned my dreams to dust. Never shall I forget these things, even if I am condemned to live as long as God Himself. Never.

WHY THE BLACK ANSWER OF HATE (Nelly Sachs) A Voice

Why the black answer of hate
to your existence, Israel?

You stranger
from a star one farther away
than the others.

Sold to this earth
that loneliness might be passed on.

Your origin entangled in weeds—
your stars bartered
for all that belongs to moths and worms,
and yet: fetched away from dreamfilled sandy shores of time
like moonwater into the distance.

In the others' choir
you always sang
one note lower
or one note higher—

you flung yourself into the blood of the evening sun
like one pain seeking the other.
Long is your shadow
and it has become late for you
Israel!

How far your way from the blessing
along the aeon of tears
to the bend of the road
where you turned to ashes

and your enemy with the smoke
of your burned body
engraved your mortal abandonment
on the brow of heaven!

O such a death!
When all helping angels
with bleeding wings
hung tattered
in the barbed wire of time!

Why the black answer of hate
to your existence
Israel?

AF AL PI CHEN V'LAMROT HAKOL (Elie Wiesel)   A Voice

To me, the whole event remains a question-mark. I still don't know
how man could have chosen cruelty. I still don't know how God
could have allowed such a choice. I still don't know why Jews kept
silent. In fact, I know nothing. And, frankly, I don't know how
one can talk about it.

As for God, I did speak about Him. I do little else in my books.
It's my problem, and His, too. I'd like to think . . . that there is now
a possibility to establish something new in theology. For I believe
that God *is* part of our experience. The Jew, in my view, may rise
against God, provided he remains within God. One can be a very
good Jew, observe all the mitzvot, study Talmud and yet be against
God. AF AL PI CHEN V'LAMROT HAKOL—as if to say: You,
God, do not want me to be Jewish; well, Jewish we shall be nevertheless, despite your will.

Our mission involves other peoples. Jews do not live alone. As a
result of what the world has done to us, it may find a way to save
itself. By now it must admit that we do have in our possession the
key to survival. We have not survived centuries of atrocities for
nothing.

This is what I think we are trying to prove to ourselves, desperately,
because it is desperately needed: in a world of absurdity, we must
invent reason; we must create beauty out of nothingness. And be-

209

cause there is murder in this world—and we are the first ones to know it—and we know how hopeless our battle may appear, we have to fight murder and absurdity, and give meaning to the battle, if not to our hope.

This is not a lesson; this is not an answer. It is only a question.

ADORATION

(Congregation rises)

CONGREGATION AND READER

Let us adore the ever-living God, and render praise unto Him who spread out the heavens and established the earth, whose glory is revealed in the heavens above and whose greatness is manifest throughout the world. He is our God; there is none else. We bow the head in reverence, and worship the King of kings, the Holy One, praised be He.

וַאֲנַחְנוּ כּוֹרְעִים וּמִשְׁתַּחֲוִים וּמוֹדִים

לִפְנֵי מֶלֶךְ מַלְכֵי הַמְּלָכִים הַקָּדוֹשׁ בָּרוּךְ הוּא.

(Congregation is seated)

READER

May the time not be distant, O God, when Thy name shall be worshipped in all the earth, when unbelief shall disappear and error be no more. Fervently we pray that the day may come when all men shall invoke Thy name, when corruption and evil shall give way to purity and goodness, when superstition shall no longer enslave the mind, nor idolatry blind the eye, when all who dwell on earth shall know that to Thee alone every knee must bend and every tongue give homage. O may all, created in Thine image, recognize that they are brethren, so that, one in spirit and one in fellowship they may be forever united before Thee. Then shall Thy kingdom be established on earth and the word of Thine ancient seer be fulfilled: The Lord will reign forever and ever.

וְנֶאֱמַר וְהָיָה יְיָ לְמֶלֶךְ עַל־כָּל־הָאָרֶץ בַּיּוֹם הַהוּא יִהְיֶה יְיָ אֶחָד וּשְׁמוֹ אֶחָד:

On that day the Lord shall be One and His name shall be One.

ANI MA'AMIN
Reader and Congregation

I believe with perfect faith in the coming of the Messiah: And though he tarry, none the less do I believe!

KADDISH

(Mourners rising)

READER

יִתְגַּדַּל וְיִתְקַדַּשׁ שְׁמֵהּ רַבָּא. בְּעָלְמָא דִּי־בְרָא כִרְעוּתֵהּ. וְיַמְלִיךְ מַלְכוּתֵהּ בְּחַיֵּיכוֹן וּבְיוֹמֵיכוֹן וּבְחַיֵּי דְכָל־בֵּית יִשְׂרָאֵל בַּעֲגָלָא וּבִזְמַן קָרִיב. וְאִמְרוּ אָמֵן:

CONGREGATION

יְהֵא שְׁמֵהּ רַבָּא מְבָרַךְ לְעָלַם וּלְעָלְמֵי עָלְמַיָּא:

READER

יִתְבָּרַךְ וְיִשְׁתַּבַּח וְיִתְפָּאַר וְיִתְרוֹמַם וְיִתְנַשֵּׂא וְיִתְהַדָּר וְיִתְעַלֶּה וְיִתְהַלָּל שְׁמֵהּ דְּקֻדְשָׁא. בְּרִיךְ הוּא. לְעֵלָּא (וּלְעֵלָּא) מִן־כָּל־בִּרְכָתָא וְשִׁירָתָא תֻּשְׁבְּחָתָא וְנֶחֱמָתָא דַּאֲמִירָן בְּעָלְמָא. וְאִמְרוּ אָמֵן:

יְהֵא שְׁלָמָא רַבָּא מִן־שְׁמַיָּא וְחַיִּים עָלֵינוּ וְעַל־כָּל־יִשְׂרָאֵל. וְאִמְרוּ אָמֵן:

עֹשֶׂה שָׁלוֹם בִּמְרוֹמָיו הוּא יַעֲשֶׂה שָׁלוֹם עָלֵינוּ וְעַל־כָּל־יִשְׂרָאֵל. וְאִמְרוּ אָמֵן:

(sitting)

211

BENEDICTION

Yossel Rackover's APPEAL TO GOD   Rabbi

God of Israel, I have fled to this place in order to worship You without molestation, to obey Your commandments and sanctify Your Name. You, however, have done everything to make me stop believing in You. Now, lest it seem to You that You will succeed by these tribulations to drive me from the right path, I notify You, my God, and God of my fathers, that it will not avail You in the least! You may insult me, You may castigate me, You may take from me all that I cherish and hold dear in the world. You may torture me to death—I shall believe in You, I shall love You no matter what You do to test me!

And these are my last words to You, my wrathful God: Nothing will avail You in the least. You have done everything to make me renounce You, to make me lose my faith in You, but I die exactly as I have lived, a believer!

Eternally praised be the God of the dead, the God of vengeance, of truth, and of law, who will soon show His face to the world again and shake its foundations with His almighty voice.

Into Your hands, O Lord, I consign my soul.

RECESSIONAL

Partizaner Lid

A SERVICE OF JEWISH GIVING

MEDITATION

We live far away from those to whom we give—many seas, great deserts, eons of unshared lives protect us from our brothers in the ancient land, and from our brothers in unhappy places who would seek out that land. Not for us the enemy massing at the water's edge, beyond the rise, or stealing, death in hand, unseen amid the market stalls or underneath the buses groaning with their peopled seats. Not for us the daily doubt if Ishmael beside us in the street is enemy or brother, is cruel oppressed or cruel oppressor; not for us the daily grief for names that are not ciphers in black borders, but are sons and brothers, children with whom we were building up a land just days ago, or yesterday . . . . These are not our life. Yet we would share that life, would give that brother be no longer enemy, that death might come with time and not with blood, that those who would seek out life and peace need find themselves no more confounded in their search.

This nightfall marks the seventh day. Within its span all men may live within one place, one life. Seas part and paths are cleared across the deserts to the ancient land which is as new as each Creation. On this day our brother is our brother, and we resolve once more that we shall help redeem our brother, no matter whether oceans roll between his life and ours, or but a finger's space divides us. For enemies mass against our lives in this land too, more complex, less visible; enemies often of the spirit more than of the flesh. For while our gift comes forth from love, from charity, from merciful sons of a merciful Creator, so also must it come from tzedakah, from a concern for justice, from a determination to restore the balance of a world where some men have too many and many not enough.

Shabbat returns to us to put our giving in perspective, to give us courage for our weeklong struggle in the world that man has bruised, by this dayful of the world that God once made, to remind us of the greatness of our task and to stir more fervor in us to ac-

complish it. To breathe Shabbat is to spend one sun's journey in
the world we want, that we might work even harder when the twilight next returns to bring that world closer to the souls we love,
with whom our souls are joined across all seas.

READER

Once each week, as afternoon turns into twilight
We open to these moments now ahead,
That we may meet
And celebrate
The world which made us
And which we are making,
To help each other know Shabbat
And greet the bride who will embrace us
With her day.

SONG

Come my beloved to meet the bride, Come welcome the Sabbath!	לְכָה דוֹדִי לִקְרַאת כַּלָה. פְּנֵי שַׁבָּת נְקַבְּלָה:
Come, let us meet the Sabbath The fountain of blessing, poured forth from of old, Last act of creation, yet first in God's thought.	לִקְרַאת שַׁבָּת לְכוּ וְנֵלְכָה. כִּי הִיא מְקוֹר הַבְּרָכָה. מֵראש מִקֶּדֶם נְסוּכָה. סוֹף מַעֲשֶׂה בְּמַחֲשָׁבָה תְּחִלָה:
Come my beloved	
Rise up, rise up, for your light has come, Arise and shine! Awake, awake, utter a song! The glory of the Lord is revealed upon you.	הִתְעוֹרְרִי הִתְעוֹרְרִי. כִּי בָא אוֹרֵךְ קוּמִי אוֹרִי. עוּרִי עוּרִי שִׁיר דַּבֵּרִי. כְּבוֹד יְיָ עָלַיִךְ נִגְלָה:
Come my beloved	

216

Enter in peace, O crown of your
    husband, in joy and exultation!
Amid the faithful of a treasured
    people,
Enter O bride! Enter, O bride!

בּוֹאִי בְשָׁלוֹם עֲטֶרֶת בַּעְלָהּ.
גַּם בְּשִׂמְחָה וּבְצָהֳלָה.
תּוֹךְ אֱמוּנֵי עַם סְגֻלָּה.
בּוֹאִי כַלָּה. בּוֹאִי כַלָּה:

Come my beloved . . . .

READER OR CONGREGATION

Praise me, says God, and I will know that you love Me.
Curse Me, I will know that you love Me.
    Praise Me or curse Me, I will know that you love Me.
Sing out My graces, says God,
Raise your fist against Me and revile, says God,
    Sing My graces or revile, reviling is also praise, says God.
But if you sit fenced off in your apathy,
    Entrenched in "I don't give a damn," says God,
If you look at the stars and yawn, says God,
    If you see suffering and don't cry out,
If you don't praise and don't revile,
    Then I created you in vain, says God.

(rising)

בָּרְכוּ אֶת־יְיָ הַמְבֹרָךְ:

Praise the Lord to Whom all praise is due.

בָּרוּךְ יְיָ הַמְבֹרָךְ לְעוֹלָם וָעֶד:

The Lord is praised; to Him all praise is due forever and ever.

(sitting)

PRELUDE TO THE SHMA: A DIALOGUE
(Two Readers)

Shabbat has come again, and with it another chance to endow
with sanctity this transient, fragile experience we call life. How

217

shall we do that? How shall we carve out of the confusion and ambiguity of living a way that makes sense, a way that brings dignity, honor, a moment of joy and triumph to this little, little world we have been given? What shall we make of this time? What can we say to each other? What can we say to our Jews?

* * *

We shall do what we have been taught. We shall go back—we shall search for the roots and causes. Buried under the thick encrustation of everything we are, buried beneath the accumulation of memory, lust, greed, love, kindness—there lurks the something out of which we have oozed. There is a way out of our confusion: a way illumined by reason, governed by compassion. Out of our tradition, out of Bible, Midrash, Talmud, come leaping a thousand familiar words: It has been told thee, O man, what is good and what the Lord doth require of thee: only to do justly, to love mercy, to walk humbly with Thy God. . . . What is hateful to thee do not do unto thy fellowman. . . . The Lord of Hosts is exalted through justice. . . . Seek justice through justice. . . . These words and countless others speak for all the redeeming moments of grandeur in the life of man.

* * *

I shall tell you of redeeming moments of grandeur! I shall tell you of horror and wrath, etched into the past and burned into the present by man's barbarism, arrogance, and stupidity. I shall tell you of cool detachment and moral sterility and the enormities they sanction. Search, search where you will, back into time and tradition and conscience, but it is always the same. It will always be the same.

* * *

That is why the Sabbath comes to us, to remind us that our world and its people, you and I, need desperately to be made whole. Our world needs Jews. It needs troubled people, men and women who care, men and women who are not ashamed to be sensitive and tender. It needs those who are willing to become members of a community dedicated to each other's fulfillment, aware that without such a community, it will be impossible to fulfill our own humanity. Our world needs men and women who have the cour-

218

age to be afraid, afraid of all the forces which have removed our humanity, which have cut us off from the unity which is mankind, the Creation we were formed to guard, and the God Whose spirit has made us men.

(rising)

שְׁמַע יִשְׂרָאֵל יְהֹוָה אֱלֹהֵינוּ יְהֹוָה אֶחָד:

Hear, O Israel: the Lord is our God, the Lord alone.

בָּרוּךְ שֵׁם כְּבוֹד מַלְכוּתוֹ לְעוֹלָם וָעֶד:

Praised be His name Whose Kingdom alone is glory forever and ever.

(seated)

וְאָהַבְתָּ אֵת יְיָ אֱלֹהֶיךָ בְּכָל־לְבָבְךָ וּבְכָל־נַפְשְׁךָ
וּבְכָל־מְאֹדֶךָ: וְהָיוּ הַדְּבָרִים הָאֵלֶּה אֲשֶׁר אָנֹכִי
מְצַוְּךָ הַיּוֹם עַל־לְבָבֶךָ: וְשִׁנַּנְתָּם לְבָנֶיךָ וְדִבַּרְתָּ
בָּם. בְּשִׁבְתְּךָ בְּבֵיתֶךָ וּבְלֶכְתְּךָ בַדֶּרֶךְ וּבְשָׁכְבְּךָ
וּבְקוּמֶךָ: וּקְשַׁרְתָּם לְאוֹת עַל־יָדֶךָ. וְהָיוּ לְטֹטָפֹת
בֵּין עֵינֶיךָ: וּכְתַבְתָּם עַל־מְזֻזוֹת בֵּיתֶךָ וּבִשְׁעָרֶיךָ:

RESPONSIVE READING

Hear, O Israel: The Lord Who links us together by His love, loves in the oneness of all.

You shall love the Lord your God with all your passions, with every fibre of your being, with all that you possess.

Let these words with which He joins Himself to you today enter your heart.

219

Pattern your days on them, that your children may discover Torah within you.

Make your life into a voice of God, both in your stillness and in your movement.

Renew these words each morning and evening in prayer and reflection.

Bind them upon your arm and head as symbols of acts and thoughts consecrated to a Godly purpose.

Write them in Mezuzot at the entrance to your home, as a sign that men may discover divinity as they enter your home and your life.

THE REDEMPTION
(Two Readers)

We, 18 religious Jewish families of Georgia, request you to help us leave for Israel. There are 18 of us who signed this letter. But he errs who thinks there are only 18 of us. There could have been many more signatures. They say there is a total of 12 million Jews in the world. But he errs who believes there are only 12 million of us. For with those who pray for Israel are hundreds of millions who did not live to this day, who were tortured to death, who are no longer here. They march shoulder to shoulder with us, unconquered and immortal, those who handed down to us the traditions of struggle and faith. That is why we want to go to Israel. We demand that the United Nations Human Rights Commission do everything it can to obtain from the Soviet Government in the shortest possible time permission for us to leave. It is incomprehensible that in the 20th century people can be prohibited from living where they wish to live. We will wait months and years, we will wait all our lives if necessary, but we will not renounce our faith or our hopes. We believe: Our prayers have reached God. We know: Our appeals will reach humanity. For we are asking little: Let us go to the land of our forefathers.

—From a letter to the Human Rights Commission of the United Nations by 18 Jewish families of the Georgian Sector of the USSR.

The survival of Judaism, not merely of a brood of suburban Bar Mitzvah boys and girls, demands a reunion between that sense of mystery, communal feeling, and tradition that we knew as children and the intellect, reason, systematization that we have learned as adults. But the burst of energy that was Chassidic is as much ours as the burst of energy that was Prophetic—and as necessary. The salvation of us all requires that the technology that is now destroying Mankind and poisoning the Earth be connected to a sense of love, joy, community.

We are Jews committed to other Jews, to the Jewish tradition, and to humanity. We believe that the American Jewish community could combine a tradition of critical social concern with real economic and political resources. The social commitment of our community must be mobilized to attack the injustices of American political and economic life. In our efforts we will seek allies among those in other traditions—Christian, Muslim, Humanist, Marxist, Existentialist, Anarchist—who have rebelled against abandoning their own ethical ideals in the face of the seductions and coercions of American practice. We will join with them to seek liberty, justice, and community for all. In the words of Hillel: "If we are not for ourselves, who will be for us? But if we are for ourselves only, what are we? If not now, when?"

—From the Statement of Principles of the National Jewish Organizing Project

PROTEST SONG OF SOVIET JEWS (*Music on p. 230*)

Pharaonu, Pharaonu *ga*varyu
Ahtpus*ti* na*rod* moy
Ahtpus*ti* na*rod* moy.

To the Pharaoh I say:
Let my people go!

Chorus:

Ahtpus*ti* na*rod* Yev*ra*yskee
Na*rod*yenu svay*u*
Ahtpus*ti* na*rod*, ahtpus*ti* na*rod*
Ahtpus*ti* na*rod* da*moy*.

Let the Jewish people go
To their homeland!

N'ustahnu, n'ustahnu paftaryat   I shall not tire of repeating,
Ahtpusti narod moy   Let my people go!
Ahtpusti narod moy.
        Chorus (repeat)

SONG OF REDEMPTION FROM EGYPT

מִי־כָמֹכָה בָּאֵלִם יְיָ מִי כָּמֹכָה נֶאְדָּר בַּקֹּדֶשׁ

נוֹרָא תְהִלֹּת עֹשֵׂה פֶלֶא:

מַלְכוּתְךָ רָאוּ בָנֶיךָ בּוֹקֵעַ יָם לִפְנֵי מֹשֶׁה זֶה

אֵלִי עָנוּ וְאָמְרוּ.

יְיָ יִמְלֹךְ לְעֹלָם וָעֶד:

וְנֶאֱמַר כִּי־פָדָה יְיָ אֶת־יַעֲקֹב וּגְאָלוֹ מִיַּד חָזָק

מִמֶּנּוּ. בָּרוּךְ אַתָּה יְיָ גָּאַל יִשְׂרָאֵל:

(As our forefathers sang on the shores of the divided Red Sea:
Who is like you, O Lord, compared to the gods men worship?
Who is like you, majestic in holiness, awesome in splendor, doing
wonders? The Lord shall reign forever and ever.)

MAIMONIDES' EIGHT STEPS OF TZEDAKA

(Antiphonal Reading)

First and lowest is to give, but with reluctance or regret. This is
the gift of the hand, but not of the heart.

> Second is to give cheerfully, but not in proportion to the
> distress of the sufferer.

Third is to give cheerfully and proportionately, but not until
solicited.

> Fourth is to give cheerfully, proportionately, and even unso-
> licited; but to put the gift in the poor man's hand, thereby
> arousing in him the painful emotion of shame.

222

Fifth is to give so the distressed may receive the gift and know the giver, without the giver knowing him. Thus our ancestors would tie up money in the corners of their cloaks so the poor might take it unperceived.

Sixth is to know the object of our bounty, but remain unknown to him. Thus our ancestors would bring their gifts into poor people's homes, taking care that the poor should not know them or their names.

Seventh is to give in such a way that the giver does not know the receiver, nor the receiver the name of his benefactor. Thus in Temple days our ancestors would secretly deposit in the Chamber of the Silent whatever they thought proper, and the poor with equal secrecy might draw money forth.

(Together)

Eighth, and most meritorious of all, is to anticipate tzedaka by preventing poverty: namely, to assist our reduced brother either by a large gift or a loan, by teaching him a trade, or enabling him to start in business, that he may earn his own way, and not be forced to hold out his hand for alms. Thus intends the Torah when it says, "If your brother becomes poor and his hand fails with you, then you shall strengthen and help him, that he may live along with you." This is the highest step in the golden ladder of tzedaka.

MEDITATIONS ON GIVING
(The Hebrew Amidah may be inserted as an alternative reading)

It is said, "If your brother becomes poor and his hand fails with you, then you shall strengthen and help him, that he may live along with you." If your brother becomes poor, you shall not allow him to fall. He is like a load resting on a wall, which one man can hold and prevent from falling, but once it has fallen to the ground, five men cannot raise it up again. And even if you have helped him four or five times, you must give him help again when he needs it.

* * *

Let your house be open; let the poor be members of your household. Let a man's house be open to the north and to the south and to the east and to the west, as Job's house was, that the poor might not have to go round the house to the back door, but each would find a door facing him as he approached. When the great suffering came upon Job, he said, "Lord of the world, have I not fed the hungry and clothed the naked?" But God said, "So far, you have not reached half the measure of Abraham, for you sat in your house and when wayfarers came to you you gave wheat bread to him whose custom it was to eat wheat bread and meat to him whose custom it was to eat meat, and wine to him who was accustomed to wine. But Abraham did not so; he went out and wandered about, and when he found wayfarers, he brought them to his house and he gave wheat bread to him who had not been able to eat wheat bread, and similarly with meat and wine. Not only this, but he built large inns on the roads, and put food and drink in them and all came and ate and drank and blessed God."

* * *

If a poor man says, "I ought not to be supported by others," then one should watch over him and support him, giving him help as a loan, and then letting him regard the loan as a gift. But other sages held that the help should be given first as a gift, and then that he should be told that it could be regarded as a loan. Rabbi Shimon said the poor man should be asked to give something as a pledge to help him preserve his self-respect.

* * *

He who needs not and takes, will find himself really needing help before he reaches old age. He who is in need and does not take, will find himself able to help others before he reaches old age. He who is not lame or blind but pretends to be so, will become blind and lame before he reaches old age.

* * *

On the way to the baths Rabbi Yochanan and Rabbi Simon ben Lakish met a poor man who asked for charity. They said, "When we come back." When they returned, they found him dead. They said, "Since we showed him no tzedaka when he was alive, let us

224

attend to him now that he is dead." When they were laying him out for burial, they found a purse full of silver pieces upon him. Then they remembered Rabbi Abbahu's words: "We must give tzedaka even to the deceivers, for we must be grateful to them: were there not some deceivers among those who call on us every day for help, we should be sinning every single time we refused."

* * *

"Open your hand wide to your brother," (Deut. 15:11). To him who needs bread, give bread; to him who needs dough, give dough; to him who needs money, give money; to him who needs the food put into his mouth, put it in.

* * *

A poor man came to Raba for sustenance. Raba asked him what he usually had for his fare. The man replied, "Fatted chicken and old wine." "But are you not concerned," Raba said, "about the burden of the community?" The man answered: "Do I eat what is theirs? I eat what is God's. Do we not read: 'The eyes of all wait for You and You give them their food in due season'? Understand by 'due season,' to mean 'each man's season'—God provides food for each man in accord with his own habits." Meanwhile there arrived Raba's sister, who had not seen him for thirteen years, and brought her brother fatted chicken and wine. "How remarkable!" Raba exclaimed; "I apologize to you," he said to the poor man. "Come and eat."

* * *

In a city where there are Jews and Gentiles Jewish alms collectors collect from both Jews and Gentiles; they feed the poor of both, visit the sick of both, bury both, and comfort the mourners whether Jew or Gentile, and they restore the lost goods of both, for the sake of peace.

* * *

One day Rabbi Hama and Rabbi Hoshaya went about among the grand synagogues of Lod. Said Rabbi Hama, "How much money my ancestors have sunk here!" Replied Rabbi Hoshaya, "How many souls your ancestors have sunk here! How many men might have used that money instead to toil in Torah!"

* * *

225

It is taught in the name of Rabbi Joshua: The poor man does more for the rich man than the rich man for the poor man. When the mother of Rabbi Tanhum bar Hiyya wanted to buy one pound of meat, she would buy two pounds, one for her son and one for the poor, because God has made each responsible for the other. Why did God create both rich and poor? That the one might be sustained by the other.

*　*　*

Loving deeds (gemilut chasadim) are greater than mere almsgiving (tzedaka). Rabbi Elazar says, "Tzedaka is greater than all sacrifice, but gemilut chasadim is greater than tzedaka, as it is said: 'Sow in righteousness (tzedaka), reap in love (chesed)' (Hosea 10:12). Of his sowing a man may or may not be able to eat, but of his reaping a man will surely be able to eat." He added: "Tzedaka becomes increasingly perfect according to the amount of love that is shown in it."

SONG

Give a Damn

If you'd take the train with me
Uptown thru the misery
Of ghetto streets in morning light,
They're always night,—
Take a window seat, put down your *Times*
You can read between the lines
Just meet the faces that you meet
Beyond the window's pane,

Chorus: And it might begin to teach you
How to give a damn about your fellowman.

Or put your girl to sleep sometime
With rats instead of nursery rhymes
With hunger and your other children
By her side.
And wonder if you'll share your bed
With something else that must be fed

For fear may lie beside you
Or it may sleep down the hall.

Chorus: And it might begin to teach you
How to give a damn about your fellow man.

Come and see how well despair
Is seasoned by the stif'ling air
See your ghetto in the good old
Sizzling summer time.
Suppose the streets were all on fire,
The flames like tempers leaping higher,
Suppose you'd lived there all your life,
D'you think that you would mind?

Last Chorus: And it might begin to reach you
Why I give a damn about my fellow man.
And I might begin to teach you
How to give a damn about your fellow man.

ALEYNU

To be a Jew in the twentieth century
Is to be offered a gift. If you refuse,
Wishing to be invisible, you choose
Death of the spirit, the stone insanity.
Accepting, take full life. Full agonies:
Your evening deep in labyrinthine blood
Of those who resist, fail, and resist; and God
Reduced to a hostage among hostages.

The gift is torment. Not alone the still
Torture, isolation; or torture of the flesh.
That may come also. But the accepting wish,
The whole and fertile spirit as guarantee
For every human freedom, suffering to be free,
Daring to live for the impossible.

(rising)

227

עָלֵינוּ לְשַׁבֵּחַ לַאֲדוֹן הַכֹּל לָתֵת גְּדֻלָּה לְיוֹצֵר בְּרֵאשִׁית שֶׁלֹּא
עָשָׂנוּ כְּגוֹיֵי הָאֲרָצוֹת וְלֹא שָׂמָנוּ כְּמִשְׁפְּחוֹת הָאֲדָמָה שֶׁלֹּא שָׂם
חֶלְקֵנוּ כָּהֶם וְגֹרָלֵנוּ כְּכָל־הֲמוֹנָם:

וַאֲנַחְנוּ כּוֹרְעִים וּמִשְׁתַּחֲוִים וּמוֹדִים
לִפְנֵי מֶלֶךְ מַלְכֵי הַמְּלָכִים הַקָּדוֹשׁ בָּרוּךְ הוּא.

CONGREGATION

May the time not be distant, O God, when Your name shall
be worshiped in all the earth, when despair shall disappear
and error be no more. We pray that the day be not far off
when all men shall find their way to calling on Your name,
when corruption and evil shall give way to integrity and
goodness, when the many kinds of men who dwell on earth
shall recognize not alone their difference but their unity, that
each people may, in its unique way, work for the coming of
God's single kingdom. Hear O Israel is only for the present;
the day will come when all the earth will hear that the Lord is
God, the Lord is One.

וְנֶאֱמַר
וְהָיָה יְיָ לְמֶלֶךְ עַל־כָּל־הָאָרֶץ בַּיּוֹם הַהוּא יִהְיֶה
יְיָ אֶחָד וּשְׁמוֹ אֶחָד:

MOURNERS' KADDISH

יִתְגַּדַּל וְיִתְקַדַּשׁ שְׁמֵהּ רַבָּא. בְּעָלְמָא דִּי־בְרָא כִרְעוּתֵהּ.
וְיַמְלִיךְ מַלְכוּתֵהּ בְּחַיֵּיכוֹן וּבְיוֹמֵיכוֹן וּבְחַיֵּי דְכָל־בֵּית יִשְׂרָאֵל
בַּעֲגָלָא וּבִזְמַן קָרִיב. וְאִמְרוּ אָמֵן:

יְהֵא שְׁמֵהּ רַבָּא מְבָרַךְ לְעָלַם וּלְעָלְמֵי עָלְמַיָּא:

228

יִתְבָּרַךְ וְיִשְׁתַּבַּח וְיִתְפָּאַר וְיִתְרֹמַם וְיִתְנַשֵּׂא וְיִתְהַדָּר וְיִתְעַלֶּה וְיִתְהַלָּל שְׁמֵהּ דְּקֻדְשָׁא. בְּרִיךְ הוּא. לְעֵלָּא (וּלְעֵלָּא) מִן־כָּל־בִּרְכָתָא וְשִׁירָתָא תֻּשְׁבְּחָתָא וְנֶחֱמָתָא דַּאֲמִירָן בְּעָלְמָא. וְאִמְרוּ אָמֵן:

יְהֵא שְׁלָמָא רַבָּא מִן־שְׁמַיָּא וְחַיִּים עָלֵינוּ וְעַל־כָּל־יִשְׂרָאֵל. וְאִמְרוּ אָמֵן:

עֹשֶׂה שָׁלוֹם בִּמְרוֹמָיו הוּא יַעֲשֶׂה שָׁלוֹם עָלֵינוּ וְעַל־כָּל־יִשְׂרָאֵל. וְאִמְרוּ אָמֵן:

Yis-ga-dal v'yis-ka-dash sh'may ra-bo,
B'ol-mo dee-v'ro hir u-say, v'yam-leeh
   mal-hu-say,
B'ha-yay-hon uv-yo-may-hon, uv-ha-yay d'hol
   bays yis-ro-ayl,
Ba-a-go-lo u-viz'man ko-reev, v'im-ru o-mayn.

Congregation and Mourners

Y'hay sh'may ra-bo m'vo-rah, l'o-lam ul-ol-may
   ol-ma-yo.

Mourners

Yis-bo-rah v'yish-ta-bah, v'yis-po-ar v'yis-ro-mam,
V'yis-na-say v'yis-ha-dar, v'yis-a-leh, v'yis-ha-lal
   sh'may d'kud-sho b'rih hu;
L'ay-lo ul-ay-lo min kol bir-ho-so v'shee-ro-so,
Tush-b'ho-so v'ne-heh-mo-so, da-a-mee-ron b'ol-mo.
V'im-ru o-mayn.
Y'hay sh'lo-mo ra-bo min sh'ma-yo,
V'ha-yeem o'lay-nu v'al kol yis-ro-ayl v'im-ru
   o-mayn.
O-se sho-lom bim-ro-mov hu ya-a-se sho-lom
O-lay-nu v'al kol yis-ro-ayl v'im-ru o-mayn.

CONCLUSION

We live far away from those to whom we give,
Yet we would share their life,
We would give that brother be no longer enemy,
That death would come with time and not with blood,
That our people who would seek out peace
Might no longer be confounded in our search.

SONG

Am Yisrael, Am Yisrael, Am Yisrael chai
Am Yisrael, Am Yisrael, Am Yisrael chai
Od avinu chai, od avinu chai
Od avinu, od avinu, od avinu chai
Am Yisrael chai . . . .
(The People Israel lives, our fathers live!)

PHARAONU

1. Pha-ra-o-nu, Pha-ra-o-nu ga-var-yu, Aht-pus-
2. N'-us-tah-nu n'-us-tah-nu paf-tar-yat,

ti-na-rod-moy, Aht-pus ti na-rod-moy.

Chorus

Aht-pus-ti na-rod Yev-ray___skee Na-

rod-ye-nu sva-yu Aht-pus-ti na-rod Yev-ray___skee Na-

rod-ye-nu sva-yu Aht-pus-ti na-rod, Aht-pus-

ti na-rod, Aht-pus-ti na-rod da-moy.

A SERVICE ON PEACE AND BROTHERHOOD

OPENING SONG

CANDLE BLESSING

The candles are lit and as the flames grow, our praying space fills with light. We are no longer separated from one another by the darkness. I cannot keep the light to myself—it escapes through my fingers and all share its benefit. Together let us thank God for the Sabbath and for His gift of light as we recite the blessing over the Sabbath candles.

בָּרוּךְ אַתָּה יְיָ אֱלֹהֵינוּ מֶלֶךְ הָעוֹלָם אֲשֶׁר קִדְּשָׁנוּ
בְּמִצְוֹתָיו וְצִוָּנוּ לְהַדְלִיק נֵר שֶׁל־שַׁבָּת:

Praised be God the author of light, who enlightens all men by the guiding flame of peace, justice, and love.

CONGREGATION AND READER

Almighty God, Ruler of the Nations, quicken our consciences that we may feel the sin and shame of war. Inspire us with courage that we may lift up our voices against private greed, social injustice, the aggression of the strong over the weak, and whatsoever works enmity between man and man, class and class, nation and nation. Grant us the wisdom so to live as a people that nations will take us for their conscience, abandon their violence and submit to Thy law of righteousness and peace. Create in us a passion for the reign of righteousness, the spread of brotherhood and good will among the nations, so that we may hasten the fulfillment of Thine ancient word: "Nation shall not lift up sword against nation, neither shall they learn war anymore."

RESPONSIVE READING

Let the mountains bear peace to the people, and the hills, through righteousness.

Let the righteous flourish and let there be an abundance of peace.

233

A king is not saved by the multitude of his host, nor a mighty man by his great strength.

Not by might nor by power but by my spirit, saith the Lord.

I will break the bow and the sword and the battle out of the land,

And will make the people to dwell in safety.

I will make thine officers peace, and righteousness thy magistrates.

The people shall abide in peaceful habitation, in secure dwellings, and in quiet havens.

I will give peace in the land, and ye shall lie down, and none shall make you afraid.

Violence shall no more be heard in the land, nor desolation and destruction within thy borders.

The Lord will give strength unto the people, the Lord will bless the people with peace.

(Congregation rises)

CANTOR

בָּרְכוּ אֶת־יְיָ הַמְּבֹרָךְ:

Praise ye the Lord, to whom all praise is due.

בָּרוּךְ יְיָ הַמְּבֹרָךְ לְעוֹלָם וָעֶד:

Praised be the Lord to whom all praise is due forever and ever.

READER

God of our fathers, we thank Thee for the dream of liberty which guided the sons of many nations to these shores. We praise Thee for the vision of a just society which inspired the fathers of this nation to establish in this land a righteous commonwealth. We pray Thee to deepen our faith in man's cooperative nature, that we may strive to preserve our heritage of equality, and labor for its extension to all men everywhere.

CANTOR AND CONGREGATION

שְׁמַע יִשְׂרָאֵל יְהֹוָה אֱלֹהֵינוּ יְהֹוָה אֶחָד:

Hear, O Israel: The Lord our God, the Lord is One.

בָּרוּךְ שֵׁם כְּבוֹד מַלְכוּתוֹ לְעוֹלָם וָעֶד:

Praised be His name whose glorious kingdom is forever and ever.

(Congregation is seated)

CONGREGATION AND READER

And Thou shalt love the Lord thy God with all thy heart, with all thy soul and with all thy might. Thou shalt love thy neighbor as thyself. Thou shalt not stand idly by the blood of thy fellow man. Depart from evil and do good; seek peace and pursue it, for the work of righteousness is peace. Quarrel with no man, but regard every man as thy brother, and teach thy children to treat all men with respect.

ANOTHER READER

And God said, "Thou Shalt Love Thy Neighbor." But do we love our neighbor?

Today there is sickness and hunger in the world in which we live. Do we help our neighbor? We see riots and destruction in the world. Do we help our neighbor? We see discrimination against people who live beside us. Do we help our neighbor? We see elderly people who are lonely and need someone to take care of them. Do we help our neighbor? We see people with mental illness who need our love and patience. Do we help our neighbor? To all these questions, most of us must answer, No. Rather than help our neighbors, more often we disdain them, or ignore them, refusing to be bothered. If God said, "Thou Shalt Love Thy Neighbor", we are separated from the will of God.

RESPONSIVE READING

To say to men, "you are my brothers", this is the whole Torah.

Brotherhood is the word of the future, and when it captures the world it will transform life utterly.

When we guard our possessions with all our might we often lose them, but when we share them with the world they may increase many fold.

The world of beasts exists on taking, but the human world is sustained by giving. Parents give to their children, the strong uphold the weak, the healthy tend to the sick.

A good man cares for his family, his community, his country, and his people.

A better man cares also for those who are not his people.

The future of mankind depends on the concern of men for those across their border and far from their country.

Brotherhood is the hope of mankind.

ALL SING

מִי־כָמְכָה בָּאֵלִם יְיָ מִי כָּמְכָה נֶאְדָּר בַּקֹּדֶשׁ
נוֹרָא תְהִלֹּת עֹשֵׂה פֶלֶא:

CANTOR

מַלְכוּתְךָ רָאוּ בָנֶיךָ בּוֹקֵעַ יָם לִפְנֵי מֹשֶׁה זֶה
אֵלִי עָנוּ וְאָמְרוּ. יְיָ יִמְלֹךְ לְעֹלָם וָעֶד:

ALL SING

וְנֶאֱמַר כִּי־פָדָה יְיָ אֶת־יַעֲקֹב וּגְאָלוֹ מִיַּד חָזָק
מִמֶּנּוּ. בָּרוּךְ אַתָּה יְיָ גָּאַל יִשְׂרָאֵל:

236

A LITANY FOR PEACE
(One or more readers)

WAR. 5,000 Americans dead. HATE. Two more riots flare up in the ghettos of America. STARVATION. Thousands on the brink of death in drought. POVERTY. Thousands unemployed. WAR. IGNORANCE. Thousands illiterate in Appalachia. HATE. NON-INVOLVEMENT. Twenty watch as girl gets stabbed on city street. REBELLION. Students invade Administration Building in new wave of demonstrations. RIOTS. March on City Hall by blacks ends in violence. WAR. REVOLT. Five hundred stop traffic, protesting new Indochina move. HATE. BIGOTRY. Southern man faces trial for murder of black teacher. HATE. SLAVERY. MILITANCY. Black panthers trade blows with police. WAR. DESTRUCTION. Two more Viet Cong villages destroyed by bombs. DISEASE. Typhoid epidemic hits southern Asia. WAR. NON-COMMUNICATION. Parents cop out on kids. DISTRUST. GENERATION GAP. HOPE. WORK. COMMUNICATION. HOPE. INVOLVEMENT. KNOWLEDGE. TOGETHERNESS. HOPE. BROTHERHOOD. EQUALITY. RENEWAL. GENEROSITY. HOPE. FREEDOM. JUSTICE. LOVE. HOPE.

And at last PEACE!

AMIDAH

Grant us peace, Thy most precious gift, O Thou eternal source of peace, and enable Israel to be its messenger unto the peoples of the earth. Bless our country that it may become a stronghold of peace, and its advocate in the council of nations. May contentment reign within its borders, health and happiness within its homes. Strengthen the bonds of friendship and fellowship among the inhabitants of all lands. Plant virtue in every soul, and may the love of Thy name hallow every home and every heart. Praised be Thou, O Lord, Giver of Peace. Amen.

CONGREGATION OR READER

A gulf of distrust divides nation from nation.
An abyss of fear separates the peoples,
And no bridge spans the chasm
To convey the truth:
That one destiny holds all the dwellers on earth.

Incline our ears, O God, to the unuttered cry
For human understanding
Which throbs in the hearts of all men everywhere.

Voice 1:	What can we do? Our world is crumbling around us!
Voice 2:	Our boys are dying in the government's war!
Congregation:	We are the government.
Voice 3:	We are surrounded by corruption!
Congregation:	Every one of us can be corrupted.
Voice 4:	The streets are filled with violence!
Congregation:	Violence is an ugliness we all understand.
Voice 1:	People are starving in all parts of the world!
Congregation:	We throw food away. How many times have we been hungry?
Voice 2:	Industry is polluting our water and air!
Voice 3:	Yes! While producing cars and cigarettes for us!
Voices 1-3:	They are spoiling our world!
Congregation:	We are spoiling our world and We must do something about it!
Voice 4:	But we can't do it merely by seeing the fault in others.
Congregation:	We must struggle against apathy and weakness in ourselves and work to make our world what we wish it to be.
Voice 3:	We must no longer laugh at virtue and wink at corruption.
Congregation:	Let us begin with ourselves that we may show the way.

Voice 2:	Self-interest is the mother of violence.
Voices 1-4:	Ignorance is the father. Together they produce not only violence, but greed, waste, hunger . . . many of the ills which are engulfing us.
Congregation:	We shall not be engulfed by despair! Let us build into our lives a passion for justice, dedication, work, self discipline, and love.

SILENT DEVOTION

We who walk in a city of unbroken walls
Have brothers who wander in cratered streets,
Searching the rubble.
We have friends who die of cold and hunger,
Whose bodies are stripped and robbed before burial
In abandoned villages.

Now we must see these others,
Now there can be no exclusion,
No place set aside,
And our houses and our minds will be invaded,
And our hearts claimed as a territory and a conquest.

We cannot bolt our doors and draw our blinds
Nor shut our hearts to the cries of the maimed and the orphaned
Nor still our voice in protest and condemnation of the desolation
Wrought by us and others in our name.
For the blood of our brothers cries to us from the reddened earth.

ALL SING

May the words of my mouth and the meditation of my heart
Be acceptable unto Thee, O, Lord, my Rock and my Redeemer.

ADORATION
(Congregation rises)

Let us adore the ever-living God, and render praise unto Him who spread out the heavens and established the earth, whose glory is revealed in the heavens above and whose greatness is manifest throughout the world. He is our God; there is none else. We bow the head in reverence, and worship the King of Kings, the Holy One, praised be He.

ALL SING

וַאֲנַחְנוּ כּוֹרְעִים וּמִשְׁתַּחֲוִים וּמוֹדִים

לִפְנֵי מֶלֶךְ מַלְכֵי הַמְּלָכִים הַקָּדוֹשׁ בָּרוּךְ הוּא.

(Congregation is seated)

READER

O Lord, the earth is Thine and the fullness thereof. Thou hast made of one blood all the families of man to inhabit the world. Unite all the nations into one brotherhood and rule Thou over us in mercy. Let each man love his native land and obey her laws, so long as obedience to the law of the state is not disobedience to Thy law. Give us the courage to bear witness to Thy word.

Forgive us for worshiping the state and offering human sacrifice to war. Forgive us for the wrongs we have done to others in the name of our country, in pride, avarice and anger. Subdue in us the pride of race and class, the vainglory of men, that lead to war. Help us to search out and destroy all the causes of war.

Grant us the wisdom to strengthen the instruments of peace in concert with all nations. Teach us to use these means not alone for the prevention of war, but in brotherly provision for the needs of all nations in a new brotherhood of men.

Remove from our hearts all enmity, contention and greed, and implant within us humility and good will toward every nation, that we may hasten the day of the establishment of Thy Kingdom on earth.

ALL SING

וְנֶאֱמַר וְהָיָה יְיָ לְמֶלֶךְ עַל־כָּל־הָאָרֶץ בַּיּוֹם הַהוּא יִהְיֶה
יְיָ אֶחָד וּשְׁמוֹ אֶחָד:

KADDISH

יִתְגַּדַּל וְיִתְקַדַּשׁ שְׁמֵהּ רַבָּא. בְּעָלְמָא דִּי־בְרָא כִרְעוּתֵהּ.
וְיַמְלִיךְ מַלְכוּתֵהּ בְּחַיֵּיכוֹן וּבְיוֹמֵיכוֹן וּבְחַיֵּי דְכָל־בֵּית יִשְׂרָאֵל
בַּעֲגָלָא וּבִזְמַן קָרִיב. וְאִמְרוּ אָמֵן:

יְהֵא שְׁמֵהּ רַבָּא מְבָרַךְ לְעָלַם וּלְעָלְמֵי עָלְמַיָּא:

יִתְבָּרַךְ וְיִשְׁתַּבַּח וְיִתְפָּאַר וְיִתְרוֹמַם וְיִתְנַשֵּׂא וְיִתְהַדַּר וְיִתְעַלֶּה
וְיִתְהַלָּל שְׁמֵהּ דְּקֻדְשָׁא. בְּרִיךְ הוּא. לְעֵלָּא (וּלְעֵלָּא) מִן־כָּל־
בִּרְכָתָא וְשִׁירָתָא תֻּשְׁבְּחָתָא וְנֶחֱמָתָא דַּאֲמִירָן בְּעָלְמָא. וְאִמְרוּ
אָמֵן:

יְהֵא שְׁלָמָא רַבָּא מִן־שְׁמַיָּא וְחַיִּים עָלֵינוּ וְעַל־כָּל־יִשְׂרָאֵל.
וְאִמְרוּ אָמֵן:

עֹשֶׂה שָׁלוֹם בִּמְרוֹמָיו הוּא יַעֲשֶׂה שָׁלוֹם עָלֵינוּ וְעַל־כָּל־יִשְׂרָאֵל.
וְאִמְרוּ אָמֵן:

CLOSING SONG

AND THE EARTH HE GAVE TO MAN

The heavens are the heavens of the Lord, but the earth He gave to man.

INDIVIDUAL READING
(A line for each member of the congregation)

Praise the Lord, my soul; You are very great, clothed in majesty and splendor, and wrapped in a robe of light.

You have stretched out the heavens like a tent and laid beams for the chambers of water; You take the clouds for chariots, and ride on the wings of the wind.

The winds are Your messengers and flaming fire your ministers; the earth you set upon its foundation, never to be shaken.

The deep covered it like a cloak, and the waters stood above the mountains. At Your call the waters ran, at the sound of Your thunder they rushed away; flowing over the hills and pouring into the valleys.

You send the springs forth into the valleys, they run between the hills. Wild beasts drink from them and asses quench their thirst; the birds of the sky nest upon their banks and sing in the leaves.

You cause the grass to grow for cattle and herbs to nourish those who toil for man, bringing bread from the earth and wine to gladden the hearts of man, and oil to make his face shine.

The cedars of Lebanon He planted; the birds nest in them; the stork makes her home in their tops.

The high mountains are the wild goats' abode; the boulders are the refuge for the badgers.

You have made the moon to establish the seasons, and taught the sun where to set.

You create the dark and it is night, the beasts of the forest creep forth; the young lions roar for prey, seeking their food from God; when the sun rises they slink away to their den; man rises to do work and labors til evening.

The sea is without end, and countless creatures move both large and small; ships sail to and fro and the great fish makes sport therein.

All depend upon You for sustenance, that You may give them food in due season; You open Your hand and satisfy all living, You hide Your face and all vanish.

May the glory of God endure forever, and may He rejoice in His works; may my prayer please the Lord, as I show joy to Him.

Let the wasteful be banished from the earth and the wicked be no more.

Praise the Lord, creator of all.

READER

Dear God, joy of earth and joy of heaven,
All things that live below that expanse
Of star and planet, whose processional
Moves ever slow and solemn over us,
All things conceived, all things that face the light
In their bright vista, the grain-bearing fields,
The marinered oceans, where the wind and cloud
Are quiet in Your presence—all proclaim
Your gift, without which they are nothingness.
For You that sweet artifice, the earth,
Submits her flowers, and for you the deep
Of ocean smiles, and the calm heaven
Shines with shoreless light.

READER

Come let us praise the Lord, maker of earth.

CONGREGATION

Praised be the Lord, creator of the universe.

READER

In the beginning God created the heavens and the earth. The earth was without form and void, and darkness was upon the face of the deep; and the Spirit of God was moving over the face of the waters.

CONGREGATION

In the beginning of the technological age, man recreated the heavens and the earth. To the earth he gave new form with dynamite and bulldozer, and the void of the heavens he filled with smog.

SONG ("Air," from *Hair*)

Welcome, sulphur dioxide,
Hello carbon monoxide
The air, the air is ev'rywhere
Breathe deep while you sleep breathe deep.

Alchohol blood stream, save me nicotine lung steam,
Incense, incense is in the air.
Breathe deep while you sleep, breathe deep,
Bless you.

Cataclysmic ectoplasm
Fallout atomic orgasm
Vapor and fume, at the stone of my tomb,
Breathing like a sullen perfume,
Eating at the stone of my tomb.

Welcome, sulphur dioxide,
Hello, carbon monoxide
The air, the air is ev'rywhere
Breathe deep while you sleep, breathe deep, (cough) deep, (cough)
deep deep (cough).

(pray together)

He creates each day and each night afresh,
Rolls light in front of darkness
And darkness in front of light
So gently
That no moment is quite like the one before
Or after.
Second by second
You make day pass into night
And You alone know the boundary point
Dividing one from the other.
Unifier of all beings is Your name.
    Timeless God,
        Be King forever.
    You Who bring the evening in
    Are praised.

READER

And God said, "Let there be a firmament in the midst of the
waters. . . . Let the waters under the heavens be gathered into one
place, and let the dry land appear."

Then man took oil from beneath the ground and spread it over
the waters, until it coated the beaches with slime. He washed
the topsoil from the fertile prairies and sank it in the ocean
depths. He took waste from his mines and filled in the valleys,
while real estate developers leveled the hills. And man said,
"Well, business is business."

ANTIPHONAL READING

I have befouled the waters and tainted the air of a magnificent land. But I have made it safe from disease.

> I have flown through the sky faster than the sun. But I have idled in streets made ugly by traffic.

I have littered the land with garbage. But I have built a hundred million homes.

> I have built a bomb to destroy the world. But I have used it to light a light.

I have outraged my brothers in the alleys of ghettos. But I have transplanted a human heart.

> I have watched children starve from my golden tower. But I have paid farmers not to plant.

I live in the greatest time in history. But I scorn the land I stand on.

SONG: *Mayim*

Ush 'avtem mayim b'sasson
Mi-mayaan-ay ha-yishuah.

(pray together)

You were God
And we were Israel,
Your shy, untutored lover
Long ago.

You loved us a great love
And you taught us
How to respond to You

Through Torah
Mitzvot
Statutes
Judgments

We go to sleep with them
And with them we awake

We shall enjoy them forever.

They give us life
They prolong our days

We form our words around them
At nighttime,
In daytime.

Now,
Long after long ago,
Do not withdraw Your love from us.

Lover of Israel,
You are praised.

שְׁמַע יִשְׂרָאֵל יְהֹוָה אֱלֹהֵינוּ יְהֹוָה אֶחָד:

בָּרוּךְ שֵׁם כְּבוֹד מַלְכוּתוֹ לְעוֹלָם וָעֶד:

Sh'ma yis-ra-ayl, A-do-nay e-lo-hay-nu, A-do-nay e-had.
Ba-ruh shaym kvod ma-l'hu-to l'o-lam va-ed.
Hear, O Israel: the Lord our God, the Lord is One.
Blessed be His name;
His glorious kingdom is for ever and ever.

וְאָהַבְתָּ אֵת יְיָ אֱלֹהֶיךָ בְּכָל־לְבָבְךָ וּבְכָל־נַפְשְׁךָ
וּבְכָל־מְאֹדֶךָ: וְהָיוּ הַדְּבָרִים הָאֵלֶּה אֲשֶׁר אָנֹכִי
מְצַוְּךָ הַיּוֹם עַל־לְבָבֶךָ: וְשִׁנַּנְתָּם לְבָנֶיךָ וְדִבַּרְתָּ
בָּם. בְּשִׁבְתְּךָ בְּבֵיתֶךָ וּבְלֶכְתְּךָ בַדֶּרֶךְ וּבְשָׁכְבְּךָ
וּבְקוּמֶךָ: וּקְשַׁרְתָּם לְאוֹת עַל־יָדֶךָ. וְהָיוּ לְטֹטָפֹת
בֵּין עֵינֶיךָ: וּכְתַבְתָּם עַל־מְזֻזוֹת בֵּיתֶךָ וּבִשְׁעָרֶיךָ.

RESPONSIVE READING

Then God said, "Let the earth put forth vegetation, plants yielding seed and fruit trees bearing fruit in which is their seed, each according to their kinds." And it was so. And God saw that it was good.

> But man was not so sure. He found that mosquitos annoyed him, so he killed them with DDT. And the robins died, too, and man said, "What a pity." Man defoliated forests in the name of modern warfare. He filled the streams with industrial waste—and his children read about fishing . . . in the history books.

If you will pay attention to My commandments which I command you today, I will free you from worry about physical sustenance so that you can devote your mind to Torah and your body to right action. I will give rain in its season for your harvest, and good pasture for your cattle. But if you open to temptations and serve other sorts of gods, I will close the heavens and there will be no rain, nor will earth yield its produce, and you shall fast disappear from the good land which God has given you.

Psalm 148—An Interpretation

> Beautiful flowers, blue & red & yellow & white, soft with the dew of the morn. Freshly cut grass, cold and green . . .
> And the rain as it dribbles off the end of my nose as I lift my head to catch glimpses of all things—
> Powdering snow, on the brown bare limbs sparkling loosely in the sky with diamonds and on the rocks and earth—
> Oh yes, oh yes, oh yes, Halleluyah, my eyes are dreaming, my voice is calling out to the sheep running in the meadow and together, we thank our God for being alive.

So God created man in his own image; in the image of God he created him. And God blessed them, and God said to them, "Be fruitful and multiply, and fill the earth and subdue it, and have dominion over . . . every living thing."

AMIDAH

In the hour when the Holy One, blessed be He, created the
    first man,
He took him and let him pass before all the trees of the Garden
    of Eden,
and said to him:
"See My works, how fine and excellent they are!
Now all that I have created for you have I created. Think
    upon this, and do not corrupt and desolate My world;
for if you corrupt it, there is no one to set it right after you."

Animals were not created merely to serve man and contribute to
his comfort, for God intends to teach us through the creatures of
the field and make us wise through the birds of the sky. He endowed
many animals with moral qualities that they might become a pattern for man. If the Torah was not given to us, we could have
learned honesty from the ant, that never takes from another's store.
We could have learned modesty from the cat, who is careful always
to wash herself. By observing the grasshopper we could learn a
zeal for life, for she sings til the moment of death. The rooster
teaches us good manners for it first coaxes, then mates. The stork
conveys a double lesson. He guards the purity of his family and is
compassionate and merciful toward his fellows.

Had we but observed the animals, we might have learned to be
gentler men, but unable to learn through the subtleties of creatures,
we sought a guide and teacher.

Our Rabbis taught: When Moses our teacher was a shepherd on the
desert, a lamb ran away to find shade and water. Moses said, "I
should have known you were thirsty. Are you tired?" He lifted her
onto his shoulders and carried her back to the fold. The all-Merciful
watched Moses and said, "This man is the man to shepherd my
flock of flesh and blood."

And so Moses, the gentle shepherd, showed us the paths of Torah
which our tradition has broadened.

"You shall not plough with an ox and ass yoked together." This teaching applies to all types of work and all animals of different species. This law teaches us to be sensitive to animals, for through our understanding of the differing capacities of living creatures we learn that two men of different temperaments and abilities should not be made to compete with each other.

"You shall not muzzle the ox when it treads out grain." An animal that helps supply nourishment for man has the right to eat while it works. Thus before man eats, he must first feed those whose labor has produced his food. Through this mitzvah we learn to be good-natured and pursue mercy. Torah, by sensitizing us to animals, hopes to teach us to be kind to our fellow man.

"When you besiege a city a long time, in making war against it, you shall not destroy the trees by wielding an axe against them." We learn that we may not destroy any fruitbearing tree during a siege, for it will cause irreparable harm to the besieged city. Our tradition learns from the destruction of trees that the needless destruction of anything, be it living or inanimate, is a distortion of creation.

We have wandered from the paths of Torah and become insensitive to the plants of the field, the beasts of the earth, and the men of the cities.

God said to Jonah, "Are you angry because of the gourd?" And Jonah said, "I am angry enough to die." And the Lord said, "You are sorry for the gourd, though you did not labor that it might grow, a plant that came in the night and perished in the night. Should I not be sorry for a great city like Nineveh, with its hundred and twenty thousand who do not know their right from their left, and cattle without number?"

Master of the universe,
grant me the ability to be alone;
  may it be my custom to go outdoors each day
  among the trees and grass, among all growing things,

and there may I be alone, and enter into prayer,
to talk with the One that I belong to.

    May I express there everything in my heart, ·
    and may all the foliage of the field
    (all grasses, trees and plants)
    may they all awake at my coming,
to send the power of their life into the words of my prayer,
so that my prayer and speech are made whole,

    through the life and spirit of growing things,
    which are made as one by their transcendent Source.
May they all be gathered into my prayer,
and thus may I be worthy to open my heart fully
in prayer, supplication and holy speech,

    that I pour out the words of my heart
    before Your Presence like water, O Lord,
    and lift up my hands to You in worship,
    on behalf of my own soul, and the souls of my children.

VAYCHULU

וַיְכֻלּוּ הַשָּׁמַיִם וְהָאָרֶץ וְכָל־צְבָאָם: וַיְכַל אֱלֹהִים

בַּיּוֹם הַשְּׁבִיעִי מְלַאכְתּוֹ אֲשֶׁר עָשָׂה וַיִּשְׁבֹּת בַּיּוֹם

הַשְּׁבִיעִי מִכָּל־מְלַאכְתּוֹ אֲשֶׁר עָשָׂה: וַיְבָרֶךְ אֱלֹהִים

אֶת־יוֹם הַשְּׁבִיעִי וַיְקַדֵּשׁ אֹתוֹ כִּי בוֹ שָׁבַת מִכָּל־

מְלַאכְתּוֹ אֲשֶׁר־בָּרָא אֱלֹהִים לַעֲשׂוֹת:

And so the heavens and the earth and all their host were completed. For with the seventh day God completed His work, ceasing all His work which He was doing. And God blessed the seventh day, setting it apart as holy time, for with it He ceased from all His work which He had created to be done.

ALEYNU

עָלֵינוּ לְשַׁבֵּחַ לַאֲדוֹן הַכֹּל לָתֵת גְּדֻלָּה לְיוֹצֵר בְּרֵאשִׁית שֶׁלֹּא

עָשָׂנוּ כְּגוֹיֵי הָאֲרָצוֹת וְלֹא שָׂמָנוּ כְּמִשְׁפְּחוֹת הָאֲדָמָה שֶׁלֹּא שָׂם

חֶלְקֵנוּ כָּהֶם וְגֹרָלֵנוּ כְּכָל הֲמוֹנָם:

וַאֲנַחְנוּ כּוֹרְעִים וּמִשְׁתַּחֲוִים וּמוֹדִים

253

לִפְנֵי מֶלֶךְ מַלְכֵי הַמְּלָכִים הַקָּדוֹשׁ בָּרוּךְ הוּא.
שֶׁהוּא נוֹטֶה שָׁמַיִם וְיוֹסֵד אָרֶץ וּמוֹשַׁב יְקָרוֹ בַּשָּׁמַיִם
מִמַּעַל וּשְׁכִינַת עֻזּוֹ בְּגָבְהֵי מְרוֹמִים: הוּא אֱלֹהֵינוּ
אֵין עוֹד. אֱמֶת מַלְכֵּנוּ אֶפֶס זוּלָתוֹ כַּכָּתוּב בְּתוֹרָתוֹ
וְיָדַעְתָּ הַיּוֹם וַהֲשֵׁבֹתָ אֶל לְבָבֶךָ כִּי יְיָ הוּא הָאֱלֹהִים
בַּשָּׁמַיִם מִמַּעַל וְעַל־הָאָרֶץ מִתָּחַת. אֵין עוֹד:
וְנֶאֱמַר וְהָיָה יְיָ לְמֶלֶךְ עַל־כָּל־הָאָרֶץ בַּיּוֹם הַהוּא
יִהְיֶה יְיָ אֶחָד וּשְׁמוֹ אֶחָד:

It is incumbent upon us to praise
The Lord of all things, The Shaper of Creation
Who has made us different from other nations,
With a different purpose from other families upon the earth.
Before Him do we bow the head and bend the knee,
Before the Source of coherence in the world,
The Source of holiness and blessing,
Who spread out the heavens and established the earth.
In Him alone, and in no human ruler, lies ultimate authority.

Therefore we hope, Lord our God,
That Your compassionate power will cut away the false gods
And repair the world in the image of Your kingdom,
That the tyrannic and the cruel might copy Your compassion
And all we live among shall know
That only before You may head be bowed and knee be bent,
And all of us, human once more,
Shall be yoked together by Your coherent power.

Let the day of Your eternal rule come soon!
With love and freedom, justice and glory,
For Your Torah has foretold it:
"The Lord will be King forever!"
Today Israel alone recites Shma,
On that day all the families on earth will affirm:

      The Lord is God,
      The Lord is One!

KADDISH

יִתְגַּדַּל וְיִתְקַדַּשׁ שְׁמֵהּ רַבָּא. בְּעָלְמָא דִּי־בְרָא כִרְעוּתֵהּ.
וְיַמְלִיךְ מַלְכוּתֵהּ בְּחַיֵּיכוֹן וּבְיוֹמֵיכוֹן וּבְחַיֵּי דְכָל־בֵּית יִשְׂרָאֵל
בַּעֲגָלָא וּבִזְמַן קָרִיב. וְאִמְרוּ אָמֵן:

יְהֵא שְׁמֵהּ רַבָּא מְבָרַךְ לְעָלַם וּלְעָלְמֵי עָלְמַיָּא:

Mourners

יִתְבָּרַךְ וְיִשְׁתַּבַּח וְיִתְפָּאַר וְיִתְרוֹמַם וְיִתְנַשֵּׂא וְיִתְהַדָּר וְיִתְעַלֶּה
וְיִתְהַלָּל שְׁמֵהּ דְּקֻדְשָׁא. בְּרִיךְ הוּא. לְעֵלָּא (וּלְעֵלָּא) מִן־כָּל־
בִּרְכָתָא וְשִׁירָתָא תֻּשְׁבְּחָתָא וְנֶחֱמָתָא דַּאֲמִירָן בְּעָלְמָא. וְאִמְרוּ
אָמֵן:

יְהֵא שְׁלָמָא רַבָּא מִן־שְׁמַיָּא וְחַיִּים עָלֵינוּ וְעַל־כָּל־יִשְׂרָאֵל.
וְאִמְרוּ אָמֵן:

עֹשֶׂה שָׁלוֹם בִּמְרוֹמָיו הוּא יַעֲשֶׂה שָׁלוֹם עָלֵינוּ וְעַל־כָּל־יִשְׂרָאֵל.
וְאִמְרוּ אָמֵן:

Conclusion

And the Lord saw all that He had created, the skies, the earth, and
all their host, that it was very good. On the seventh day, His work
complete, God rested and gave a blessing to the seventh day that
it might be holy. For on this day rest came into the world: for God
and for the newborn, fragile universe now ours to care for and
protect.

It could be very good.

SONG

O Lord, my God, may these never end: The sand and the sea, the
rush of the waters, the flash of the heavens, the prayer of man.

Eli, eli, shelo y'gamer l'olam: hachol v'hayam rishrush shel hamayim
b'rak hashamayim, t'filat ha' adam.

SERVICES FOR MINOR FESTIVALS

AN ANTICIPATION OF PURIM

(Worshippers turn and introduce themselves to those near them)

SILENT MEDITATION

We look, on this Shabbat, toward Purim—on the Day of Rest we look to the holiday of Unrest, of mirth and laughter, foolish kings and dazzling queens, virtuous heroes and murderous villains. Shabbat brings us joy, but the profound joy that follows days of satisfying work, or that permits us to close a book of weeklong struggles for that blissful infinity between a day's two sunsets.

That is not the joy of Purim, whose style is rather playfulness than deep abiding joy—but that is useful too in lives we seem to live always at the edge of an abyss of despair and fear and brooding doubts about our worth and purpose. Purim solves no problems, but forces us to laugh in the midst of them, that reassuring laughter that puts anguish in perspective, that peers out through the darkness and sees the beam of light on the other side. Amidst the threats that have for centuries engulfed our people, Purim lets us thumb our nose at enemies and banish them from thought. To shake a gregger at an enemy reduces him to manageable size, reminds us that he is a man after all, and men can deal with men. To shake a gregger at him even helps us think that he is not even a man, and so our confidence that we can manage him grows with every rattle of the noisemaker.

But Purim confidence is also Purim danger. To shake a gregger at a man does make him less than a man—it reduces him to a thing, deprives him of his humanity by destroying his detractors. To say "pig" to a man in a uniform armed with awesome weapons, may reduce the awe of his weapons but it will also increase his desire to reject the epithet by showing his power to do what no animal can do. Even worse, to call him names, to shake greggers at him, is to mask his humanity, preventing us from understanding why he acts as he does and why we respond to him as we do, and so discover a way in which we each can act for each other's benefit. Instead, we *all* become less than human, our humanity invisible behind the rigid masks our minds invent of Evil, Goodness, Right, and Wrong.

261

Masks make Purim fun, but masks rob men of their humanity and life of its profundity. Some moments ago we turned and introduced ourselves to each other, yet all we met were the masks of names, of years in school, of punch-card details from whose narrow slits we all peer out to see but be unseen, to observe but hide ourselves, preventing anyone from finding out that we're not sure who we are—preventing *us* from finding out that no one else is sure who he is either. Could we only spindle our masks, we might discover the faces of our being which we share with others and the very special face which is our own, which no one can destroy, over which no one else has power, which can laugh in times of danger and drink deeply of the joy which is our rightful portion now at week's end, with the time between the sunsets ours to savor and the mirth of Purim but another Sabbath sunset from our sight.

SONG: *Purim Day*

Hag Purim, hag Purim,	Purim day, Purim day,
Hag gadol hu lay'hudim.	Gladsome, joyous holiday.
Masehot raashanim,	Happy throngs, singing songs,
Z'mirot, rikudim.	Masked and dancing gay.
Hava narisha rash, rash, rash,	Let's make clamor, rah, rah, rah,
Hava narisha rash, rash, rash,	Lusty noises, grah, grah, grah,
Hava narisha rash, rash, rash,	Loudly cry and shout hurray!
Bara' ashanim.	With your gregers play.
Hag Purim, hag Purim	Purim day, Purim day,
Ze el ze shol-him ma-not.	Gladsome, joyous holiday.
Mah-ma-dim, mam-ta-kim,	Happy throngs, singing songs,
Tu-fi-nim, mig-da-not.	Masked and dancing gay.

ANTIPHONAL READING

Is it right to come here seeking Purim, to seek mirth when men are dying, sweetmeats when men starve, costumed gaiety when beggars go about their sooty streets in rags?

Is it right to come here seeking Shabbat, to seek the joy of work fulfilled when some men are jobless and others do meaningless tasks for pay, while still others build machines of war and others earn their bread by exploitation?

We must laugh not to drown out the cries of suffering, but to remind us that there is another song, that suffering is not all we can expect, that a melody exists to which we can tune the notes of weeping men, that all might one day sing together.

We must rejoice in work fulfilled that we may broaden our perception of work, that each of us may form a vision of the world we want and strive to see what each of us may do to win that world, to work in six days for the world we celebrate on the seventh.

Purim and Shabbat, mirth and joy and satisfaction, costume us in the clothing of the life we want all men to live, that for a moment we might experience what that life might be, and what the men who live within that world might become. In such a world are Esther Queens and Sabbath Queens, heroines and lovers, justice, joy, and peace, and a festive, soothing darkness that embraces all our quiet longings with the promise of fulfillment.

> Out of the land of heaven
> Down comes the warm Sabbath sun
> Into the spice-box of earth.
> The Queen will make every Jew her lover.
> In a white silk coat
> Our rabbi dances up the street,
> Wearing our lawns like a green prayer-shawl,
> Brandishing houses like silver flags.
> Behind him dance his pupils,
> Dancing not so high
> And chanting the rabbi's prayer,
> But not so sweet.
> And who waits for him

On a throne at the end of the street
But the Sabbath Queen.
    Down go his hands
Into the spice-box of earth,
And there he finds the fragrant sun
For a wedding ring
And draws her wedding finger through.
    Now back down the street they go,
Dancing higher than the silver flags.
His pupils somewhere have found wives too,
And all are chanting the rabbi's song
And leaping high in the perfumed air.
    Who calls him Rabbi?
Cart-horse and dogs call him Rabbi,
And he tells them:
The Queen makes every Jew her lover.
And gathering on their green lawns
The people call him Rabbi,
And fill their mouths with good bread
And his happy song.

בָּרְכוּ אֶת־יְיָ הַמְבֹרָךְ:

(Praise the Lord to whom all praise is due.)

בָּרוּךְ יְיָ הַמְבֹרָךְ לְעוֹלָם וָעֶד:

(Praised be the Lord to whom all praise is due forever and ever.)

READER

To praise God is to seek Him, but men have cloaked Him in so many various disguises that none can find Him underneath the human masquerade. For His part, God creates all men in His single image, but He works not as the coinmakers, who must stamp out each piece identical with its mold, but rather forms each man unique, expressing in the ultimate totality of mankind the infinite possibility that is God. And so we move amidst the masquerade, finding only difference, only good here and evil there, hurting men and helpful men, each behind his mask, each playing his own role, and the end will be that either good will triumph, or evil. But harmony is what we seek, not victory: we are determined that the Haman forces and the Esther forces shall not strive forever, but that the passion which, subverted, turns to evil might instead be turned to deeper goodness, so that evil might be purged and goodness made profound. For finding God must somehow enable us as well to find the unifying source and purpose of evil and of good, and permit us all to find our place within the world as whole, integrated persons, no longer playing roles, no longer wearing masks, perceiving in our different forms the single image from which all we divers humans spring. The call to oneness is thus an affirmation and a goal, and to speak of God as One is to commit ourselves once more to our people's ancient quest:

שְׁמַע יִשְׂרָאֵל יְהוָֹה אֱלֹהֵינוּ יְהוָֹה אֶחָד:

(Hear, Israel: the Lord our God, the Lord is One.)

בָּרוּךְ שֵׁם כְּבוֹד מַלְכוּתוֹ לְעוֹלָם וָעֶד:

(Praised be His name whose glorious kingdom is forever and ever.)

וְאָהַבְתָּ אֵת יְיָ אֱלֹהֶיךָ בְּכָל־לְבָבְךָ וּבְכָל־נַפְשְׁךָ
וּבְכָל־מְאֹדֶךָ: וְהָיוּ הַדְּבָרִים הָאֵלֶּה אֲשֶׁר אָנֹכִי
מְצַוְּךָ הַיּוֹם עַל־לְבָבֶךָ: וְשִׁנַּנְתָּם לְבָנֶיךָ וְדִבַּרְתָּ
בָּם. בְּשִׁבְתְּךָ בְּבֵיתֶךָ וּבְלֶכְתְּךָ בַדֶּרֶךְ וּבְשָׁכְבְּךָ
וּבְקוּמֶךָ: וּקְשַׁרְתָּם לְאוֹת עַל־יָדֶךָ. וְהָיוּ לְטֹטָפֹת
בֵּין עֵינֶיךָ: וּכְתַבְתָּם עַל־מְזֻזוֹת בֵּיתֶךָ וּבִשְׁעָרֶיךָ:

265

RESPONSIVE READING

Hear, O Israel: The Lord Who links us together by His love, loves in the oneness of all.

You shall love the Lord your God with all your passions, with every fibre of your being, with all that you possess.

Let these words with which He joins Himself to you today enter your heart.

Pattern your days on them, that your children may discover Torah within you.

Make your life into a voice of God, both in your stillness and in your movement.

Renew these words each morning and evening in prayer and reflection.

Bind them upon your arm and head as symbols of acts and thoughts consecrated to a Godly purpose.

Write them in Mezuzot at the entrance to your home, as a sign that men may discover divinity as they enter your home and your life.

THE PARADOXES OF REDEMPTION
(Antiphonal Reading)

It is true and certain that but one God can rule the world, one Power and one purpose, which at the end of time all men shall understand.

Yet within the realm of One God are many peoples, each with its own perception of true power, each convinced that God has chosen only its believers to carry truth to the world.

Each people has its truth, but if one truth ever tries to conquer others, God will ultimately protect each facet of His truth from extinction.

Yet before that struggle ends, many tyrants will blind the eyes of the unknowing, and simple men will slaughter others for reasons few can fathom.

It is fitting to praise God who ultimately delivers truth out of the hands of its enemies, and sends to their doom the Hamans and the Pharaohs who arise in every age.

Yet it is not fitting to utter praise while men, however cruel they have become, are banished from the sight of God in whose image they were innocently born.

Oppressors must suffer if the oppressed are to be freed; and in a land of unclean hands, even the innocent may suffer for the evils of their rulers.

Only God, therefore, is the proper "man of war"; only that redemption can be absolutely just which is achieved through other means than man's.

מִי־כָמֹכָה בָּאֵלִם יְיָ מִי כָּמֹכָה נֶאְדָּר בַּקֹּדֶשׁ
נוֹרָא תְהִלֹּת עֹשֵׂה פֶלֶא:
מַלְכוּתְךָ רָאוּ בָנֶיךָ בּוֹקֵעַ יָם לִפְנֵי מֹשֶׁה זֶה
אֵלִי עָנוּ וְאָמְרוּ.
יְיָ יִמְלֹךְ לְעֹלָם וָעֶד:
וְנֶאֱמַר כִּי־פָדָה יְיָ אֶת־יַעֲקֹב וּגְאָלוֹ מִיַּד חָזָק
מִמֶּנּוּ. בָּרוּךְ אַתָּה יְיָ גָּאַל יִשְׂרָאֵל:

(At the shores of the Red Sea, our forefathers, redeemed from bondage, sang this song of praise to God:

Who is like You, O Lord, compared to the gods men worship? Who is like You, majestic in holiness, awesome in splendor, doing wonders? The Lord will reign forever and ever.)

267

AMIDAH

Praised be the God of our fathers,
The God of Abraham, of Isaac, of Jacob,
And of Mordecai.
Praised be the God of our mothers,
Of Sarah, of Rebecca, of Leah and of Rachel,
And of Esther.
Praised be the source of strength and awe,
The source of exaltation and good deeds.
Praised be the source of gentleness and love,
Of softness and kind words.
Praised be the man who transcends strength
Through gentleness,
Praised be the woman who perfects gentleness
Through strength.
Praised be the person who acts according to the best that
    is within,
Praised be the person who reaches out to touch the best
    in others.
Praised be the tender loyalty of Mordecai
And the valiant courage of Esther.
Praised be the God Who created with divinity a woman
    and a man.

Mighty is the Lord forever,
Restoring life to those marked out for death,
Liberating peoples once destined for defeat,
Returning hopeful springtime breezes to a silent winter's
    world.

Mighty is the Lord forever,
Banishing despair through the loving acts of human
    beings,
Reviving barren hopes within the womb of weary
    dreamers,
Cutting loose the fetters of the victims

Fallen underneath the sickness of our days,
Remembering those passed over by the dust of time.

May He extend His mighty hand to us,
Restoring us,
Banishing our despair,
That from the dust of this uncaring time
We might bring to bud those loving acts that make us
   human.

אַתָּה קָדוֹשׁ וְשִׁמְךָ קָדוֹשׁ וּקְדוֹשִׁים בְּכָל־יוֹם
יְהַלְלוּךָ סֶּלָה. בָּרוּךְ אַתָּה יְיָ הָאֵל הַקָּדוֹשׁ:

Praised be the source of holiness
In every human masquerade,
In every joyous song,
In every laughing moment,
In every yearning silence.

A Motivation for Reflection

The Jewess, Hadassah, takes the name of the moon-goddess, Esther;
her kinsman, Mordecai, whatever his Hebrew name,
has the name of the Babylonian god.
If you have intelligence and beauty, Esther,
"tell no one of your people or your kindred,"
and you will live in the king's palace and be a queen.

"We are sold, I and my people, to be destroyed, to be slain, and to
   perish!"
The hands, heavy with rings, are Esther's
but the voice is the voice of Hadassah.

SILENT PRAYER

THE PURIM STORY

(Worshippers may be encouraged to share in the telling of the Purim story as they remember it, each person adding on to the account of those who have already spoken. Greggers may be provided for appropriate accompaniment when the infamous name is mentioned. Alternatively, an abridged or updated Megillah may be read aloud.)

SONG

Oh once there was a wicked wicked man, and Haman was his name, sir,
He would have murdered all the Jews, though they were not to blame, sir.

CHORUS: Oh today we'll merry merry be (repeat twice more)
            And nash some hamantashen.

Now Esther was the lovely queen of King Ahasuerus;
When Haman said he'd kill us all, oh my how he did scare us!
   (Chorus)

But Mordecai, her cousin bold, said, "What a dreadful chutzpah!
If guns were but invented now, this Haman I would shoot, sir."
   (Chorus)

When Esther, speaking to the king, of Haman's plot made mention,
"Ha, ha," said he, "oh no, he won't! I'll spoil his bad intention."
   (Chorus)

"The guest of honor he shall be, this clever Mr. Smarty,
And high above us he shall swing at a little hanging party."
   (Chorus)

Of all his cruel and unkind ways this little joke did cure him,
And don't forget: we owe him thanks for the jolly feast of Purim.
   (Chorus)

ALEYNU
(rising)

עָלֵינוּ לְשַׁבֵּחַ לַאֲדוֹן הַכֹּל לָתֵת גְּדֻלָּה לְיוֹצֵר בְּרֵאשִׁית שֶׁלֹּא

עָשָׂנוּ כְּגוֹיֵי הָאֲרָצוֹת וְלֹא שָׂמָנוּ כְּמִשְׁפְּחוֹת הָאֲדָמָה שֶׁלֹּא שָׂם

חֶלְקֵנוּ כָּהֶם וְגֹרָלֵנוּ כְּכָל הֲמוֹנָם:

וַאֲנַחְנוּ כּוֹרְעִים וּמִשְׁתַּחֲוִים וּמוֹדִים

לִפְנֵי מֶלֶךְ מַלְכֵי הַמְּלָכִים הַקָּדוֹשׁ בָּרוּךְ הוּא.

May the time not be distant, O God, when Your name shall be
worshipped in all the earth, when despair shall disappear and error
be no more. We pray that the day be not far off when all men shall
find their way to calling on Your name, when hatred and evil shall
give way to understanding and goodness, when the many kinds of
men who dwell on earth shall recognize not alone their difference
but their unity, that each people may, in its unique manner, work
for the coming of God's single purpose. On that day no people
need live in fear for its survival, but the joy which is ours at this
Purim season shall reign throughout the year and throughout the
world, for all the earth shall have come to know that the Lord is
God, the Lord is One.

וְנֶאֱמַר וְהָיָה יְיָ לְמֶלֶךְ עַל־כָּל־הָאָרֶץ בַּיּוֹם הַהוּא יִהְיֶה

יְיָ אֶחָד וּשְׁמוֹ אֶחָד:

MOURNERS' KADDISH

יִתְגַּדַּל וְיִתְקַדַּשׁ שְׁמֵהּ רַבָּא. בְּעָלְמָא דִּי־בְרָא כִרְעוּתֵהּ.

וְיַמְלִיךְ מַלְכוּתֵהּ בְּחַיֵּיכוֹן וּבְיוֹמֵיכוֹן וּבְחַיֵּי דְכָל־בֵּית יִשְׂרָאֵל

בַּעֲגָלָא וּבִזְמַן קָרִיב. וְאִמְרוּ אָמֵן:

Congregation and Mourners

יְהֵא שְׁמֵהּ רַבָּא מְבָרַךְ לְעָלַם וּלְעָלְמֵי עָלְמַיָּא:

271

יִתְבָּרַךְ וְיִשְׁתַּבַּח וְיִתְפָּאַר וְיִתְרֹמַם וְיִתְנַשֵּׂא וְיִתְהַדָּר וְיִתְעַלֶּה
וְיִתְהַלָּל שְׁמֵהּ דְּקֻדְשָׁא. בְּרִיךְ הוּא. לְעֵלָּא (וּלְעֵלָּא) מִן־כָּל־
בִּרְכָתָא וְשִׁירָתָא תֻּשְׁבְּחָתָא וְנֶחֱמָתָא דַּאֲמִירָן בְּעָלְמָא. וְאִמְרוּ
אָמֵן:

יְהֵא שְׁלָמָא רַבָּא מִן־שְׁמַיָּא וְחַיִּים עָלֵינוּ וְעַל־כָּל־יִשְׂרָאֵל.
וְאִמְרוּ אָמֵן:

עֹשֶׂה שָׁלוֹם בִּמְרוֹמָיו הוּא יַעֲשֶׂה שָׁלוֹם עָלֵינוּ וְעַל־כָּל־יִשְׂרָאֵל.
וְאִמְרוּ אָמֵן:

CONCLUDING SONG

אדון עולם

בְּטֶרֶם כָּל יְצִיר נִבְרָא:	אֲדוֹן עוֹלָם אֲשֶׁר מָלַךְ
אֲזַי מֶלֶךְ שְׁמוֹ נִקְרָא:	לְעֵת נַעֲשָׂה בְחֶפְצוֹ כֹּל
לְבַדּוֹ יִמְלוֹךְ נוֹרָא:	וְאַחֲרֵי כִּכְלוֹת הַכֹּל
וְהוּא יִהְיֶה בְּתִפְאָרָה:	וְהוּא הָיָה וְהוּא הֹוֶה
לְהַמְשִׁיל לוֹ לְהַחְבִּירָה:	וְהוּא אֶחָד וְאֵין שֵׁנִי
וְלוֹ הָעֹז וְהַמִּשְׂרָה:	בְּלִי רֵאשִׁית בְּלִי תַכְלִית
וְצוּר חֶבְלִי בְּעֵת צָרָה:	וְהוּא אֵלִי וְחַי גּוֹאֲלִי
מְנָת כּוֹסִי בְּיוֹם אֶקְרָא:	וְהוּא נִסִּי וּמָנוֹס לִי
בְּעֵת אִישַׁן וְאָעִירָה:	בְּיָדוֹ אַפְקִיד רוּחִי
יְיָ לִי וְלֹא אִירָא:	וְעִם רוּחִי גְּוִיָּתִי

272

A HANUKKAH SERVICE OF LIGHTS

OPENING CHANUKAH SONG

READER: Light is the emblem of joy. If we have no joy, how shall we bless the candles of our feast? How shall we light the symbol of our faith in this dark world?

Though the midnight of sorrow is past, the hours are long until the dawn. Our eyes are weary of the dark and we long for light and warmth, courage and hope. To withhold our feet from the bog of disillusion, to press onward and retain integrity—this is our Maccabean task.

בָּרְכוּ אֶת־יְיָ הַמְבֹרָךְ׃

Praise the Lord to whom all praise is due.

בָּרוּךְ יְיָ הַמְבֹרָךְ לְעוֹלָם וָעֶד׃

Praised be the Lord to whom all praise is due forever and ever.

FIRST LIGHT

READER: When the eyes are blind and the lips silent;
When the hands are fallen empty to a man's side and his knees bend beneath him;
When he has forgotten hope and his thoughts no longer turn to God; then God has prepared for him a final goal.

CONG: God does not bring the Jew to a haven of rest nor fold his hands in the peace of death; God blows through his soul the breath of a last courage.

READER: The thin, high wind of courage which is beyond reason, beyond emotion, this God blows into his nostrils.

CONG: It is the breath of life and not of death. In its name we shall kindle the first light.
Baruch alta Alonay, Eloheynu melech ha-olam, asher

275

kidd'shanu b'mitzvotav v'tzivanu l'hadlik ner shel
Hanukah. Baruch Atta Adonay, Eloheynu melech
ha-olam she-asa hissim la'avoteynu bayamim haheym
baz'man hazeh.

בָּרוּךְ אַתָּה יְיָ אֱלֹהֵינוּ
מֶלֶךְ הָעוֹלָם אֲשֶׁר קִדְּשָׁנוּ
בְּמִצְוֹתָיו וְצִוָּנוּ לְהַדְלִיק
נֵר שֶׁל חֲנֻכָּה:

בָּרוּךְ אַתָּה יְיָ אֱלֹהֵינוּ
מֶלֶךְ הָעוֹלָם שֶׁעָשָׂה נִסִּים
לַאֲבוֹתֵינוּ בַּיָּמִים הָהֵם
בַּזְּמַן הַזֶּה:

(Light First Light)

SECOND LIGHT

READER: Each people finds its own road to mankind's final
truth. There is only one Truth, though ignorance and
stubbornness may keep man from its light.

CONG: No man hates if truth becomes his way of life. Neither
is pain an enemy of truth but rather the lens which
gives it focus and intensity.

READER: We have learned the futility of hatred, and of striving
to escape pain; the one falls like a worn-out cloak from
our shoulders, the other clings like a companion to our
hand. God has not spared us insight; may He also give
us courage to accept his truth.
We shall light this light, as a beacon to the single Truth
which will one day guide all people.

שְׁמַע יִשְׂרָאֵל יְהֹוָה אֱלֹהֵינוּ יְהֹוָה אֶחָד:

Hear O Israel, the Lord our God, the Lord is One.

בָּרוּךְ שֵׁם כְּבוֹד מַלְכוּתוֹ לְעוֹלָם וָעֶד:

Praised be His name Whose glorious Kingdom is forever and ever.

(Light Second Light)

276

THIRD LIGHT

READER: We cannot long endure alone in solitary search for truth and God. We seek, also, the rich and varied companionship of all our past—our own lives, our fathers' and our people's woven and interwoven in warm and beautiful companionship.

CONG: Sometimes we think of Israel's history as a long series of events fading into a distant past, and we look back seeking to suffer our people's suffering, and to joy in their rejoicing.

READER: Yet merely the backward glance is wrong. As the tree holds within itself the rings of growth, so also, by acting as Jews today, do we embody the history of our people. In a chain a link may break, but so long as a tree lives the rings of its life remain inviolate within it.

CONG: We stand, not one upon another's shoulder, but arms entwined together, our truths woven as one fabric upon our bodies, one spirit in our souls.

God grant us the comfort of our inheritance and the strength to bear our people's immortality together.

(Light Third Light)

FOURTH LIGHT

READER: Bound up as we are with our people's life, in the great moments of existence, ultimately each man stands alone in terrible isolation. He may live and work with his fellow man but his moments of solitude are illimitable and timeless.

CONG: How powerfully is this known to every Jew! He craves constant companionship and is by his own nature thrown back constantly into the loneliness of his own self. Within his own individual being he recognizes an expression of God's will.

READER: He seeks no ecclesiastical authority; he shuns the herd in persuasion and often in deed. Even to a fault he stands alone and by some dangerous and secret

alchemy he makes of pride (that serpent among vices)
a humble virtue.

CONG: God grant to every Jew the pride to stand alone, to
think alone, to act alone, and then the strength to suffer
for his pride—alone.

We shall light this light, O Maccabee, in memory of
heroes.

(Light Fourth Light)

מִי־כָמֹכָה בָּאֵלִם יְיָ מִי כָּמֹכָה נֶאְדָּר בַּקֹּדֶשׁ
נוֹרָא תְהִלֹּת עֹשֵׂה פֶלֶא:

מַלְכוּתְךָ רָאוּ בָנֶיךָ בּוֹקֵעַ יָם לִפְנֵי מֹשֶׁה זֶה
אֵלִי עָנוּ וְאָמְרוּ.

יְיָ יִמְלֹךְ לְעֹלָם וָעֶד:

וְנֶאֱמַר כִּי־פָדָה יְיָ אֶת־יַעֲקֹב וּגְאָלוֹ מִיַּד חָזָק
מִמֶּנּוּ. בָּרוּךְ אַתָּה יְיָ גָּאַל יִשְׂרָאֵל:

(As our fathers sang at the Red Sea: Who is like Thee, O Lord
among the gods of men? Who is like Thee, glorious in holiness
awesome in praise, doer of wonders? The Lord will reign foreve
and ever.)

FIFTH LIGHT

READER: Hope is not housed in shallow vessels. It dwells in a
deep chalice, so deep that if all be spilt there yet re
mains a bitter dreg within.

CONG: Hope is not fresh and sweet and blissful. It is the last
essential residue of life. It far outreaches the uphill
spurt of our desires. It is resilient and enduring. For
Israel's hopes are hardened by the salt of tears. If our
people can still hope, all is not lost. It is the bitter and
the grim, the close-lipped hope of Israel to which we
silently pay honor.

(Light Fifth Light)

SILENT PRAYER

SIXTH LIGHT

READER: There is no escape from the past; from the grim reality of war there is no escape for any man. The dragnet of war has been cast over us many times, and even when our cause is just, we may not rest at ease.

CONG: If it shall be again required of us that we empty our hearts of peace that justice might ensue, let our hearts remain sore until true peace shall be established.

READER: Now when we recall the Maccabees, let us not adorn ourselves with the dross and tinsel of their victory. Let us not glorify war nor ever pray for war.

CONG: Lord, mend our insufficiencies; grant us, soon and in our days, a whole and perfect peace.

(Light Sixth Light)

SONG

לֹא־יִשָּׂא גוֹי אֶל־גּוֹי חֶרֶב וְלֹא־יִלְמְדוּ עוֹד מִלְחָמָה:

(Let nation not lift up sword against nation, neither shall they learn war any more.)

SEVENTH LIGHT

READER: When men grow fat on the hunger of their fellowmen there can be no peace. Such peace is but the harbinger of other wars.

CONG: When any man goes hungry (and there are no national boundaries to hunger), when any man is cold, is homeless or is without proper honor in his community (and there are no racial prerogatives to honor), we as Jews sin twice.

READER: If out of self-interest our lips are closed, we sin. If out of fear we bid ourselves be silent, then we sin.

There was a prophet who said, "Do justly and love mercy." This is our duty and our dignity and if we fail in justice and in mercy there is no mystic hiding place, no cultural half-truth, no homeland that will shelter us.

As we light this seventh light, we rise in prayer for a new and just merciful and courageous time for all mankind.

(Light seventh light)

עָלֵינוּ לְשַׁבֵּחַ לַאֲדוֹן הַכֹּל לָתֵת גְּדֻלָּה לְיוֹצֵר בְּרֵאשִׁית שֶׁלֹּא

עָשָׂנוּ כְּגוֹיֵי הָאֲרָצוֹת וְלֹא שָׂמָנוּ כְּמִשְׁפְּחוֹת הָאֲדָמָה שֶׁלֹּא שָׂם

חֶלְקֵנוּ כָּהֶם וְגֹרָלֵנוּ כְּכָל הֲמוֹנָם:

וַאֲנַחְנוּ כּוֹרְעִים וּמִשְׁתַּחֲוִים וּמוֹדִים

לִפְנֵי מֶלֶךְ מַלְכֵי הַמְּלָכִים הַקָּדוֹשׁ בָּרוּךְ הוּא.

וְנֶאֱמַר

וְהָיָה יְיָ לְמֶלֶךְ עַל־כָּל־הָאָרֶץ בַּיּוֹם הַהוּא יִהְיֶה

יְיָ אֶחָד וּשְׁמוֹ אֶחָד:

EIGHTH LIGHT

READER: May our last words be prayer, for man's last strength is not within himself, nor is a man's power for himself, nor is his life only unto himself. Lord, we have spoken many words, yet only in silence can we come before Thee.

CONG: There is the silence of the individual who in his heart bows down before Thee. And there is the silence of the group who with closed lips bows down before the altar of Thy silence.

UNISON: It is seldom that we come together with thoughts at one, turned toward one goal, desiring but one purpose.

280

Grant that we may feel the power of our united prayer, the only power which cannot be misused; for it is laid down in silence before Thee.

(Light Eighth Light)

MOURNER'S KADDISH

יִתְגַּדַּל וְיִתְקַדַּשׁ שְׁמֵהּ רַבָּא. בְּעָלְמָא דִי־בְרָא כִרְעוּתֵהּ. וְיַמְלִיךְ מַלְכוּתֵהּ בְּחַיֵּיכוֹן וּבְיוֹמֵיכוֹן וּבְחַיֵּי דְכָל־בֵּית יִשְׂרָאֵל בַּעֲגָלָא וּבִזְמַן קָרִיב. וְאִמְרוּ אָמֵן:

יְהֵא שְׁמֵהּ רַבָּא מְבָרַךְ לְעָלַם וּלְעָלְמֵי עָלְמַיָּא:

יִתְבָּרַךְ וְיִשְׁתַּבַּח וְיִתְפָּאַר וְיִתְרֹמַם וְיִתְנַשֵּׂא וְיִתְהַדַּר וְיִתְעַלֶּה וְיִתְהַלָּל שְׁמֵהּ דְּקֻדְשָׁא. בְּרִיךְ הוּא. לְעֵלָּא (וּלְעֵלָּא) מִן־כָּל־ בִּרְכָתָא וְשִׁירָתָא תֻּשְׁבְּחָתָא וְנֶחֱמָתָא דַּאֲמִירָן בְּעָלְמָא. וְאִמְרוּ אָמֵן:

יְהֵא שְׁלָמָא רַבָּא מִן־שְׁמַיָּא וְחַיִּים עָלֵינוּ וְעַל־כָּל־יִשְׂרָאֵל. וְאִמְרוּ אָמֵן:

עֹשֶׂה שָׁלוֹם בִּמְרוֹמָיו הוּא יַעֲשֶׂה שָׁלוֹם עָלֵינוּ וְעַל־כָּל־יִשְׂרָאֵל. וְאִמְרוּ אָמֵן:

READER: The midnight of sorrow is past, yet the hours are long until the dawn. In the darkness we have kindled light and warmth, courage and hope. With thoughts at one, turned toward one goal, to press onward and retain integrity—this is our Maccabean task.

CLOSING HANUKKAH SONG

281

A SERVICE FOR SHABBAT HANUKKAH

OPENING MEDITATION

The year's dark time has come again, when shadows start to fall not long past noon, and long before our day is done the sun has gone. How taunting is this early darkness! For now the sun turns twilight before our eyes have drunk their fill, and distance sinks into the darkness, leaving us again with no world but our own to meet our sight. This darkness in the afternoon descends uneasily upon our minds . . . is life itself like winter days? Shall our lives peak before our noon, and then with death sink prematurely in oblivion's sea? Such thoughts intrude upon our minds at this dark time, for this is the contrast season, when we mark the winter solstice, the longest nights and the darkest days; how dark our world appears beneath the solstice sky, as war snuffs out more lives each day than our benighted souls can count; as injustice and oppression dim the possibilities that whole races of mankind might grow to personhood and purpose. But this night is as well a time when we lift a flickering candle to the darkness, that we might lure the sun back from its sleep to light our world, when the darkness of the nights of suffering, of death, oppression, and injustice might shrink before the healing light of love, of life, redemption, and of peace.

THE CONTRAST SEASON: TRIUMPH AND CONSECRATION

Mi yemalel gvurot Yisrael	מִי יְמַלֵּל גְּבוּרוֹת יִשְׂרָאֵל
Otan mi yimne	אוֹתָם מִי יִמְנֶה (2)
Hein b'chol dor yakum hagibor	הֵן בְּכָל דּוֹר, יָקוּם הַגִּבּוֹר
Goel haam.	גּוֹאֵל הָעָם.
Shma!	שְׁמַע !
Bayamim haheim bazman haze	בַּיָּמִים הָהֵם בַּזְּמַן הַזֶּה
Makabi moshia ufode	מַכַּבִּי מוֹשִׁיעַ וּפוֹדֶה
Uvyameinu kol am Yisrael	וּבְיָמֵינוּ כָּל עַם יִשְׂרָאֵל
Yitached yakum veyigael.	יִתְאַחֵד, יָקוּם וְיִגָּאֵל.
Mi yemalel	מִי יְמַלֵּל . . . .

285

(Who can retell Israel's deeds of strength,
Who can count them?
In every generation a hero arises, a redeemer of the people.
Hark! In ancient days at this season
The Maccabee was a savior and deliverer
And in our days the entire people Israel
Shall arise to be united and redeemed.)

Hanukah is a time of heroes. The Maccabees felt they had to fight to win their people's right to live as a separate culture. Nor is this the first time that the issue of violence has faced us in our struggle to survive. The fight against the Romans and the battle for Israel have all demanded that people give their lives. In the dark months of 1942, Emanuel Ringelblum wrote from the Warsaw ghetto: "Most of the populace is set on resistance. It seems to me that people will no longer go to the slaughter like lambs. They want the enemy to pay dearly for their lives. . . . We have seen the confirmation of the psychological law that the slave who is completely repressed cannot resist. The Jews appear to have recovered somewhat from the heavy blows they have received; they have shaken off the effects of their experiences to some extent, and they calculate now that going to the slaughter peaceably has not diminished the misfortune, but increased. . . . We must put up a resistance, defend ourselves against the enemy, man and child."

ZOG NIT KAYNMOL
(Song of the Vilna Ghetto Partisans)

Zog nit keynmol az du geyst dem letstn veg,
Chotsh himlen blayene farshteln bloye teg;
Kumen vet noch undzer oysgebenkte sho,
S'vet a poyk ton undzer trot: mir zenen do!

Oh, never say that you have reached the very end,
Though leaden skies a bitter future may portend.
Because the hour for which we yearned will yet arrive
And our marching steps will thunder: We survive!

From land of palm trees to the land of distant snow,
We are here, with our pain, with our woe,
And wherever our blood was shed in pain,
Our fighting spirits will resurrect again.

Not lead, but blood, inscribed this song we sing,
It's not a caroling of birds upon the wing.
It was a people midst the crashing barricades,
Who sang this song, in time with pistols and grenades.

(repeat first verse in Yiddish)

ANTIPHONAL READING

Can survival come only in marching steps, announced by songs of pistols and grenades? Is the real celebration of this day the triumph of an ancient war or the new consecration of an altar?

> How vain, in that day, was the strife of the factions, how futile the wars of the nations, how barren the victor's gain! Even as the Maccabees, according to their vision did the right, their foe also, according to his vision, did the right. In the end, the light that was needed shown.

No strife can be in Heaven's name; no strife is of that which endures. In those ancient struggles, may we see the model of our own dissensions and grow in the wisdom of peace. May we prefer the endurance of injury to the inflicting of injury, rejecting every pretext wrought of passion which masks as a just reason to harm our fellowmen.

> The old law of an eye for an eye leaves everybody blind. It destroys community and makes brotherhood impossible. It creates bitterness in the survivors and brutality in the destroyers. But the principle of nonviolent resistance seeks to reconcile the truths of two opposites—acquiescence and violence. The nonviolent resister rises to the noble height of opposing the unjust system while loving the perpetrators of

the system. In winning our freedom, they say, we will so appeal to your heart and conscience that we will win you in the process.

May new altars and nobler resolves be ever consecrated within us, that the inward light of conscience might shine with an eightfold splendor in this time of dedication.

SONG

לֹא־יִשָּׂא גוֹי אֶל־גּוֹי חֶרֶב וְלֹא־יִלְמְדוּ עוֹד מִלְחָמָה:

(Nation shall not lift up sword against nation,
Nor shall they learn war any more.)

O Infinite Sunlight, return Thou to us. Be Thou our soul's springtime prepared for in the empty days of winter. Be Thou our soul's summer, for the summer of eternity art Thou, in which vigor will blossom forth no more through blood and torment, but in life and beauty and joy, flawless and everlasting.

(rising)

בָּרְכוּ אֶת־יְיָ הַמְבֹרָךְ:

(Praise the Lord to whom all praise is due.)

בָּרוּךְ יְיָ הַמְבֹרָךְ לְעוֹלָם וָעֶד:

(Praised be the Lord to whom all praise is due forever and ever.)

THE CONTRAST SEASON: THE ONE AND THE MANY

Antiochus thought to make his kingdom one, and unite by force all the disparate sects and factions underneath his sway. And so the ancient Mattathias and his sons opposed him, and his collaborators among the Jews as well. No man may institute the rule of One, they cried; in man's world, One has not yet come, and so there must be room for many, that the One may take root and spread abroad; the lives of many must be cultivated, lest a part of Oneness be cut off before its time has come. God is One, and some day His unity will be the sole existence for all men; but man is also one—the ancients tell us that the world was formed with but one man to teach us that one man's life is like the life of the whole world. And so each person and each unique belief must be protected, for in each one is a breath of the ultimate One. Through the many, One may be obscured, yet only through the many may One become reality.

שְׁמַע יִשְׂרָאֵל יְהֹוָה אֱלֹהֵינוּ יְהֹוָה אֶחָד:

(Hear, Israel: the Lord our God, the Lord is One.)

בָּרוּךְ שֵׁם כְּבוֹד מַלְכוּתוֹ לְעוֹלָם וָעֶד:

(Praised be His name whose glorious kingdom is forever and ever.)

(seated)

THE SHMA OF A CONSCIENTIOUS OBJECTOR

I believe that human life is sacred, sacred to mankind, to each individual, and to myself as an individual within mankind. I believe that man has a meaning to his life and that each person has a responsibility to his fellow man. I believe that we are all God's children. This is the meaning I attach to life; we belong to the family of man. Because we are all tied together by this human thread, anything and everything we do will affect all people.

I feel very strongly the oneness of all people. We are all human beings living on this earth, sharing common experiences. We all live, die, love, hate, and have the same fears of life and death.

I see this common bond as the relationships all people have with each other, based on love, care, understanding, and commitment.

This common bond is the motivating factor in our world; it makes everything happen. This bond is what I understand to be the meaning of God.

If I take a human life, then I am not fulfilling my responsibility to God, because I will be taking away one of the components that make up the common bond. My taking of another person's life would also be taking a part of my own life.

To affirm life means right now and right here. It is to say "Yes" to existence, to ourselves, to others with whom we share our lives. It is to become a person who can save even a single soul from the depths of despair and self-negation, a person who can be alive.

(As our forefathers sang on the shores of the divided Red Sea: Who is like you, O Lord, compared to the gods men worship? Who is like you, majestic in holiness, awesome in splendor, doing wonders? The Lord shall reign forever and ever.)

מִי־כָמֹכָה בָּאֵלִם יְיָ מִי כָּמֹכָה
אֶדָּר בַּקֹּדֶשׁ נוֹרָא תְהִלֹּת עֹשֵׂה
פֶלֶא:
מַלְכוּתְךָ רָאוּ בָנֶיךָ בּוֹקֵעַ יָם
לִפְנֵי מֹשֶׁה. זֶה אֵלִי עָנוּ וְאָמְרוּ.
יְיָ יִמְלֹךְ לְעֹלָם וָעֶד:
וְנֶאֱמַר כִּי־פָדָה יְיָ אֶת־יַעֲקֹב
וּגְאָלוֹ מִיַּד חָזָק מִמֶּנּוּ. בָּרוּךְ אַתָּה יְיָ
גָּאַל יִשְׂרָאֵל:

THE CONTRAST SEASON: THE HELLENE
AND THE JEW

This season is as much a struggle of two cultures as a struggle of two powers: that which other people have seems always more seductive than our own—more pleasurable, less burdensome. Nor can we always distinguish clearly between the culture of those we live among and the culture of our own people, for each lends to the other and soon what we are becomes impossible to distinguish from the way our neighbors live.

READERS

Come, therefore, let us enjoy the good things that exist
    and make use of the creation to the full as in youth.
Let us take our fill of costly wine and perfumes,
    and let no flower of spring pass by us,
Let us crown ourselves with rosebuds before they wither.
Let none of us fail to share in our revelry,
    everywhere let us leave signs of enjoyment,
    because this is our portion, and this is our lot.

(Parody of contemporary mores from the
Wisdom of Solomon, 1st century BCE)

*   *   *   *

What else, I ask you, were all those prohibitive . . . rules and regulations all about to begin with, what else but to give us little Jewish children practice in being repressed? Practice, darling, practice, practice, practice. Inhibition doesn't grow on trees, you know—takes patience, takes concentration, takes a dedicated and self-sacrificing parent and a hard-working attentive little child. . . . Why else the two sets of dishes? Why else the kosher soap and salt? Why else, I ask you, but to remind us three times a day that life is boundaries and restrictions if it's anything, hundreds of thousands of little rules laid down by none other than None Other, rules which either you obey without question, . . . or you transgress . . . , only with the strong likelihood . . . that comes next Yom Kippur and the names are written in the big book . . . , and lo, your own precious name ain't among them.

(From Roth, *Portnoy's Complaint*, 20th Century CE)

*   *   *   *

For man is not merely an animal, even a *rational* animal . . . , but a "religious" animal, one which has the wonderful power to take his animal functions and turn them into something holy. The glory of man is his power to hallow. We do not live to eat; we eat to live. Even the act of eating can be sanctified; even the act of eating can become a means for achieving holiness.

(Dresner, The Jewish Dietary Laws:
Their Meaning for Our Time)

* * * *

The most important thing about the food laws seems to be that a pattern exists in the daily act of eating, a pattern that Jews have shared since Sinai. It is a community bond and a reminder of personal identity that comes whenever a man gets hungry. It is a daily commitment in action to one's faith, a formal choice, a quiet self-discipline.

(Wouk, This Is My God)

* * * *

TOGETHER

Leave this chanting and singing and telling of beads.
Come out of thy meditations and leave aside thy
    flowers and incense.
What harm is there if thy clothes become tattered and stained
Meet him and stand by him in toil and in sweat of thy brow.

(Rabindranath Tagore)

THE STANDING PRAYER

(in silence)

"Had they but abandoned Me," says God, "and kept faith with My Torah!"

This must be interpreted as follows: The end-all of knowledge is to know that we cannot know anything. But there are two sorts of not-knowing. The one is the immediate not-knowing, when a man does not even begin to examine and try to know, because it is impossible to know. Another, however, examines and seeks, until he comes to know that one cannot know. And the difference between

292

these two—to whom may we compare them? To two men who wish to see the king. The one enters all the chambers belonging to the king. He rejoices in the king's treasure rooms and splendid halls, and then he discovers that he cannot get to know the king. The other tells himself: "Since it is impossible to get to know the king, we will not bother to enter, but put up with not knowing." This leads us to understand what those words of God mean. They have abandoned Me, that is, they have abandoned the search to know Me, because it is not possible. But oh, had they but abandoned Me with searching and understanding, so keeping faith with My Torah!

(Israel Baal Shem)

May the will come from thee,
Adonai, my God, and God of my fathers,
shaper of origins,
as thou hast called thy universe into being this day,
and thy unity proclaimed in thy universe,
and hast hung therein worlds above and worlds below
at thy word,
so with thy multiple compassion
unify my heart,
and the heart of all thy folk, Israel,
to love and to revere thy name.
And our eyes enlighten
in the light of thy Torah,
for with thee is the source of life:
in thy light shall we see light.

(Shaare Zion)

Our God and God of our fathers,
May the rest we choose for this Shabbat
    be pleasing.
May the mitzvot we undertake bring us near
    to holiness.
May the portion which is ours in Torah
    remain with us as a loved one's gift.

Let us sense the joy of mastering our own
    lives.
Yet know the purity of a heart which reaches
    out to serve our brothers.
Let us touch the love and holiness of this day
    as we would caress a precious heirloom,
And from its touch find rest.
God, who leads men into the holiness of Shabbat,
You are blessed.

> Guard us
> from vicious leanings and from haughty ways,
> from anger and from temper,
> from melancholy, talebearing,
> and from all the other evil qualities.
>
> Nor let envy of any man rise in our heart,
> nor envy of us in the heart of others.
>
> On the contrary:
> put it in our hearts that we may see our comrades' virtue,
> and not their failing.

(Elimelekh of Lizhensk)

TOWARD THE UNITY OF CONTRASTS

If God is hidden in the darkness of our winter times, we must go in search of Him with the candle of conviction, that we might cleanse our altars without blood, preserve the many and yet find the One, make use of the creation to the full and yet give flesh to that creation by the disciplines through which we share our people's life. In the darkness we must kindle light.

That light is but a symbol of ourselves and of all mankind. The gentle flame that gives us life knows no differences of place or color, or the stature of its transient wick of flesh. Each flame dehumanized steals the glow from another, each smoldering wick robs another man of warmth.

Let the flames we kindle in this week of Dedication live on as a
sign that we are one, that we are fragile, that we possess the spark
of warmth and deep humanity. Praised be the Lord our God who
makes us holy in the act of lighting candles, who lets us share the
miracle of our people's life through light.

בָּרוּךְ אַתָּה יְיָ אֱלֹהֵינוּ מֶלֶךְ הָעוֹלָם שֶׁעָשָׂה נִסִּים לַאֲבוֹתֵינוּ בַּיָּמִים הָהֵם בַּזְּמַן הַזֶּה:

בָּרוּךְ אַתָּה יְיָ אֱלֹהֵינוּ מֶלֶךְ הָעוֹלָם אֲשֶׁר קִדְּשָׁנוּ בְּמִצְוֹתָיו וְצִוָּנוּ לְהַדְלִיק נֵר שֶׁל חֲנֻכָּה:

ALEYNU

עָלֵינוּ לְשַׁבֵּחַ לַאֲדוֹן הַכֹּל לָתֵת גְּדֻלָּה לְיוֹצֵר בְּרֵאשִׁית שֶׁלֹּא
עָשָׂנוּ כְּגוֹיֵי הָאֲרָצוֹת וְלֹא שָׂמָנוּ כְּמִשְׁפְּחוֹת הָאֲדָמָה שֶׁלֹּא שָׂם
חֶלְקֵנוּ כָּהֶם וְגֹרָלֵנוּ כְּכָל הֲמוֹנָם:

וַאֲנַחְנוּ כּוֹרְעִים וּמִשְׁתַּחֲוִים וּמוֹדִים
לִפְנֵי מֶלֶךְ מַלְכֵי הַמְּלָכִים הַקָּדוֹשׁ בָּרוּךְ הוּא.

May the time not be distant, O God, when Your name shall be
worshipped in all the earth, when unbelief shall disappear and
error be no more. We fervently pray that the day may come when
all men shall feel capable of calling on Your name, when corruption and evil shall give way to integrity and goodness, when all
who dwell on earth shall know the single Purpose in the world,
before which every knee may bend. May the many, created in
God's single image, recognize that they are one, and so announce
the coming of His kingdom upon earth, when the Lord will reign
forever and ever, and all the earth will hear that the Lord is God,
the Lord is one.

וְנֶאֱמַר

וְהָיָה יְיָ לְמֶלֶךְ עַל־כָּל־הָאָרֶץ בַּיּוֹם הַהוּא יִהְיֶה
יְיָ אֶחָד וּשְׁמוֹ אֶחָד:

MOURNERS' KADDISH

יִתְגַּדַּל וְיִתְקַדַּשׁ שְׁמֵהּ רַבָּא. בְּעָלְמָא דִי־בְרָא כִרְעוּתֵהּ.
וְיַמְלִיךְ מַלְכוּתֵהּ בְּחַיֵּיכוֹן וּבְיוֹמֵיכוֹן וּבְחַיֵּי דְכָל־בֵּית יִשְׂרָאֵל
בַּעֲגָלָא וּבִזְמַן קָרִיב. וְאִמְרוּ אָמֵן:

Congregation and Mourners

יְהֵא שְׁמֵהּ רַבָּא מְבָרַךְ לְעָלַם וּלְעָלְמֵי עָלְמַיָּא:

Mourners

יִתְבָּרַךְ וְיִשְׁתַּבַּח וְיִתְפָּאַר וְיִתְרוֹמַם וְיִתְנַשֵּׂא וְיִתְהַדָּר וְיִתְעַלֶּה
וְיִתְהַלָּל שְׁמֵהּ דְּקֻדְשָׁא. בְּרִיךְ הוּא. לְעֵלָּא (וּלְעֵלָּא) מִן־כָּל־
בִּרְכָתָא וְשִׁירָתָא תֻּשְׁבְּחָתָא וְנֶחֱמָתָא דַּאֲמִירָן בְּעָלְמָא. וְאִמְרוּ
אָמֵן:

יְהֵא שְׁלָמָא רַבָּא מִן־שְׁמַיָּא וְחַיִּים עָלֵינוּ וְעַל־כָּל־יִשְׂרָאֵל.
וְאִמְרוּ אָמֵן:

עֹשֶׂה שָׁלוֹם בִּמְרוֹמָיו הוּא יַעֲשֶׂה שָׁלוֹם עָלֵינוּ וְעַל־כָּל־יִשְׂרָאֵל.
וְאִמְרוּ אָמֵן:

SONG: Maoz Tzur

MAOZ TZUR Y'SHUATI
LCHA NA-EH L'SHABEACH
TIKON BEYT TFILATI
V'SHAM TODA NZABEACH.
L'EYT TACHIN MATBEACH
MIZOR HAMNABEACH
AZ EGMOR B'SHIR MIZMOR
CHANUKAT HAMIZBEACH
  (repeat last two lines)

מָעוֹז צוּר יְשׁוּעָתִי
לְךָ נָאֶה לְשַׁבֵּחַ
תִּכּוֹן בֵּית תְּפִלָּתִי
וְשָׁם תּוֹדָה נְזַבֵּחַ.
לְעֵת תָּכִין מַטְבֵּחַ
מִצָּר הַמְנַבֵּחַ
אָז אֶגְמוֹר בְּשִׁיר מִזְמוֹר
חֲנֻכַּת הַמִּזְבֵּחַ.

296

Y'VANIM NIKB'TZU ALAY
AZAY BIMEY CHASHMANIM
UFARTZU CHOMOT MIGDALAY
V'TIM'U KOL HASH'MANIM.

UMINOTAR KANKANIM
NAASEH NEYS L'SHOSHANIM
BNEY VINAH Y'MEY SHMONAH
KAV'U SHIR UR'NANIM.
(*repeat last two lines*)

יְוָנִים נִקְבְּצוּ עָלַי

אֲזַי בִּימֵי חַשְׁמַנִּים

וּפָרְצוּ חוֹמוֹת מִגְדָּלַי

וְטִמְּאוּ כָּל הַשְּׁמָנִים

וּמִנּוֹתַר קַנְקַנִּים

נַעֲשָׂה נֵס לַשּׁוֹשַׁנִּים,

בְּנֵי בִינָה יְמֵי שְׁמוֹנָה

קָבְעוּ שִׁיר וּרְנָנִים.

FIVE SETTINGS FOR CREATIVE WORSHIP

FIVE SETTINGS FOR CREATIVE WORSHIP

The following section describes several campus services which illustrate the variety of settings which can be designed for experimental Sabbath worship. At the same time they demonstrate once more the spectrum of possible formats for such services, ranging from a slight modification of the conventional structure and text of a service to a radical restructuring of its form, content, and environment.

Richard Levy's suggestions for advance preparation and for conducting an Erev Shabbat service, although originally designed for "New Windows on an Ancient Day," describe arrangements and approaches which can be fruitfully used or adapted for other services, whether traditional or experimental. The "Preparation," conducted in a different room from that in which the service itself is held, may precede any service. If the preparatory reading is of sufficient length, it may even develop into a completely "unstructured" service by itself which can, in turn, be embellished by group singing.

Albert Axelrad and Richard Israel describe experimental *Friday evening* services at Brandeis University and Yale University respectively. Raphael Zahler's report on "The Upstairs Minyan" describes an experimental approach to *Shabbat morning* worship at Hillel at the University of Chicago; and Joseph Polak outlines an approach to a *total Shabbat* experience from Friday afternoon until after Havdalah, developed at Ohio and Boston Universities.

CREATING THE SETTING

(With specific reference to 'New Windows on an Ancient Day')

Richard N. Levy

I. ARRANGING THE SERVICE

1. The following persons may be utilized:
   - (a) A song leader, preferably with guitar, to lead one or two lively Shabbat tunes.
   - (b) One or two readers to read aloud the Preparation paragraph (see below) and to comment on it.
   - (c) A reader for candle-lighting.
   - (d) (optional) One or two readers to prepare in advance to offer an original prayer during the Sharing of Prayer section of the Amidah.
   - (e) (optional) People to participate in Sharing of Prayer and/or the Torah and Haftarah portions in dance, song, or mixed media.

     NOTE: The parashah might serve as a basis for both Preparation paragraph and original prayer, giving the service a unifying theme.

2. To be distributed to each worshipper:
   - (a) The prayer service.
   - (b) A Preparation reading of approximately one or two paragraphs to set a Shabbat mood (perhaps from A. J. Heschel's *The Sabbath*).
   - (c) A song sheet with words of all songs to be sung.
   - (d) (optional) Torah and Haftarah selections to serve as bases for discussion.
   - (e) (distributed or placed on chairs) Slips of blank paper and pencils, unless the traditional nature of the congregation should make this inappropriate.

II. CONDUCTING THE SERVICE

1. *The Preparation:*
   - (a) The congregation should gather in a preparation room

302

(lounge, study, library), the smaller the better, to increase the sense of closeness.

(b) After distributing the prayer booklet, a song sheet, and the separate Preparation reading, the Reader may wish to convey some of these ideas in mood-setting remarks:

—Worship consists of both the shared experience and the evoking of private thoughts. This service is intended to stimulate both, and as a result, the content of the service will depend as much on the individual contributions (shared and private) of the worshippers, as on the printed service.

—The preparation room symbolizes the transition from weekday to Shabbat.

—Worshippers, the Reader should remind them, are not really ready for a Shabbat service. He may draw attention to their feelings of the moment: weariness, the harassments of the week, uneasiness in a house of worship, etc.—hence the need for a period of transition to and preparation for Shabbat.

—To share the experience of prayer and Shabbat through the Jewish people, we must first know at least those with whom we are worshipping. Everyone should be asked to introduce himself to those in his immediate vicinity, with the Reader setting an example.

(c) To restore order, a musical leader, preferably with a guitar, should play a lively Shabbat melody and encourage the group to welcome the Sabbath in song.

(d) A prearranged reader should be called on to read the Preparation paragraph from the middle of the group.

(e) That person should then be asked to express his reaction to the Preparation statement. The group should then be invited to discuss their feelings informally with people near them or with the whole group if it is small enough, expressing innermost feelings if possible (the Reader should try gently to discourage mere conversation) to create an appropriate mood in anticipation of the service. The Reader may conclude with some mood-setting remarks of his own.

(f) When the desired mood has been set, the Reader should lead the group into the sanctuary (or other prayer room), encouraging them to sit as close to the pulpit and to each other as possible. Guitar music and silence or soft singing should accompany the move.

2. *The Service:*
The conduct of the service should proceed as the Reader determines, with the following specific suggestions:

(a) After the introductory blessings of the Amidah, the worshippers should be invited to express their own prayers. If appropriate, paper and pencils provided in advance can be used to write a prayer, jot down prayer words, or sketch a prayerful feeling. A designated individual can offer an original prayer.

(b) (optional) Prayers may be expressed through dance, music, or mixed media.

(c) At a designated point in the Amidah, worshippers should be invited to share their prayer or inner feelings with their neighbors. Worshippers in alternate rows may be invited to turn around to face congregants behind them. This is possible whether movable chairs or fixed pews are used.

3. *Torah Service:*
This should introduce a less formal mood into the service, allowing for some study of the parasha, with free translation and congregational and Reader's commentary.

(a) Techniques suggested above may again be used (i.e. mixed media, original prepared comments, free discussion from the congregation).

(b) The "Prophetic Reading" may either be the traditional Haftarah or a contemporary prophetic statement.

4. *Concluding Portions:*
(a) After Kaddish or a concluding reading, worshippers should

be invited each to bestow a Shabbat blessing on his neighbor. The Reader might set the example with others on the pulpit.

(b) Space permitting, the congregation should be invited to come forward to link arms as they sing a closing song, led by guitar and soloist.

(c) Worshippers should be led singing to the place where Kiddush is sung and refreshments served. Words to the Kiddush might be posted or distributed.

(d) A talk or action workshop, emphasizing the ethical imperative of the service, might conclude the evening.

JEWISH FELLOWSHIP SERVICE AT BRANDEIS UNIVERSITY

Albert Axelrad

At Brandeis University, like elsewhere, the nature of the Sabbath services, conducted by the B'nai B'rith Hillel Foundation, is determined by the background and interests of those who attend. Consequently, there is a continual experimentation and modification of both content and structure in order to meet student needs. Both traditional and liberal services are planned and conducted by students every Friday evening, and a traditional Sabbath dinner usually follows the services. Sabbath observance on Saturday follows the traditional pattern and includes traditional morning services, a Sabbath lunch, a study session, *Minchah, Se'udah sh'lishit, Ma'ariv* and *Havdalah.*

However, in addition to the traditional and liberal services, a creative and experimental service, known as "Jewish Fellowship" (Havurah) also meets every Friday in a lounge on campus in order to welcome and honor the Sabbath. The origin of the project and its approach are described in the following report by Rabbi Albert Axelrad, Director of the B'nai B'rith Hillel Foundation at Brandeis University.

I initiated this project a few years ago, partly because of my own dissatisfaction with non-traditional worship services, but mainly in order to reach out to the many serious-minded Jews on campus who are altogether unattracted to conventional worship of any kind, yet seriously want to remain Jews and to find some ways of expressing their commitment. I invited all interested students to an open meeting in a lounge to discuss what was on my mind and to see how they felt. I proposed a weekly meeting in a lounge in honor of Shabbat, and I stressed that both content and format should be open and flexible, but that the elements should be appropriate to the spirit of Shabbat and should seek to combine spiritual elevation and intellectual stimulation. Together we evolved the following initial format:

1. The lighting of the Sabbath candles and the chanting of the blessing in unison.
2. The reading of certain parts of the Torah portion of the

week by students or by me, interspersed with comments utilizing relevant rabbinic commentaries.

3. A creative or experimental element, to be introduced each week by a different student or group of students. So far, this aspect has included poetry readings, readings from other religious (especially oriental) traditions, readings on peace, non-violence, and human dignity, records and folk music, sometimes recorded, sometimes presented live. Occasionally some program elements were dramatically juxtaposed—for instance by two sound tracks running simultaneously, one presenting a song of quiet and serenity, the other presenting a news broadcast with its report of brutality and savagery.

4. Meditation and discussion based either on the Torah portion, the commentary, or the experimental element.

5. The chanting of the Kiddush by the entire group and the sharing of wine from the same cup.

This year we have made several changes. The Torah portion is no longer read by me aloud, but by all of us silently. When someone feels stimulated to raise a question or to make a comment, he is free to do so. Above all, I have tried to get the students to participate more than in the past. During the first year I was the dominating figure. Now I am trying to serve more as an advisor. Right now we are also considering additional projects besides the weekly "service," e.g., we plan to spend a whole Sabbath together on or away from campus and to create a new Sabbath liturgy on the theme of *Shabbat Shalom*—of peace between people and nations. Students continue to take on the responsibility for the experimental or creative element. Sometimes they consult with me, sometimes they don't. The first time when a student, on his own initiative, prepared a commentary, he brought in a scholarly and professional presentation which did not fit in with the mood of the occasion. The experience taught all of us a lesson.

The response has been good although limited. At present the *havurah* consists of 15 students, all of whom are regulars. However, as the project becomes more widely known, additional students are expected to join.

SOME SABBATH EXPERIMENTS AT YALE
Richard J. Israel

An experimental approach developed and used by the B'nai B'rith Hillel Foundation at Yale University is described in the following report by Rabbi Richard Israel:

We have long felt a need for a non-traditional worship experience. Those students who want to pray but can't daven do not necessarily find themselves satisfied with the Union Prayer Book. We have been experimenting with a service based on the Sabbath meal rather than the *Kabbalat Shabbat* liturgy.

At the present time, it takes the following form:

1. Candles are lit beforehand. They are the only light in the room. Hallot are on a plate on the floor between the candles along with a large kiddush cup.

2. As people come in, they sit quietly on the floor in a circle.

3. Shalom Aleichem is quietly sung.

4. Kiddush: The cup is passed around and everyone drinks.

5. The "content:" This has variously been a story, a poem, or readings. The students have been encouraged to bring in their own "gifts" or readings or thoughts that are really important to them. Sometimes they have brought in flowers. One evening, we shared fantasies we had about what it was like as we imagined the world immediately after the creation was finished. On another evening, after I had told them the legend, we fantasied about what was on the other side of the Sambation. Still another time was dedicated to viewing a rose until we saw it in all of its absolute uniqueness. Sometimes there are just good discussions. On one evening that turned out to be particularly rewarding, we looked at a daisy until we could see it in its connections with all life. Our goal was to see it in its contiguity with all creation, rather than its discreteness.

6. A period of silence.

7. A niggun.

8. A one-line *birkhat ha-mazon.*

The "service" lasts about 45 minutes. There is much silence between the segments. Though I don't think we are ready for it yet, I hope to institute a *n'tilat yadayim,* with each person washing the hands of the one next to him using a massive cup and bowl. We also may take to using incense if it does not make it all too much of a "put-on." I would discuss both of these matters with the participants before bringing them in.

Another dimension of our Shabbat program should be noted: For several years we have announced "Sabbath Suppers" within university dining halls. The students who are interested take over a given table or two. We provide them with halah and wine. Someone is there who will hold things together, and who can make kiddush and lead a short *birkhat hamazon*. Perhaps there is a song or two during the meal, depending on the people who are at the table. Most of the meal is spent in informal conversation.

The response has been quite remarkable in terms of what I would have expected. We have already reached the point where we have had to utilize several dining halls simultaneously, since no single one could permit all the students who wanted to, to commandeer the tables they needed. There is a significant group of non-halachic students for whom the Sabbath is a viable symbol and who enjoy a low-pressure recognition of its presence.

THE UPSTAIRS MINYAN:
AN EXPERIMENTAL PRAYER COMMUNITY
Raphael Zahler

By now there is no reason to discuss the sterility of normative non-Orthodox American Judaism.* It has all been said before. The lush building filled with empty seats, the services purged of all beauty or impact, the dominance of fund-raising and social activities, the absence of real commitment to social action—these familiar symptoms of *rigor mortis* exist in all but a few of our congregations. The many Jewish youth who have been turned on to their tradition, whether by Zionism, an exciting Jewish atmosphere in college, or an encounter with a great personality, are faced with a serious "re-entry" problem when they leave school, find a job, and attempt to join a local congregation. For this synagogue is almost always the same hollow institution that helped alienate them and their friends in post-Bar-Mitzvah years.

Jewish youth have tried several modest solutions to this problem. In a few congregations scattered across the country there are stirrings of political or religious concern. Havurot and Jewish communal groups, like those in Boston, New York, Washington, and Berkeley, have also attracted wide attention, like the underground church and religious communes of contemporary Christianity. I will describe another effort to solve the re-entry problem in Judaism, an experimental community at the University of Chicago Hillel Foundation, known simply as the "Upstairs Minyan."

* * * * * * *

Shabbat, Oct. 4, 1969: Shemini Atzeret
Gandhi: On Truth
Sing: *Shabbat m'nucha*
Silverman, pp. 46, 47, 58 (*Berachot ha-shachar, shir ha-kavod*)
"I was resolved to do his will"—Judah Leon Moscato
(black notebook)
Baruch Sh'amar—paraphrase by Art Green (black notebook)
P'suke d'zimra (individually)

* * * * * * *

---

*Since I am not qualified to treat Orthodox Judaism on its own terms, I want to direct my attention to those Jews who permit themselves some halachic leeway in their behavior.

316

From week to week its members may pray sitting on the floor or through dance, exclusively in English or exclusively in Hebrew, with rock music and contemporary poetry, or hassidic chant and Yehuda Halevi. Yet despite the searching, the constant liturgical flux, the Upstairs Minyan has evolved into a closely-knit community, and its religious experimentation has sharpened its members' understanding of themselves and of Judaism.

The youngest members of the Minyan are college freshmen and high-school seniors. The oldest are the two rabbis and their wives, and other couples, in their late twenties or early thirties, some with children. The Minyan links these re-entering couples to the younger people, whose Jewish re-awakening is just beginning. Out of about forty "regulars" (twenty-five on the average attend the Shabbat morning service), ten or so are undergraduates, twenty are graduate students, and another ten are post-doctoral age; about half the regulars are married; and the overall ratio of men to women is roughly 60-40. There are three faculty couples as well as several ex-students. The Upstairs Minyan is definitely a university-oriented group. This does not make it atypical, of course, considering the pervasiveness of college training in the Jewish community and the recent growth of strongly intellectual sub-communities outside a college setting, like Boston's Route 128, parts of the San Francisco area, and Chicago's north shore suburbs.

Of course, different kinds of subcommunities of *klal Yisrael* also exist: religious groups, study groups, activist groups. In a sense the Minyan exemplifies all of these: it has led to the formation of the University of Chicago Jewish Radical Action Group; it has stimulated its members to study traditional texts, and it has motivated them to study more both at Hillel and outside. Trying to move in all of these seemingly different directions at once often leads to strain and an undesirable compartmentalization of interests.

Just as the Minyan has influenced activities outside of the religious sphere, the Minyan itself has been influenced greatly by people entering from the outside. Five or six members are converts to Judaism. Rita, a student of Mircea Eliade, is deeply interested in the religious tone of the service. Marion comments forcefully on social problems from an anarchist perspective, and on history of religion (in which she did her graduate work). Joel prefers to listen most of the time, yet Joan is one of the most active contributors to the discussion (and the refreshments). Statistically, most of our converts are married to native-born Jews, but nearly all of them had a strong interest in Judaism before their marriage. In any case, the relaxed tone of the Minyan allows them to enter the group more gracefully than they might in more formal surroundings.

Yet there are other members of the Minyan who also come from outside Judaism: the *baaley teshuvah* who either left the Jewish community early in life, or else were never really there. Paradoxically, many of those who returned after many years have clear memories of what services are supposed to be. Those with strongly reform or orthodox backgrounds often have trouble justifying their participation in the Minyan, for even though no one is coerced into leading any particular kind of service, the overall group attitude carries unmistakable elements of respect for tradition and insistence on individuality and innovation.

The Minyan is six years old, and its "alumni" can already be found at Hebrew Union College, the Jewish Theological Seminary, and Havurat Shalom. Several have settled in Israel, and of those who remain here, many are conscientious objectors. The Minyan has experienced marriages, *bar mitzvahs,* and *brisses;* it has had its share of dissension, and there were months when it seemed the group would dissolve. Strangely enough, at this writing it is as vigorous as ever.

* * * * * * *

All hold hands and sing *Pithu li* (Carlebach melody)
Silverman, pp. 84-88 (*Nishmat, shochen ad*)
"Bright is the earth"—ancient Egyptian prayer to
       God the creator (black notebook)
Silverman, pp. 92 ff. (*Shema* through end of *amidah*)

* * * * * * *

The Upstairs Minyan is founded on two principles of equality: equality of participation and equality of the sexes. Ten adults of any sex form a quorum; no distinctions are made in granting *aliyot* and other honors, and women are encouraged to lead prayers. One issue still has not been resolved: women do not wear the *talit,* although several ingenious substitutes have appeared. Yet some women members still refuse to read the Torah, and others have begun only after much thought. Such subtle group pressures towards conformity are often (but not always) brought out into the open during the weekly discussion.

Equality of participation means that each service is planned and led by a member or a group of members. The rabbis are available if needed for consultation; in addition they usually assume the responsibility of preparing a short introduction to each week's *Torah* and *Haftarah* readings.

The core of each *Shabbat* morning service is always the traditional Hebrew text for *shacharit,* although any of several prayer books may be used—orthodox, conservative, reform, or reconstructionist; ashkenazic or sefardic. Over the years the members of the Upstairs Minyan have taught each other the inner rhythms of the traditional service, the reasons for the order of the prayers and the layers of significance interweaving each passage. When a new member feels that he has acquired such an appreciation of the traditional text, he is ready to introduce his own additions and modifications. Many media are possible: music, for instance. The "Electric Prune" 's version of *Kol Nidre,* a psalm of Josquin des Pres, Simon and Garfunkel, and Aretha Franklin sometimes say things that open new areas of *kavvanah.* Hillel's music room, equipped with tape and record players, has been helpful; live instrumental music is much more difficult to get. Visually, wall posters, photographs and prints are sometimes passed around or displayed. How many synagogues have likewise adapted the bright banners found in many churches to our needs? Dancing is also popular at the Minyan, but restrained—the floor is weak. Many of the methods of sensitivity training have also been introduced.

The most common additions are readings. Members have introduced excerpts from the Kabbalah and the Qumran manuscripts, ancient Egyptian religious texts and passages from the Midrash, pueblo prayers and Biblical psalms. People have used works of hasidim like Levi Yitzhak of Berdichev, poets ranging from ibn

319

Gabirol to George Herbert, Saul Tschernichovsky, e. e. cummings and Nelly Sachs, and of course passages from philosophers like Heschel and Buber. Contemporary writers are well represented: Leonard Cohen, Loren Eisely, Malcolm Boyd, Tuvia Rivner, and of course Bob Dylan and the Beatles. Many of these readings have been collected in looseleaf form, and each member has a copy of this "black notebook" available during the service. People feel free to drop out of the organized ritual and respond to the notebook; prayer leaders try to allow time for individual musings in their services.

* * * * * * *

"Pied Beauty"—Hopkins (black notebook)
Silverman, pp. 110-116 (Hallel)
Prayer—from the Manual of Discipline, Qumran
      Torah Service
      Prayer for the U. S. and Israel
      Mussaf

* * * * * * *

The members of the group appreciate good (but not florid) hazzanut, and each year a few hesitant amateurs are prodded into making their cantorial debuts. Of course English is important in the services, since only about one-fifth of the members have a solid knowledge of prayer-book Hebrew. But just how English is used matters a great deal. Responsive readings frequently put people to sleep; instead, the leader may chant in English, or have each person read a section in turn, or use new translations where he finds that the prayer book is uninspiring or even dishonest. One of the most successful experiments was a three-part spoken fugue on Psalm 150 in English. The effect of the fugue is different each time, but the result is a very appropriate ending for the *p'suke d'zimra*.

Most beloved are the nigunim. Each new melody is sung not once, but again and again, until the rhythm of *ha-tov* or *v'kulam m'kablim* makes the room shake, and professors, housewives, and freshmen close their eyes, sway, dance. Sometimes a whole service is nothing but nigunim and, equally important, the silence between nigunim.

The group has been less successful in coping with the Torah service. A triennial cycle is used: the first three *aliyot* of the weekly portion are read the first year; the third, fourth, and fifth the year after; and the fifth, sixth and seventh during the third year. But experiments in the service for taking out and returning the Torah, or varying the pattern of the reading, have not caught on. Some members believe that the Torah is one thing you don't experiment with; others think that the content of the particular week's reading should determine its treatment. Different approaches to the *haftarah* are more readily accepted, perhaps because it is traditionally treated with less respect.

After the Torah is returned to the ark, the chairs are rearranged into a circle, and an hour or so is spent in discussion. It is a period of freedom as compared to the tightly structured liturgy, and it also fortifies the sense of community through face-to-face interchange. The hardest job for the service planner is to find a good discussion topic. God and man, prayer, *kavvanah*, ethics—these "theoretical" topics are close to many people in the Minyan, but they are also the hardest for people to articulate in personal terms. "Practical" discussions about the state of Israel, interfaith understanding and the like are livelier but sometimes not very illuminating. One type of compromise topic has been the text-centered discussion: a close reading of a chapter of Samuel, for example, or of a contemporary philosopher. Another possibility is a theoretical topic with much practical interest: universalism versus particularism, in its many guises, has led to some fierce discussions, with roughly equal amounts of light and heat. Finally, some weeks are given to evaluation sessions, to chart the path of the Minyan in preceding months and plan for the future.

The weekly discussion owes its seriousness and depth to the presence of our Elders: Max, Esther, and Danny. They are able to clarify the discussion's course by picking out critical themes as well as the nuances of feeling. Having thought out many of the moral and social questions which are relatively new to the rest, they help us avoid rhetorical traps, easy answers, and ego tripping. Danny is experienced in Bible scholarship, the history of Jewish mysticism, and the relationship between religion and issues of peace and the draft; Max and Esther's knowledge encompasses clinical psychology and encounter groups, as well as modern Hebrew literature. It would be hard to find a better combination. And their own nuances of personality often stimulate further discussion: Esther's basically traditional outlook, Danny's flinty restlessness, Max's openness to new ideas (combined with a talent for incredibly gruesome puns). They participate on a first-name basis, so one does not think of them as The Rabbis (and Rebbetzin), but as exceptionally valuable *haverim*.

The weekly discussions have revealed fundamental differences among the members of the Minyan. One, a mystic and storyteller, feels very strongly that *kavvanah* is the only thing and that intellectual discussion only over-rationalizes the basic mysteries. Another, more businesslike, dislikes efforts to probe his personal feelings deeply. Some enjoy attending services but are put off by the pressure to help lead and innovate. On balance, though, the discussions are a useful learning experience.

Let me not forget the kiddush. Here the spirit of both participation and competition leads to more and better goodies each week. The *kiddush*, in fact, is more important to the success of the Minyan than some people may think.

On the High Holy Days the Upstairs Minyan is submerged in a much larger congregation drawn from the University area. Yet the Minyan members plan and lead these services too, and, remarkably, the sense of community and intimacy is greatly strengthened. Rosh Hashanah and Yom Kippur prayer in this setting is moving and powerful, for the best of the Upstairs Minyan crystallizes because of the grander ritual, and gains intensity from the larger group and the sense of solemnity that is shared. Thus the small activist Minyan is able to energize a much larger group of more casual worshippers.

But it has been difficult to extend the Upstairs Minyan community beyond the spare-time limits of the Hillel chapel on Saturday mornings. Week-night get-togethers and evaluation sessions sometimes work, and outside activities like the Jewish Radical Action Group and Israeli folk dancing draw a large Upstairs Minyan clientele. But the dreams some members have of a quasi-*havurah* experience based on the Minyan are unlikely to be realized, because most members are heavily committed to the outside world. What is so remarkable about the Minyan, in fact, is the intensity of shared feeling it manages to achieve in just four hours a week.

What does the experience of the Upstairs Minyan mean for the mass of spiritually impoverished American Jewish congregations? Here are some tentative conclusions. First, continuity and community are necessary for living worship, and these are two of the strengths of the Upstairs Minyan. Occasional folk-rock services will not revitalize a congregation. Moreover, a community of creating, involved worshippers is very different from the routine daily or weekly minyan whose sole purpose is the mourners' *kaddish* or *oneg-shabbat* socializing. This is simultaneous prayer, not communality. The members of a group need not share the same beliefs or biases; what is needed instead of superficial unity are open minds and common goals.

Members must be knowledgeable about the tradition. Being knowledgeable must not be confused with knowing Hebrew. The worshipper gets more out of each reader's *kaddish* if he knows where it comes from and what it means and can mean, even if he can't pronounce every word. The reverse is equally true. Finally, and most important, the members must take prayer seriously—not merely as a halachic obligation, nor as an impressive ritual, but as a basic, necessary attempt to understand oneself, others, and God.

With these foundations, groups like the Upstairs Minyan should be able to grow in many places. At least I hope they do, because I am troubled by the quality of American Jewish existence. Communities like this *must* spread—I see no other way to renew our religious energy.

* * * * * * *

Yiskor service
"Ten Rungs" excerpt—Buber (Black notebook)
Discussion
"I do believe that, where there is only a choice between cowardice and violence, I would advise violence. I would rather have India resort to arms in order to defend her honor than that she should, in a cowardly manner, become or remain a helpless witness

to her own dishonor. But I believe that nonviolence is infinitely superior to violence, forgiveness is more manly than punishment . . . Strength does not come from physical capacity. It comes from an indomitable will."—M. K. Gandhi

"Ben Zoma says . . . who is mighty? He who conquers his urges, as it is said: better is a patient man than a mighty one; better one who controls his spirit than he who takes a city."

—*Pirke Avot*

Geshem
Aleynu
Kaddish
Yah Ribon

A COMPLETE SHABBAT EXPERIENCE: THE SHABBAT RETREAT

Joseph Polak

Rabbi Joseph Polak, Director of the B'nai B'rith Hillel Foundation at Boston University (formerly at Ohio University), has repeatedly experimented with approaches designed to introduce students to a deepened understanding and appreciation of the religious dimension of Jewish life. The following excerpts from Rabbi Polak's reports on two such "Retreats" present the highlights of his approach.

By far the most exciting religious program I have ever conducted was a "Retreat" held the second Sabbath of January. It was developed in response to a request by a dozen students for a more intensely Jewish religious and spiritual experience than they could get from our regular services; but it was also stimulated by some conversations and meetings I had with some students at my Foundation and at the National Hillel Summer Institute.

Forty students participated in the Retreat—twenty boys and twenty girls. Some were of the Joe College variety, others were more or less hip. The Retreat had several purposes. First, it was intended to be a way of experiencing the holiness of the world—based on the assumption that all things in the world are inherently sacred and that this fact is reflected and emphasized in the Sabbath's preoccupation with creation. Secondly, we wanted to demonstrate that this experience can be achieved only through discipline in general, and through halachic discipline in particular. Thirdly—an allied point—we wanted to show that halachic discipline can do marvelous things for human relations.

The Retreat roughly followed a model set up some years ago by Rabbi Zalman Schachter. Our retreatants spent 26 hours in worship and study, eating and sleeping at Hillel. Some highlights will give you an idea of the program and impact of the retreat.

Immediately after the Friday evening service, everyone was asked to bless everyone else in as warm and as human a way as he could. The *mechitza* was removed, more tables were set up and combined, and place settings were laid. Retreatants then gathered around the one long dinner table for *shalom aleichem,* which was sung facing the front door. Following the kiddush, I told all retreatants that there was to be no talking whatsoever during the meals, except for a brief dedication of each course to the Sabbath. The meal lasted about an hour; the silence was interspersed with *zemirot*. The meal was followed by an evaluation of what the silence had accomplished. Briefly: the students were amazed at how well and how rapidly they had come to know each other without talking. Most of them felt that the trite, ordinary day-to-day conversation of the "what's your name?" or "what courses are you taking?" variety was actually an impediment to true dialogue. A humorous but not insignificant observation by the students was that they had become very sensitive to sound during the silence; hearing oneself eat was an awesome experience, hearing twenty soup spoons clacking was at once hilarious and somewhat unnerving. A study session followed the discussion.

On Saturday morning, at 9:15, after a snack, the students studied once again, this time the Lurianic Table Hymns. This was followed by the morning service. The major difference between the morning service and that of Friday evening was that there was no cantor for the *p'sukei dezimrah*. Services formally began with *shokhein ad*. From here on, the full traditional service was followed. As had been the case on the previous evening, considerable emphasis was placed on speaking rather than reading the prayers.

Dinner was once again silent except for song and ended about 1:45 p.m. It was followed by a rest period. At 4:30 the retreatants were sent out for a walk, with the instruction to walk by themselves and to avoid any conversation with other persons, though not at the price of discourtesy. We reassembled at 5:45, and the students reported on their walks. . . . Common to all retreatants was the feeling that the Sabbath was present even outside of Hillel and that it was actually a painful experience to see people violating it. . . .

At 6:30, a snack was served, followed by another communal reading session, the afternoon prayer and, 'finally, the third Sabbath meal. . . . Havdalah and an evaluation session (in my home) concluded the retreat.

* * * * * * *

Last week another Retreat was held. Several important differences between our past Retreats and that of last week merit attention.

(1) We had a more sophisticated intake procedure: any student who wished to participate was interviewed by me. The following is more or less what they were told: "The Retreat is an effort on the part of the 40 people who are going to participate to create a temporary monastic community dedicated to peace and the kind of mutual liking that you don't find in your day-to-day dormitory life. We shall use the Sabbath as a medium and the techniques of ancient and contemporary Jewish mysticism.

"The Retreat is a powerful experience, a kind of strong 'mind-blowing' affair that is so intense that, to judge by past Retreats, a person who has participated in a retreat is generally not the same person he was before the Retreat. We have often noticed a re-structuring of values on the part of the Retreatants, a new interpretation of their life style. Some students have changed their majors, while adults may change their family relations.

"Because the Retreat has a powerful impact, we have developed two basic controls that are employed to prevent the situation from getting out of hand.

"The sole purpose of these controls is to give you, the Retreatant, some modicum of self-control throughout the weekend, and to prevent you from blowing your mind in the wrong way. The first control we call the 'inner control;' it consists of your understanding of the basic philosophy of the Retreat, which is in essence that the Retreat is a game. A group of people have decided to get together and play a game for a weekend. Nothing more. When the Retreat ends, the game will be over, and you can continue or not continue playing, as you please. This realization will help keep you in control of things throughout the Retreat. The second control, which we call the 'outer control,' is in the guise of the Retreat Master. The Retreat Master is not a dominant figure, but he will keep a constant eye on you, help you get into things, and make sure that you do not get into things which he feels he cannot handle. In order for his guidance to be effective, however, you will have to be able to commit yourself to unequivocally *obeying* (and I use this strong word very advisedly) the Retreat Master, no matter *what* he tells you to do. Thus, for example, I might ask you at 2:00 in the afternoon in the middle of a session, to walk upstairs and lie down.

At this point, you would simply get up, humbly walk upstairs, crawl into a corner, and go to sleep. Before you give us a commitment on this, the question you have to ask yourself, of course, is whether or not you can accept me in this kind of a role.

"Because the Retreat is a game, it has rules. If you break one rule, you can ruin the Retreat not only for yourself; you can blow it for all the players as well as those who are only spectators.

"Finally, on Sunday before the Retreat you will receive a detailed letter on how to prepare yourself throughout the week for the Retreat." (See below).

It should be noted that before each of these interviews, each retreatant was questioned in the hope of assessing his general state of mental well-being. If he appeared particularly depressed about anything at that time, he was generally encouraged not to go on the Retreat.

(2) Let me add a word about the study materials. We used two selections: "Customs of the Maggid of Mezritch, according to a manuscript by Rabbi Shmelkeh of Nicholsburg," and "Customs for Men according to Rabbi Elimelech of Lizensk." I had translated them, partly for use in the Retreat, partly for use in my credit course in Hasidism. In addition to being provocative documents in themselves, they lend themselves to interesting literary comparisons. Students were asked to speculate on whether the differences in the two documents were based on the different temperaments of the two men, the different historical situations and social needs that each experienced in his time; whether the different priority ratings of each could be given any special meaning, etc. All in all, they proved to be excellent sources for the analysis of social and historical conditions critical to Hasidic thought in those times by quick reference to a primary source.

* * * *

Letter to Retreatants:

Our Retreat will be an effort on our part to achieve a sense of total Shabbos and total community, using techniques culled from a mystic tradition that goes back 3,000 years. For this reason it is important that you come prepared.

Each day of the week keep a diary of the things that happen

to you, especially beautiful things. A good time to review them each day is in the evening while lying in bed just before going to sleep. Be prepared to share some of these experiences with some of the other retreatants during the Friday evening service.

Be at Hillel House no later than 3:30 p.m. Be completely showered before you come. When showering, bear in mind that you are doing this for the Sabbath and as a religious rite for self-purification *(T'vila)*. When you emerge from the water you will want to experience rebirth. Eat well before coming to Hillel; we will probably not eat until about 11:00 p.m.

When you arrive at Hillel you should be dressed in casual clothes that are completely fresh and clean—just back from the laundry or dry-cleaner. (The same for underwear.) Although you will be wearing this outfit until just before services, be sure that it is not too fancy, as these will also be your sleeping clothes. Just before services you will change into your second set of clothes; this should be what you consider to be your (a) favorite and (b) your finest set of clothes—again, completely fresh and unworn since the time that it was last cleaned. You may bring as many of these outfits as you please, but remember that physical comfort is an extremely high priority. Also, bear in mind that Hillel is a concrete building that tends to get cold.

Do *not* bring the following: Watch or clock, keys, wallets, smoking supplies, pens, pencils, notebooks, textbooks, newspapers, magazines, or money. It is in fact imperative that your pockets be empty when you arrive at Hillel so that we will all be poor and equal at least in this symbolic way. Immediately before candle-lighting however, you will be asked to place a voluntary amount of money in the charity box, so have this ready. Women may use any kind of make-up they like before 4:30 p.m. on Friday, but they are restricted to cold cream and powder until 5:45 p.m. on Saturday. Women should have their finest jewelry to enhance the Sabbath. As there are a limited amount of sofas at Hillel, most of which will be used by the women, it is recommended that everyone bring an excess of blankets, a pillow (if you use one) and a clean towel.

Please call me if you have any questions. Remember that the most important thing about the Sabbath is your preparation for it.

SOURCES AND ACKNOWLEDGMENTS

CONTRIBUTORS

Rabbi Alfred Jospe is National Director of the B'nai B'rith Hillel Foundations

Rabbi Richard N. Levy is the Director of the Hillel Council at UCLA

    *   *   *   *   *

Rachel Adler is a doctoral candidate at Northwestern University. She lives in the Los Angeles area where she writes and teaches.

Rabbi Albert Axelrad is the Director of the B'nai B'rith Hillel Foundation at Brandeis University

Rabbi David Berner is Associate Director of the Hillel Council at UCLA

Rabbi Theodore Falcon is the on-campus rabbi at California State University, Northridge

Robert Ganz, a member of the class of 1973 at the University of Rochester, is a political science major with an allied field in religion

Rabbi Richard Israel is coordinator of Hillel affairs in the Boston area

Rabbi Joel Poupko is Associate Hillel Director at the University of Michigan

Rabbi Stanley Ringler is the Director of the B'nai B'rith Hillel Foundation at the University of Miami

Debra Sowald is a junior in elementary education at Mather College of Case-Western Reserve University, Cleveland, Ohio

Raphael Zahler graduated from Harvard, received a Ph.D. (math.) from the University of Chicago, and currently teaches at Rutgers State University

Members of the Shabbat Workshop of the Hillel Council at UCLA: Mitch Corber, Bruce and Monica Devons, Gerald Fisch, Karen Fox, Evelyn Graziani, David Rosner, Carrie Small, and Suzanne Weiss.

INTRODUCTION

NEW WINDOWS ON AN ANCIENT DAY

THE SABBATH BRIDGE

Page	Selection	
79	Reader C	The reference is to a story in William James, *Essays on Faith and Morals,* New York 1962, pp. 260-263.

SILENCE

85	Reader 1	H. N. Bialik, "Throbs the Night," transl. by Bertha Beinkinstadt, *Complete Works of Hayyim Nahman Bialik,* ed. with an introduction by Israel Efros, New York 1948, pp. 101-102. © 1948 by The Histadruth Ivrith of America, publishers, and used with their permission.
85	All	"Solitude" by Henry David Thoreau, *Walden V* (Quoted from John Bartlett, *Familiar Quotations,* New York 1955, p. 590. © 1955 by Little, Brown and Company and used with their permission.)
86	Reader 3	"Silence," by Charles Hanson Towne, from *Masterpieces of Religious Verse,* ed. by J. D. Morrison, 1948. Reprinted by permission of Harper and Row, publishers.

NOAH'S SABBATH

HAVDALAH

A SERVICE FOR ISRAEL

A DAY OF WITNESS:
A SERVICE FOR SOVIET JEWS

A SERVICE OF REMEMBRANCE
FOR THE SIX MILLION

A SERVICE OF JEWISH GIVING

A SERVICE ON PEACE AND BROTHERHOOD

Prayers on pages 234 Praise ye the Lord)
235 (Hear O Israel)
237 (Grant us peace) (adapted)
240 (Let us adore)
are taken from *Union Prayerbook for Jewish Worship,* Vol. I, © by Central Conference of American Rabbis, and used with their permission.

Several prayers (on pp. 233, 234, 235, 236, 238, 239, 240-241) were written by Rabbi Aaron Opher and are reproduced with his permission.

343

AND THE EARTH HE GAVE TO MAN

345